Beyond the Panama Papers.
The Performance of EU Good Governance Promotion
The Anticorruption Report
Volume 4

Alina Mungiu-Pippidi
Jana Warkotsch (editors)

Beyond the Panama Papers. The Performance of EU Good Governance Promotion

The Anticorruption Report 4

written by
Alina Mungiu-Pippidi
Ramin Dadašov
Sindy Natalia Alvarado Pachón
Christopher Norman
Simone Dietrich
Eliska Drapalova
Miroslav Beblavý
Emília Sičáková-Beblavá
Martin Mendelski
Digdem Soyaltin
Justine Louis
Jana Warkotsch
Max Montgomery

Barbara Budrich Publishers
Opladen • Berlin • Toronto 2017

All rights reserved. No part of this publication may be reproduced, stored in or introduced into a retrieval system, or transmitted, in any form, or by any means (electronic, mechanical, photocopying, recording or otherwise) without the prior written permission of Barbara Budrich Publishers. Any person who does any unauthorized act in relation to this publication may be liable to criminal prosecution and civil claims for damages.

You must not circulate this book in any other binding or cover and you must impose this same condition on any acquirer.

A CIP catalogue record for this book is available from
Die Deutsche Bibliothek (The German Library)

The information and views set out in this publication are those of the author(s) only and do not reflect any collective opinion of the ANTICORRP consortium, nor do they reflect the official opinion of the European Commission. Neither the European Commission nor any person acting on behalf of the European Commission is responsible for the use which might be made of the following information.

© 2017 by Barbara Budrich Publishers, Opladen, Berlin & Toronto
www.barbara-budrich.net

ISBN 978-3-8474-0582-5 (Paperback)
eISBN 978-3-8474-0405-7 (e-book)

Das Werk einschließlich aller seiner Teile ist urheberrechtlich geschützt. Jede Verwertung außerhalb der engen Grenzen des Urheberrechtsgesetzes ist ohne Zustimmung des Verlages unzulässig und strafbar. Das gilt insbesondere für Vervielfältigungen, Übersetzungen, Mikroverfilmungen und die Einspeicherung und Verarbeitung in elektronischen Systemen.

Die Deutsche Bibliothek – CIP-Einheitsaufnahme
Ein Titeldatensatz für die Publikation ist bei Der Deutschen Bibliothek erhältlich.

Verlag Barbara Budrich Barbara Budrich Publishers
Stauffenbergstr. 7. D-51379 Leverkusen Opladen, Germany

86 Delma Drive. Toronto, ON M8W 4P6 Canada
www.barbara-budrich.net

Jacket illustration by Bettina Lehfeldt, Kleinmachnow, Germany – www.lehfeldtgraphic.de

Contents

For a More Effective Link Between EU Funds and Good Governance . . 7

1. EU Democracy Promotion, Conditionality and Judicial Autonomy . . 34
2. Spain: Roads to Good Governance? How EU Structural Funds Impact Governance across Regions 46
3. Slovakia: The Impact of EU Good Governance Aid 2007–2013 58
4. Romania: Europeanisation of Good Governance Where and why does it fail, and what can be done about it? 68
5. Turkey: The Paradoxical Effects of EU Accession 79
6. Egypt: The Failed Transition 89
7. Tunisia: Great Expectations 104
8. Tanzania: The Cosmetic Anticorruption 116

Acknowledgements 128

For a More Effective Link Between EU Funds and Good Governance

ALINA MUNGIU-PIPPIDI[1], RAMIN DADAŠOV[2], SINDY NATALIA ALVARADO PACHÓN[3], CHRISTOPHER NORMAN[4]

This introduction examines the EU's influence over governance in EU aid recipient countries[5]. The results find a small positive effect of total aid, no effect on corruption of specialised aid (anticorruption, public sector) and a strong divergence between countries which manage to progress on governance and countries which receive the most aid. The main explanations as to why no real success case has been found for governance improvement are the excessive reliance on formal regulation in non-rule of law environments and the continuous degradation over the last ten years of essential components for control of corruption, such as freedom of the press, from the Balkans to sub-Saharan Africa. However, when checking for targeted aid's influence we find that countries receiving anticorruption aid in the end do better on average than those not receiving it in terms of evolving perception of judicial independence and freedom of the press.

Changing the norm of corruption

The main research question here is how an external actor (the EU) can influence the transition of a society from corruption as a governance norm – where public resource distribution is systematically biased in favour of authority holders and those connected with them – to corruption as an exception, resulting in a state that is largely autonomous vis-à-vis private interest and an allocation of public resources based on ethical universalism (everyone treated equally and fairly). We ask if EU aid has succeeded in changing governance for the better in recipient countries and we test what theories of change explain progress in good governance and how the EU's good governance promotion relates to them.

We call a country "corrupt" when we find a governance regime where corruption is institutionalised as a rule of the game, and we call the opposite "control of corruption" when a society reaches the capacity to constrain corrupt behaviour in order to enforce the norm of individual integrity in public service and politics, to prevent state capture by particular interests and thus to promote the public interest and social welfare. Control of corruption and rule of law overlap within a complex equilibrium that includes a government subject to the law, the equality of citizens before the law, respect for individual rights, equal and fair distribution of

---

[1] Hertie School of Governance, pippidi@hertie-school.org
[2] Hertie School of Governance, dadasov@hertie-school.org
[3] Hertie School of Governance, alvarado-pachon@hertie-school.org
[4] Hertie School of Governance, c.norman@mia.hertie-school.org
[5] The text is based on the work package 8 in EU FP7 ANTICORRP and several online materials published on the site of the project, www.anticorrp.eu, most notably the policy paper from February 2017. Full models can be found in Dadašov 2017.

public resources and corresponding societal norms, such as respect for rules and widespread observation of the ethical universalism norm. These optimal equilibria are grounded in a social order which is based on individualism and low power distance (Eisenstadt and Roniger 1984; Hofstede 1999; Husted 1999; Mungiu-Pippidi 2015). On the contrary, institutionalised corruption is based on particularism (individuals treated differently according to status), an exchange mode of collectivistic and status based societies (Parsons 1997: 80–82; Mungiu-Pippidi 2006; Mungiu-Pippidi 2015, Chs. 1–2), which in relation to public office feeds patrimonialism, the lack of private-public separation for authority holders (Weber 1981). Particularism encompasses a variety of interpersonal and personal-state transaction types, such as clientelism, bribery, patronage, nepotism and other favouritisms – all of which imply, when an authority holder is concerned, some degree of patrimonialism. Particularism defines not only the relations between a government and its subjects but also between individuals in a society, and it explains why advancement in a given society is based on merit or, on the contrary, status or particular connections with influential people. If particularistic exchanges, which are carried out on the basis of status and connections versus impersonal factors (such as merit of product, price and rules), are the dominant mode in a society, markets cannot evolve from a state of imperfect competition. Similarly, particularism of transactions between state and citizens makes democracy a mere façade, as resources are systematically spoiled by authority holders and the state never manages to become autonomous from private interest, with bureaucrats and rulers colluding in the public resources spoliation game. The existence of particularism limits access to public resources (some applicants are favoured and some are discriminated against) resulting in unfair treatment. Particularism is a broader concept than corruption, as it includes both criminalised forms of corruption (favour in exchange for undue profit) and what Daniel Kaufmann labelled "legal corruption" (Kaufmann and Vicente 2011). In its extreme form (most government transactions are particularistic) a state can be entirely "captured" by private interest. If we picture governance as the set of formal rules and informal practices determining who gets what in terms of public resources, we can then imagine a continuum of public resource allocations with full particularism at one end and full ethical universalism at the other.

To place a country on the continuum, we use the Control of Corruption (CoC) indicator of the Worldwide Governance Indicators (WGI) World Bank project, which has recorded basically all corruption ratings for 192 countries in the world since 1996. Thus we obtain a range from closed access with particularistic exchanges at one end to open access with universalistic exchanges at the other. This shows a compact group of ten countries with the best quality of governance in the world, with another thirty or so in the upper tercile, but the majority of countries score five or less. Simply put, the evidence seems to indicate that the world is more particularistic than universalistic. Very few developing countries are to be found in the upper tercile and with the exception of Japan the "achieving" group is composed of early European modernisers and early Anglo-Saxon colonies such as Canada, the US, New Zealand and Australia. Exceptions to the rule come only in the form of small islands or city-states.

Figure 1. The 2015 distribution of countries on the particularism-ethical universalism continuum.

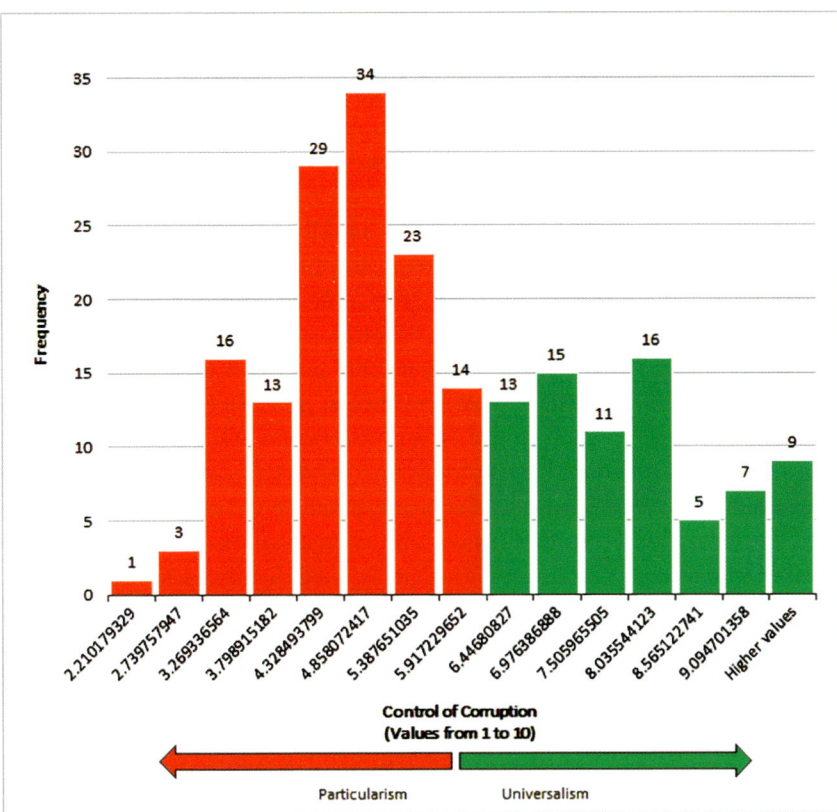

Source and legend: WGI Control of Corruption frequency distribution, recoded 1–10 with Denmark 10. Red areas show particularism to be the norm.

The transition away from a regime based on particularistic governance and the evolution to governance based on universalism does not come easily. Both public opinion polls and expert surveys concur in the assessment that few countries have made it and even fewer seem to have succeeded on this path in recent times, since we have collected data allowing comparisons across countries and time (North et al. 2009; Mungiu-Pippidi 2015). Furthermore, the efforts of the anticorruption community since the international promotion of good governance has been born have yet to produce a final undisputed success case, rather than what self-promoters report in general as incremental evolution (Klitgaard 2014). Many anticorruption policies and programmes have been declared successful, but no country has yet achieved control of corruption due to international assistance and its standard prescriptions, though a few have succeeded on their own. The definition of success also needs clarification. "Success" can only mean a consolidated dominant norm of ethical universalism and public integrity. Exceptions, in the form of corrupt acts, will always remain, but as long as they are as numerous as to make the rule virtually indistinguishable, a country cannot be seen as an achiever. A successful transformation requires both the dominance of the norm of public integrity (the majority of acts and public officials are not corrupt) and its resilience against an eventual backslide, as happened in some Eastern European countries after EU accession. Reducing corruption to the status of exception in a sustainable way thus defines a successful evolution. Quite a few developing countries seem to be presently struggling in a borderline area, where the old norm and the new norm confront one another; hence the anticorruption headlines from such countries, where popular demand for integrity of leaders has increased substantially over the years (India, Brazil, Bulgaria, Romania).

EU aid and good governance promotion

The EU institutions are collectively the largest multilateral donor of foreign aid and the second largest donor overall behind the United States providing development assistance to every region in the world. Between 2002 and 2014, Official Development Assistance (ODA) dispersed from EU institutions to developing countries tripled from above USD 5 billion to over 16 billion. Compared with USD 41 billion in 2002 and 94 billion in 2014 from all OECD Development Assistance Committee (DAC) members, multilateral aid from the European Union regularly comes in between 10 and 20% of the annual DAC total. Moreover, around 12% of the total ODA from the EU institutions in 2014 was allocated to the government and civil society sector that includes, among other areas, development of public sector and administrative management, development of anticorruption organisations and institutions, and legal and judicial development. Only humanitarian aid received slightly greater contributions.

Types of EU aid

The substantial material funds devoted to the promotion of good governance and civil society reflect the relevance of this area in the European development policy of recent times. As noted by Hout (2013, 1), driven by the consensus among practitioners and academics about the importance of governance quality for development, European aid "has been subject to the governance turn of the late 1990s". Since then, good governance has been assigned to serve as a fundamental principle and its promotion has become a key priority in designing European development policy. In practical terms, new development instruments were created that use the principles of positive conditionality for allocation of financial assistance. For example, since 2008 the European Development Fund financing the development assistance to the group of countries in Africa, Caribbean and Pacific (ACP) has included an instrument called "governance incentive tranche". Within this mechanism, additional funds can be allocated to countries that adopt or credibly commit themselves to governance reforms. Similarly, the European Neighbourhood Policy Instrument (ENPI), which governs a group of countries in the Middle East and North Africa as well as some former Soviet republics, contains the specific "governance facility" instrument, which was introduced in 2007, to reward countries with progress in good governance reforms. The European Commission has identified institutional indicators on democratic accountability, rule of law, control of corruption, government effectiveness, economic governance, and internal and external security as key factors for evaluation and monitoring of countries' reforms in this area (Hout 2013).

The data used for this analysis covers more than 120 developing countries, which are net recipients of EU official development aid (ODA), and the period between 2002 and 2014, for which most of the listed disaggregated data is available.

Our sample of 127 countries spans five continents with populations ranging from less than one million to 1.3 billion. EU development policy can be categorised in a number of different ways: by sector, geographical region, type of aid, funding instrument grouping, how aid is channelled to recipients, income grouping, and the relative size of aid to a country compared to its economy. The differences in these categories may explain differences in governance outcomes and the effectiveness of aid overall. Empirical literature on foreign aid specifically emphasises the importance of the sectorial allocation, and the types and channels of ODA in analysing its effectiveness (see, e.g., Wright and Winters 2010).

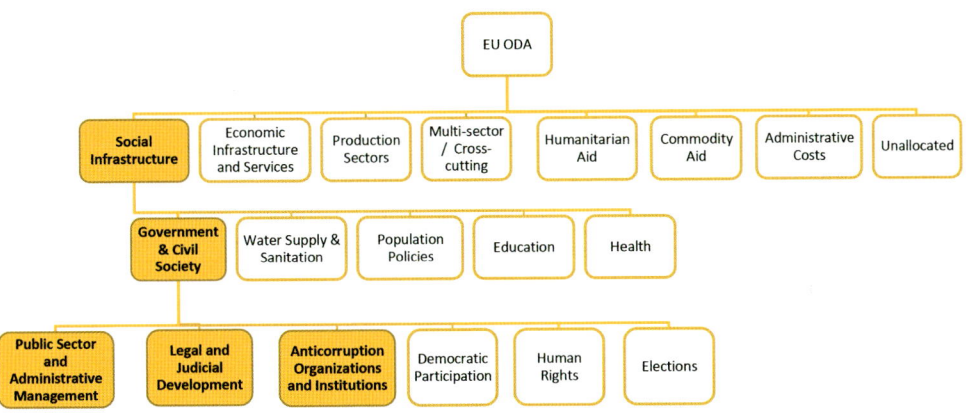

Figure 2. Types of EU aid.

Source: OECD - QWIDS Official Development Aid

Sector classifications specifically track the share of ODA to each specific purpose in a recipient country. The sector of destination is assigned by answering the question "which specific area of the recipient's economic and social structure is the transfer intended to foster".[6] Sectors are labelled with purpose codes for these specific areas.

The "type" of aid is presumed to impact the outcomes as well. The OECD started to collect data for the type of aid in 2010 "to distinguish between the various modalities of aid".[7] Between 2006 and 2009, ODA was retroactively assigned to certain types based on an automatic mapping, which used the purpose codes. This means that for our sample years, aid type is partly uncategorised (2002 to 2005), partly categorised using a mapping formula (2006 to 2009), and categorised regularly (starting 2010). According to the OECD[8], types can include 1. budget support, 2. "core contributions and pooled programs and funds", 3. project-type interventions, 4. experts and other technical assistance, 5. scholarships and student costs in donor countries, 6. debt relief, 7. administrative costs not included elsewhere, and 8. other in-donor expenditures. The first four types listed are the largest and most relevant to our chapter.

Budget support is distinctive in the fact that the donor relinquishes exclusive control of its funds by sharing responsibility with the recipient. Budget support can be sector-specific but can also be a transfer to the national government's treasury. Funds for which the responsibility is shared with another stakeholder, such as NGOs, other donors or multilateral organisations, fall under the "core contributions and pooled programmes and funds". Project-type interven-

---

[6] http://www.oecd.org/dac/stats/dac-glossary.htm#Sector_Class
[7] stats.oecd.org/qwids
[8] http://www.oecd.org/dac/stats/type-aid.htm

tions are for more narrowly defined projects that have specific outcomes. The label "exports and other technical assistance" covers the provision of personnel, training and research in private and public bodies, including university courses, exchanges and publications.

Multilateral aid can also be categorised by channel. Channels include the public sector, NGOs and civil society, public-private partnerships and multilateral organisations. Public sector includes not only national governments but also local governments and public corporations or "third countries" with delegated cooperation on a certain ODA project. NGO examples include Transparency International, International Women's Tribune Center, and the African Medical and Research Foundation. In certain countries, government-operated organisations that mimic NGOs (GONGOs) are also recipients of ODA. Multilateral organisations may include such groups as UN agencies, the IMF, the International Organisation for Migration, or the Nordic Development Fund.

In 2002, the EU allocated nearly one third of its funds in the commodity aid/general programme assistance sector, but by 2014 this sector represented only 7%. The increased emphasis on other sectors by 2014 mainly contributes to "economic infrastructure and services" and "social infrastructure and services". Figure 3 shows sectorial differences between 2002 and 2014.

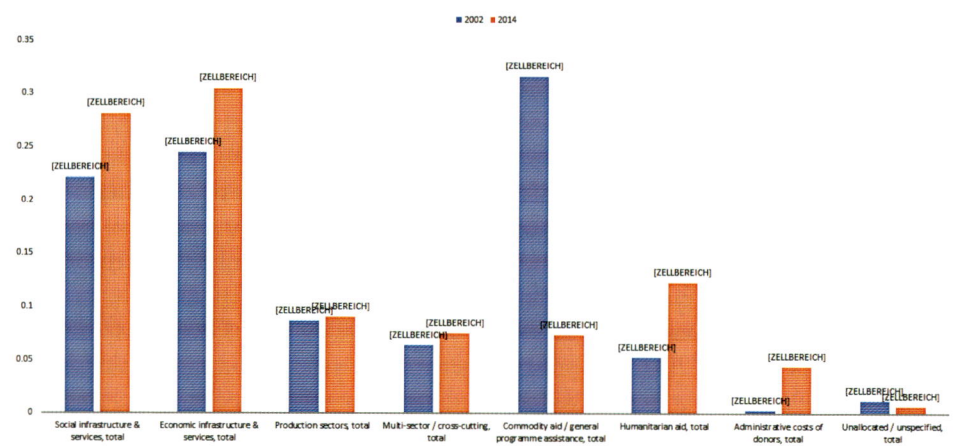

Figure 3. Total aid by sector

Source: OECD - QWIDS Official Development Aid, own calculations

As a share of total aid within the social infrastructure and services sector, government and civil society increased from 2002 to 2014, remaining the largest category within this grouping. In 2014, it occupied nearly half of all social infrastructure and services aid.

Figure 4. Social infrastructure and services Aid as % Total Aid

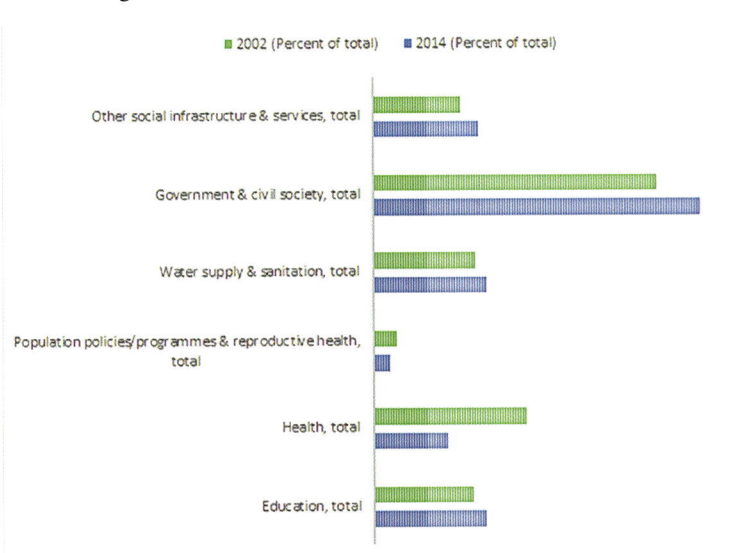

Source: OECD - QWIDS Official Development Aid, own calculations

In 2002, "public sector policy and administrative management" received the majority of government and civil society funding, but in 2014 a much wider range of subsectors received funding, including decentralisation, human rights, democratic participation, and legal and judicial development. Anticorruption organisations and institutions are not recorded in 2002 as a recipient of government and civil society sector aid, and are relatively small in 2014 as well.

Figure 5. Government and civil society sector Aid as % Total Aid

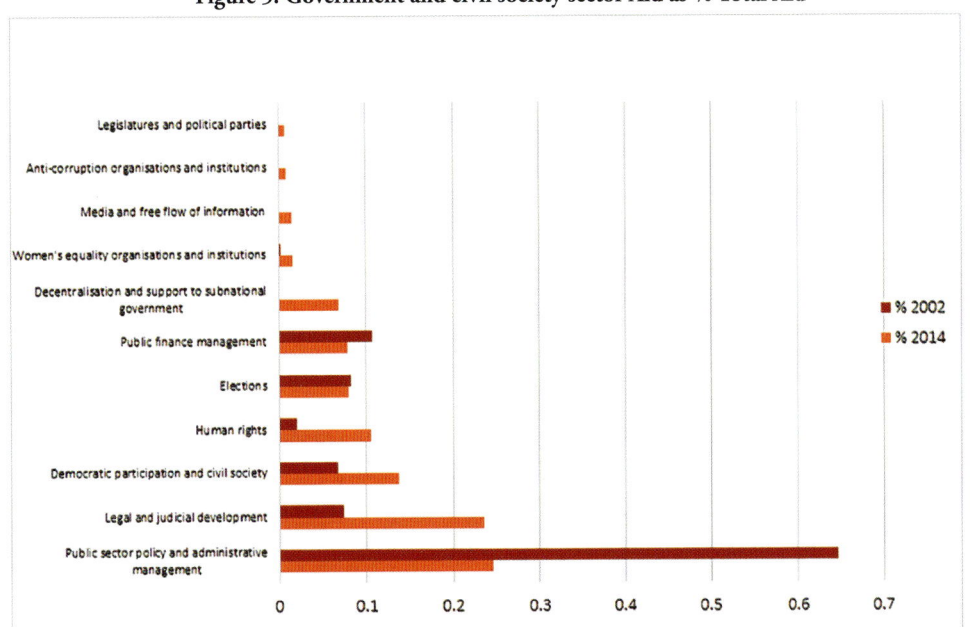

Source: OECD - QWIDS Official Development Aid, own calculations

ODA type is mostly composed of "project type" aid, increasing over the course of this timeframe. The category, "Experts and technical assistance" was first recorded as a type of funding post-2010, where it maintained a presence between 5 and 10% of all aid types. The "core contributions and pooled programmes and funds" type is not represented in the table below.

Table 1. Types of aid (2006–2014)

	2006	2007	2008	2009	2010	2011	2012	2013	2014	Total
Budget support (USD)	843	833	825	1220	2309	2306	2253	2285	2221	15095
Budget support (%)	8%	7%	6%	9%	18%	13%	12%	13%	12%	10.3%
Project type (USD)	5117	5660	5516	5760	7753	13103	13180	12181	13333	81603
Project type (%)	51%	49%	43%	44%	61%	73%	73%	71%	72%	55.5%
Experts/tech (USD)	0	0	0	0	1285	1142	995	1016	929	5367
Expert/tech (%)	0%	0%	0%	0%	10%	6%	5%	6%	5%	3.7%

Source: OECD - QWIDS Official Development Aid, own calculations

Distribution of Aid by Country and Region

Recipients of EU multilateral aid can be classified in multiple ways. The focus of European aid over the course of this time period shifted a number of times, and its instruments changed repeatedly as well. Some ODA recipients physically closest to the European Union itself are candidates for EU membership. These countries, including Albania, Bosnia-Herzegovina, Montenegro, FYR Macedonia, Serbia and Turkey, receive money through the Instrument for Pre-Accession (IPA) assistance. Immediately surrounding the EU and its membership candidates are the countries under the European Neighbourhood Policy (ENP). These include countries to the South such as Algeria, Egypt, Jordan, Lebanon, Libya, Morocco, Syria, Tunisia, and the West Bank and Gaza Strip. To the East, Armenia, Azerbaijan, Belarus, Georgia, Moldova and the Ukraine also fall under the ENP instrument. The Africa, Caribbean and Pacific (ACP) instrument covers the largest number of and most geographically widespread recipients. Finally, Other Developing Countries (ODC) refers mostly to countries on the Asian Continent outside of the countries already categorised. The instrument used is relevant because research by Dadašov (2017) finds that the positive effect of multilateral EU aid is statistically significant throughout the ACP region and the ENP, excluding outliers. These instrument regions also have relatively poor governance quality compared to others, suggesting that such instruments are useful categories for this study.

Apart from instruments, the World Bank uses a common regional classification. Europe and Central Asia (ECA) consists of the IPA countries, the East ENP countries, and the Central Asian region. The Middle East and North Africa (MENA) consists of countries that are in the South ENP and other Arabian Peninsula states. South Asia (SA) is Afghanistan, Bangladesh, Bhutan, India, Maldives, Nepal, Pakistan and Sri Lanka. Sub-Saharan Africa (SSA) refers to countries to the south of the MENA region on the African continent. The East Asia and Pacific (EAP) as well as Latin America and the Caribbean (LAC) are self-explanatory geographical regions. Although these geographical regions are similar to the instrument, this chapter makes sure to distinguish between both methods of representing aid recipients.

Another interesting way to categorise ODA recipients is by their income group. Income groups differ from geographic or instrument groups because countries change groups over time. A country that is considered low income in one year might be considered low middle income the next. For 2015, the World Bank uses GNI per capita (Atlas Method) to define Low Income (LC) as USD 1,185 or less, Lower Middle Income (LMIC) as USD 1,026 to USD 4,035, Upper Middle Income (UMIC) as USD 4,036 to USD 12,475, and High Income (HIIC) as USD 12,476 or more[9].

The largest recipient of EU aid over the 2002–14 time periods is Turkey. With USD 14 billion, it receives over twice the funding of the next largest recipient, Serbia. Of the highest nominal recipients, there are only three Low Income countries in the top ten, and countries such as Turkey and Serbia fall within the Upper Middle Income Group.

Table 2. Largest recipients of EU ODA in millions of USD

Country Name	Total Aid (millions USD)	Income Group	Instrument	Region
1. Turkey	14326.30	UMIC	IPA	ECA
2. Serbia	5122.11	UMIC	IPA	ECA
3. West Bank & Gaza Strip	4739.61	LMIC	ENP	MENA
4. Morocco	4237.52	LMIC	ENP	MENA
5. Afghanistan	3607.53	LIC	ODC	SA
6. Congo DR	2963.63	LIC	ACP	SSA
7. Tunisia	2814.33	UMIC	ENP	MENA
8. Ethiopia	2801.91	LIC	ACP	SSA
9. Egypt	2605.02	LMIC	ENP	MENA
10. Sudan	2463.36	LMIC	ACP	SSA
11. South Africa	2257.28	UMIC	ACP	SSA
12. Ukraine	2238.82	LMIC	ENP	ECA
13. Bosnia Herzegovina	2183.02	UMIC	IPA	ECA
14. Mozambique	2032.05	LIC	ACP	SSA
15. Tanzania	1943.47	LIC	ACP	SSA

Source: OECD - QWIDS Official Development Aid, own calculations

[9] http://data.worldbank.org/about/country-and-lending-groups

When considering the size of a country's economy, however, we may divide the amount of aid received by the country's total GNI. Relative to its GNI, the largest recipient is Somalia, which at 13% of aid relative to its GNI from EU institutions, receives over twice as much as the next highest recipient, Liberia. All but three of the top 15 recipients relative to GNI receive aid through the Africa, Caribbean and Pacific instrument.

Table 3. Largest recipients of EU ODA as a percentage of their GNI

	Country Name	Total Aid (% GNI)	Income Group	Instrument[1]	Region
1.	Somalia	13%	LIC	ACP	SSA
2.	Liberia	6%	LIC	ACP	SSA
3.	Djibouti	5%	LMIC	ACP	SSA
4.	Burundi	5%	LIC	ACP	SSA
5.	West Bank & Gaza Strip	5%	LMIC	ENP	MENA
6.	Guinea-Bissau	4%	LIC	ACP	SSA
7.	Kosovo	3%	LMIC	IPA	ECA
8.	Central African Rep.	3%	LIC	ACP	SSA
9.	Sierra Leone	3%	LIC	ACP	SSA
10.	Niger	3%	LIC	ACP	SSA
11.	Malawi	3%	LIC	ACP	SSA
12.	Afghanistan	2%	LIC	DCI	SA
13.	Eritrea	2%	LIC	ACP	SSA
14.	Haiti	2%	LIC	ACP	LAC
15.	Mali	2%	LIC	ACP	SSA

Source: OECD - QWIDS Official Development Aid, own calculations

In 2002, the most EU aid went to the least developed countries, but as aid increased over the past 12 years, nominal disbursements to other income groups increased, such as to the Upper Middle Income Group.

Figure 6. Total EU aid by income group

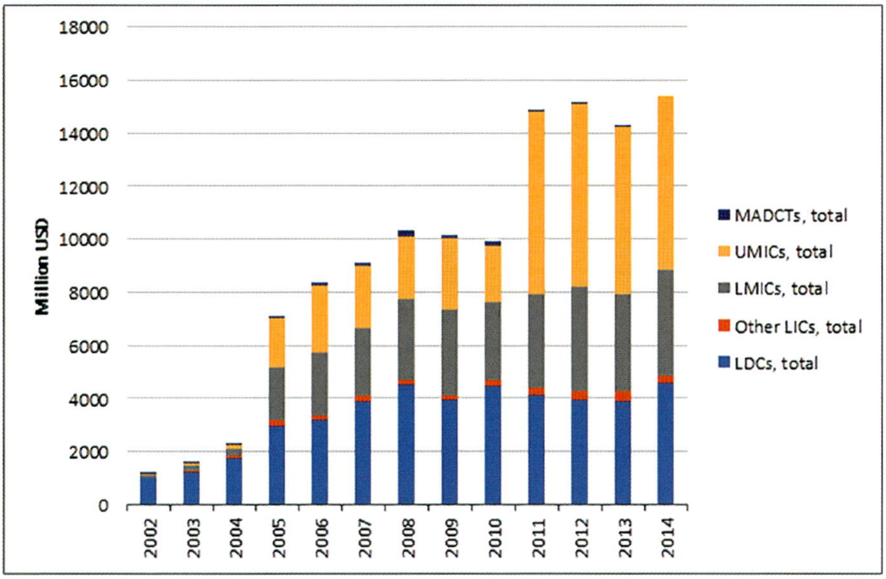

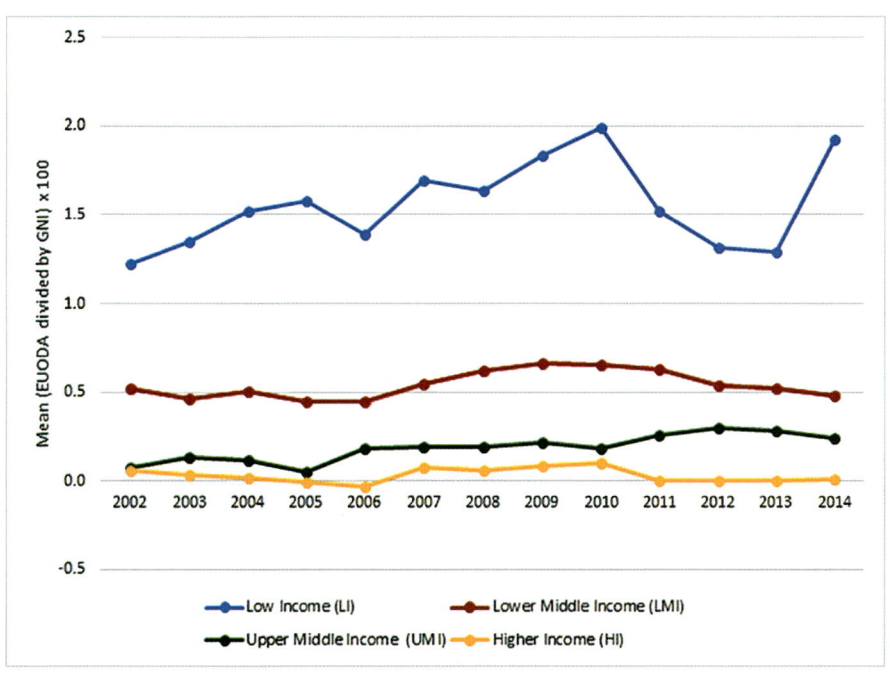

Source: OECD - QWIDS Official Development Aid, own calculations

Figure 7. EU aid relative to GNI by income group

Source: OECD - QWIDS Official Development Aid, own calculations

The average ODA per region was less varied in 2002, increasing for all regions except for Latin America/Caribbean and East Asia/Pacific. By 2014, the ECA region has the largest average aid disbursements, followed by MENA. The gap remains, albeit less starkly, when Turkey is removed in 2011, with the MENA region surpassing it thereafter. Since 2010, Turkey receives a far higher amount of aid than any other countryOf the four instruments, the pre-accession instrument consistently received the most ODA.

When aid is calculated relative to GNI, a different picture emerges. The Instrument for Pre-Accession funding decreased from 2002 to 2008, but sharply increased thereafter. Aid consistently composes around 1% of GNI to Africa, Caribbean and Pacific instrument countries and usually less than .5% of ENP and ODC regions. When grouped by region, aid composes the largest share of GNI for sub-Saharan African countries, and post-2008, the second highest share of GNI is the Europe and Central Asia region.

The link between governance change and EU aid

The Direct Evidence and its Puzzles

As stated above, the world changed little in control of corruption over this interval, so it was not a very favourable period in general. The only region where the average change is significant is South-Eastern Europe where the pre-accession instrument IPA is in operation, while countries in the Africa, Caribbean and Pacific region have, on average, regressed. No statistically significant change was registered for the European Neighbourhood Area, and other developing countries report, on average, a small progression (see Figure 8).

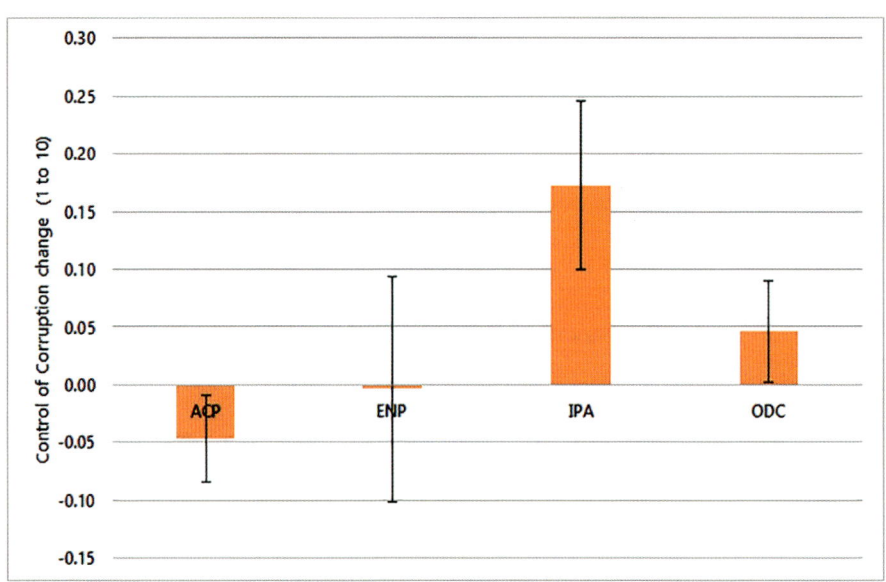

Figure 8. Corruption evolution across instruments

Source: WGI Control of Corruption

Upon examination of the performance of the largest aid recipients (Table 4), we find that their performance is not always rewarding – again, only IPA countries did well (not accounting for the recent backslide on Turkey on all counts).

Table 4. Top general aid recipients and their performance

EU Aid (2002–2014)			
Country	Total Aid (mill. USD)	Change in CoC	Change in JI
Turkey	14326.30	1.06	-1.24
Serbia	5122.11	0.50	
West Bank & Gaza Strip	4739.61	0.72	
Morocco	4237.52	-0.14	0.34
Afghanistan	3607.53	0.18	
Congo, DR	2963.63	-0.05	
Tunisia	2814.33	-1.15	-2.03
Ethiopia	2801.91	0.54	0.84
Egypt	2605.02	-0.54	-1.23
Sudan	2463.36	-0.77	

Source: OECD - QWIDS Official Development Aid, WGI Control of Corruption and World Economic Forum, own calculations

From the countries receiving the most specialised aid (see Tables 5 to 7), most did not register any significant progress on control of corruption. Egypt, Ukraine, Colombia and South Africa regressed, and some IPA countries – Montenegro, Albania and Serbia – progressed by around a half point on a scale of one to ten (which is not a big change, but that's what's driving the regional average up), on both judicial independence and anticorruption. Macedonia progressed the most, although it has less governance, but its progress was questioned in more recent times. Algeria also progressed. Kosovo, with a staggering 35% of aid share for governance reforms (public sector and civil society combined) and Ukraine (16%) or Bosnia, with 15% targeted aid, have really not managed to take off, and the strategies to improve their governance need urgent revisiting.

Table 5. Performance of top Public Sector Aid recipients

Public Sector Aid					
Country	Aid (% GNI)	Aid (% ODA)	Change in CoC	Change FOP	Change JI
Somalia	0.34	2.55	-0.94	0.09	
Guinea-Bissau	0.24	6.53	-1.19	-1.8	1.17
Djibouti	0.21	3.98	0.40	-0.54	
Comoros	0.19	10.58	0.61	-0.18	
Afghanistan	0.18	7.81	0.18	0.27	
Mali	0.16	8.10	-0.34	-1.17	-1.02
Burundi	0.14	2.90	-0.45	0	-0.31
Kosovo	0.10	2.58	0.20		
Malawi	0.09	3.66	0.45	0.36	5.50
Sierra Leone	0.09	3.44	-0.36	0.9	3.71

Source and legend: OECD - QWIDS Official Development Aid, WGI Control of Corruption, Freedom House and World Economic Forum, own calculations. Note: Changes in Freedom of the Press are recorded for the period 2005 to 2014, and changes in Judicial Independence are recorded for the period 2006 to 2014.

Table 6. Performance of top Legal and Judicial Aid recipients

Legal and Judicial Aid					
Country	Aid (% GNI)	Aid (% ODA)	Change in CoC	Change FOP	Change JI
Kosovo	1.09	0.20	0.20		
Moldova	0.08	0.18	0.18	1.08	2.43
Afghanistan	0.07	0.18	0.18	0.27	
Albania	0.07	0.56	0.56	0.09	-0.16
Rwanda	0.07	2.32	2.32	0.54	6.83
West Bank & Gaza Strip	0.05	0.72	0.72		
Georgia	0.05	3.38	3.38	0.81	2.41
Guinea-Bissau	0.04	-1.19	-1.19	-1.8	1.17
Eritrea	0.04	-1.66	-1.66	-0.27	
Malawi	0.04	0.45	0.45	0.36	5.50

Source and legend: OECD - QWIDS Official Development Aid, WGI Control of Corruption, Freedom House and World Economic Forum, own calculations. Note: Changes in Freedom of the Press are recorded for the period 2005 to 2014, and changes in Judicial Independence are recorded for the period 2006 to 2014.

Table 7. Performance of top Anticorruption Aid recipients

Anticorruption Aid					
Country	Aid (% GNI)	Aid (% ODA)	Change in CoC	Change FOP	Change JI
Liberia	0.039	0.70	0.70	0.54	0.00
Guinea-Bissau	0.018	-1.19	-1.19	-1.8	1.17
Montenegro	0.014	0.67	0.67		4.55
Kosovo	0.010	0.20	0.20		
Burundi	0.006	-0.45	-0.45	0	-0.31
Albania	0.003	0.56	0.56	0.09	-0.16
Comoros	0.002	0.61	0.61	-0.18	
Bosnia-Herzegovina	0.002	0.13	0.13	-0.45	-3.92
Mozambique	0.002	-0.45	-0.45	-0.18	0.01
Cameroon	0.001	-0.11	-0.11	-0.09	0.92

Source and legend: OECD - QWIDS Official Development Aid, WGI Control of Corruption, Freedom House and World Economic Forum, own calculations. Note: Changes in Freedom of the Press are recorded for the period 2005 to 2014, and changes in Judicial Independence are recorded for the period 2006 to 2014.

The list of top aid recipients is thus quite different from the list of top achievers, with only a few countries in common. Turkey, the top recipient, first progressed on control of corruption, but in more recent times it regressed on both COC and judicial independence, for which it received the largest amount of aid in the world. Georgia and Rwanda progressed the most, disproportionately with the aid received, driven by domestic factors. At around 10% progress (1 of 10) we also find countries such as the Maldives, Senegal, Ivory Coast, Laos, Bhutan and Korea. Tunisia registered a spectacular improvement on freedom of the press, which has also driven control of corruption positively, but far less than expectations, and far less than its potential.

The top achievers do have some EU funding, but their progress is disproportional to funds- for instance Georgia, Rwanda, Macedonia, Vanuatu, Uruguay, Indonesia and Chile (see also Figure 9, green circle). Others, like Mauritius and Zambia, do not have governance aid but a considerable part of their budget comes from donors.

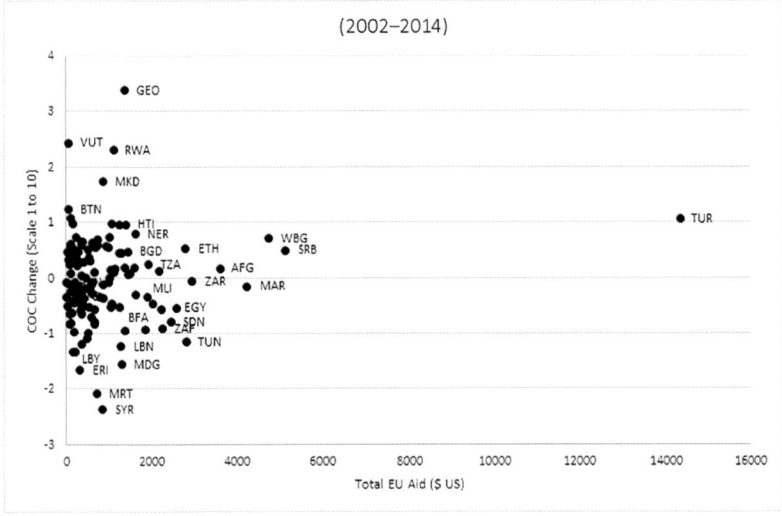

Figure 9. Change in Control of Corruption and total EU ODA.

Sources: WGI Control of Corruption and OECD - QWIDS Official Development Aid

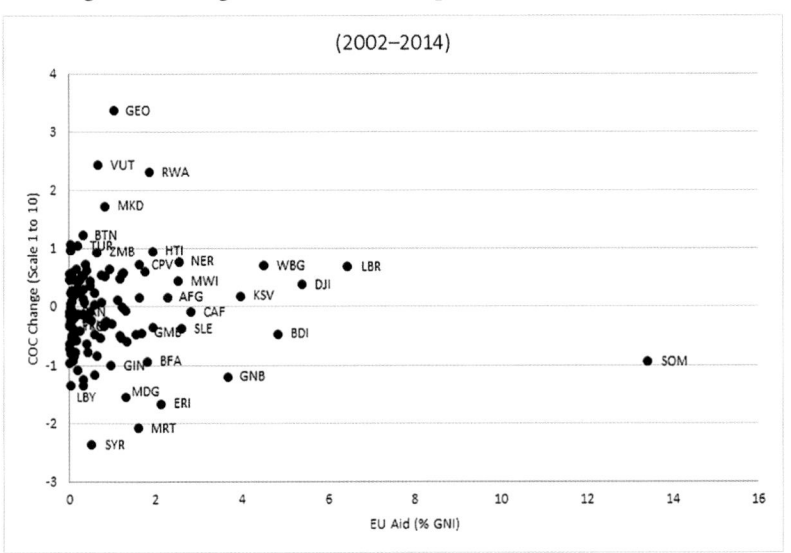

Figure 10. Change in Control of Corruption and EU ODA as % GNI.

Sources: WGI Control of Corruption and OECD - QWIDS Official Development Aid OECD - QWIDS Official Development Aid

Table 8. Achievers on Control of Corruption and their EU aid

Country	Change in CoC	Average of total aid (%GNI)	Average governance aid (%GNI)
Georgia	3.38	0.91	0.19
Vanuatu	2.45	0.82	0.14
Rwanda	2.32	2.15	0.15
Macedonia	1.75	0.87	0.15
Bhutan	1.24	0.35	0.06
Uruguay	1.08	0.03	0.01
Turkey	1.06	0.16	0.02
Belarus	0.99	0.03	0.01
Indonesia	0.99	0.02	0.00
Haiti	0.97	1.88	0.14

Sources: WGI Control of Corruption and OECD - QWIDS Official Development Aid

Countries which receive more aid than the average present on the average worse performances in Control of Corruption and Judicial Independence (WEF) over time (see figures 10–11).

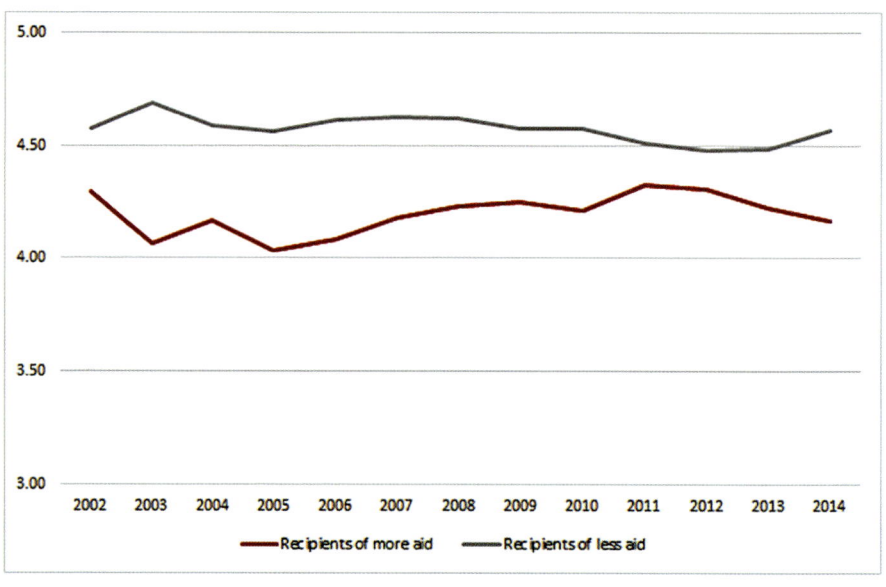

Figure 11. Progress on Control of Corruption by aid (below or above average recipient).

Sources: WGI Control of Corruption and OECD - QWIDS Official Development Aid

The same descriptive analysis is performed for countries receiving anticorruption aid compared to countries which do not report aid from the EU for anticorruption. The number of recipient countries for this sample is no more than 22 countries with registered disbursements from 2009 to 2014. Countries receiving anticorruption aid also perform worse on Control of Corruption, however, it seems that the difference between recipients and non-recipients diminishes in the observed time period. Nevertheless, the difference between recipients and non-recipients and the change from 2002 to 2014 are not significant at the 95% confidence error. So in the best-case scenario, the targeted governance aid made no significant contribution.

Modernisation

We presume that the theory of change that the EU operates under is overall modernisation, for general aid, and state modernisation, for governance and civil society aid, and we test first the evolution of two key indicators in these areas. Figure 12 shows the evolution of education compared with the evolution of control of corruption for aid recipient countries for the years that HDI data is available. While education ends significantly higher up, control of corruption ends nearly at the same point. Simply put, the influence of education on governance in the short and medium term does not exist. In the long term it is mainly through demand for good governance that education works (this is why education in the 1900s can help explain corruption today, but we find no robust relationship between current education and control of corruption), and the clear improvement in education is insufficient to drive up control of corruption in the short and medium term. It is however a worthwhile investment in the long term.

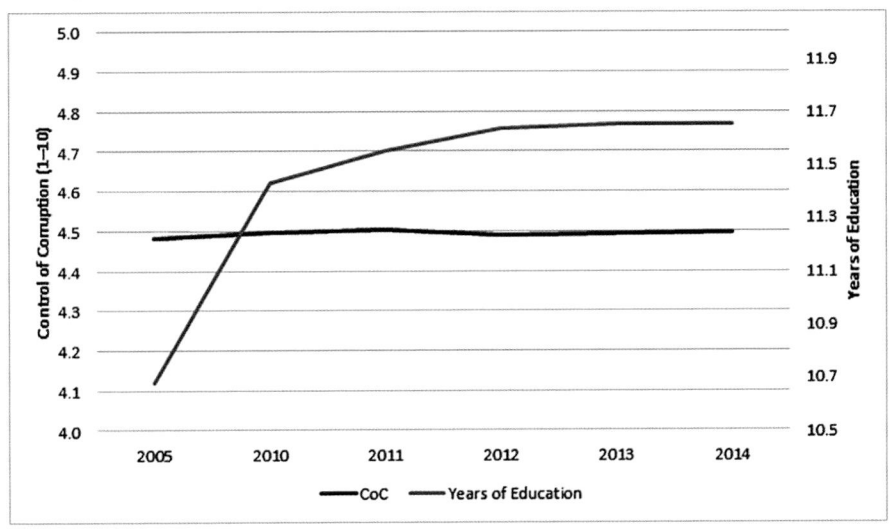

Figure 12. Years of education (HDI component) and WGI Control of Corruption.

Sources: WGI Control of Corruption and Human Development Index (years of education)

The evolution of bureaucracy for the 80 countries for which we have data is somewhat similar. ICRG's Bureaucratic Quality indicator finds some improvement over this period – as predicted by theory, in MENA countries mostly, so not in democracies (see Mungiu-Pippidi 2015 chapter 3 on a larger argument on why traditional monarchies develop bureaucracies as a means of performance and control, while democracies do not). This is insufficient to drive control of corruption (see Figure 13).

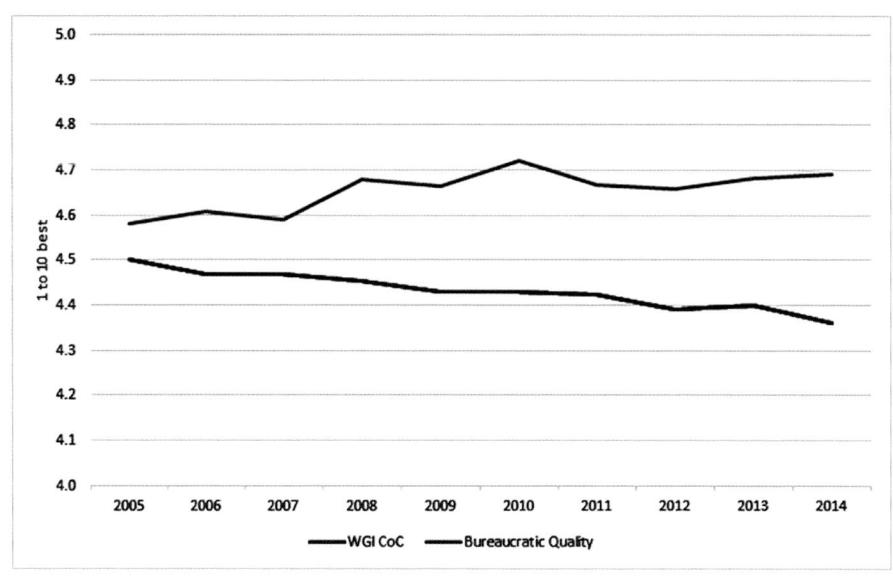

Figure 13. Bureaucratic Quality (ICRG) and WGI Control of Corruption.

Sources: WGI Control of Corruption and ICRG's Bureaucracy

Institutional transfer

The more corrupt countries have the most laws, an old Latin saying goes, and so it is empirically. Most instruments associated with control of corruption and promoted by consultants – whistleblower legislation, anticorruption agencies, ombudsmen, party finance restrictions and so forth bring no significant change. The exceptions are fiscal transparency and public financial disclosures of officials, in other words transparency which allows civil society monitoring of government works, not legal tools that have to be implemented by the same government or even by the judiciary, which is seldom independent in such countries.

Independence of the judiciary is a strong predictor of control of corruption even in complex time-series (Ades and Tella 1996; Mungiu-Pippidi 2015). However, independence of the judiciary depends very much on the decision of politicians to let the magistrates be free – it's a political, not a technical issue. Using the Global Competitiveness Report expert survey, we discover that independence of the judiciary could not have driven much control of corruption in the last ten years (since it has been monitored), because there was just too little of it (CESifo 2014). Many countries where corruption was not perceived as a big problem regressed (countries as different as Austria and Turkey), many countries with a corruption problem have further declined over these ten years (India, Bulgaria, Mexico, Greece, Slovakia and Spain) and very few have progressed but are still far from the level required (Latvia, Brazil, China and Romania).[10]

---

[10] The Executive Opinion Survey, administered each year in over 140 economies, captures valuable information on a broad range of factors that are critical for a country's competitiveness and sustainable development, and for which data sources are scarce or, frequently, non-existent on a global scale. Among several examples of otherwise unavailable data are the quality of the educational system, indicators measuring business sophistication, and labour market variables such as flexibility in wage determination. The survey results are used in the calculation of the Global Competitiveness Index (GCI) and other indexes of the World Economic Forum.

Control of corruption on average declined in the group of countries which do not enjoy rule of law or freedom. Slight progress was registered only in the groups of rule of law, free and partly free countries (see Figure 14). As we have a very close correlation between rule of law and control of corruption (at over 90% in World Governance Indicators), it results that wherever corruption is high, rule of law is also poor, so legal approaches to anticorruption can hardly be expected to work: *the solution cannot be the same as the problem*. Furthermore, change in control of corruption in countries with an anticorruption agency (ACA) but without rule of law is on average (marginally) lower than in those which introduced an ACA and reached a certain level of rule of law[11]. There is no mystery in these results: sub-Saharan African countries, for instance, have poor judicial independence, state capture is in the open and officials amass lavish fortunes because impunity reigns (see the case of President Zuma in South Africa and his use of the public purse for his personal expenses), and yet they were pushed to introduce legislation, such as protection for whistleblowers, by very advanced rule of law and exceptional corruption countries. Corruption is not hidden in South Africa, and this is why statistical tests find that none of these instruments managed to trigger some change. And creating anticorruption agencies where the judiciary is not impartial is a waste of time and money.

Figure 14. Average changes in Control of Corruption across Democracy and the Rule of Law (2002–2014)

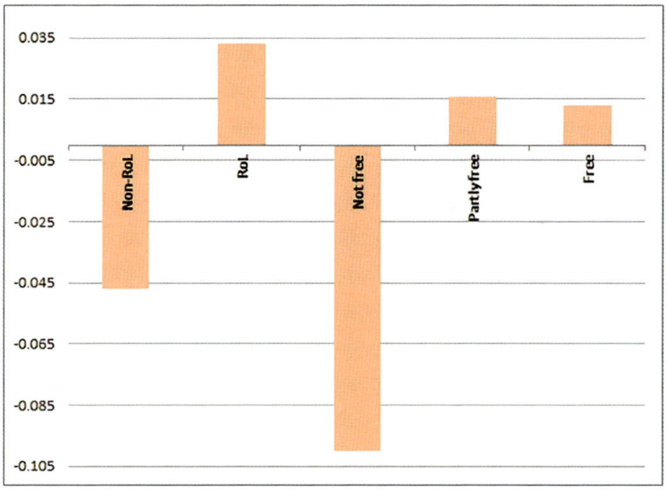

Source: Worldwide Governance Indicators; Freedom House.
Legend: non-RoL/RoL: countries with WGI "rule of law" scores below/above the sample median; not free/ partly free/ free – corresponding freedom status by Freedom House

Equilibrium

As we have proven in our previous work (Mungiu-Pippidi 2015), control of corruption is best described as an equilibrium between *opportunities (or resources)* for corruption, such as

---

[11] There are many types of ACA. We investigated those described in OECD 2008, the separate types as well as an aggregate of all definitions. In principle we consider an ACA just the type modelled after Singapore and Hong Kong, in other words a relatively autonomous prosecutorial agency.

natural resources, unconditional aid, lack of government transparency, administrative discretion and obstacles to trade, and *constraints*, such as legal (an autonomous judiciary and audit) and normative (by the media and civil society)[12]. Not only has each element high explanatory power of corruption in statistical regression models, but the statistical interactions between resources and constraints, between red tape and independence of the judiciary, between transparency in any form (fiscal, existence of a FOI, financial disclosures) and civil society activism or press freedom are highly significant. Using this model, a parsimonious composite index for public integrity for 105 countries was built by an ANTICORRP team based on policy determinants of control of corruption, which should be seen as the starting point of any country diagnosis, as it shows at a first glance where the balance goes wrong (see Figure 15).

Figure 15. Control of corruption as interaction between resources and constraints

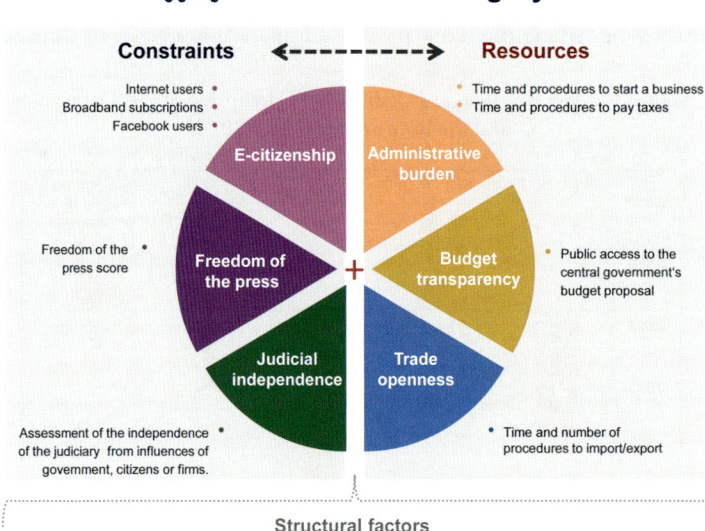

The explanations of stagnation across the EU aid recipient countries become evident if we check the elements of the IPI. From the six elements, we find progress in the non-political areas, such as broadband Internet connections (a component of the e-citizens indicator in the Index of Public Integrity), reduction of red tape for business creation and trading.

---

[12] For the full models, see *The Quest*, chapter 4, and Alina Mungiu-Pippidi and Ramin Dadasov, Measuring Control of Corruption by a New Index of Public Integrity, (*European Journal on Criminal Policy and Research*, 2016), 22.3: 415–438.

Figure 16. Governance evolution of countries with least and most aid compared

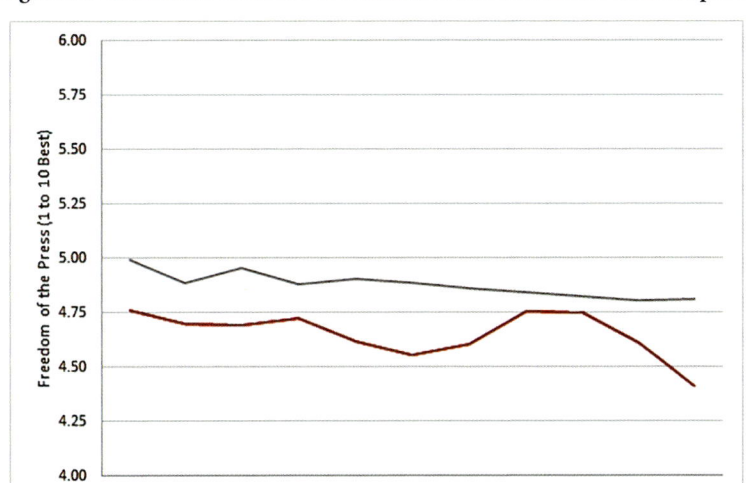

Sources: Freedom House – Freedom of the Press and OECD - QWIDS Official Development Aid

Figure 17. Evolution of recipients and non-recipients of anticorruption aid.

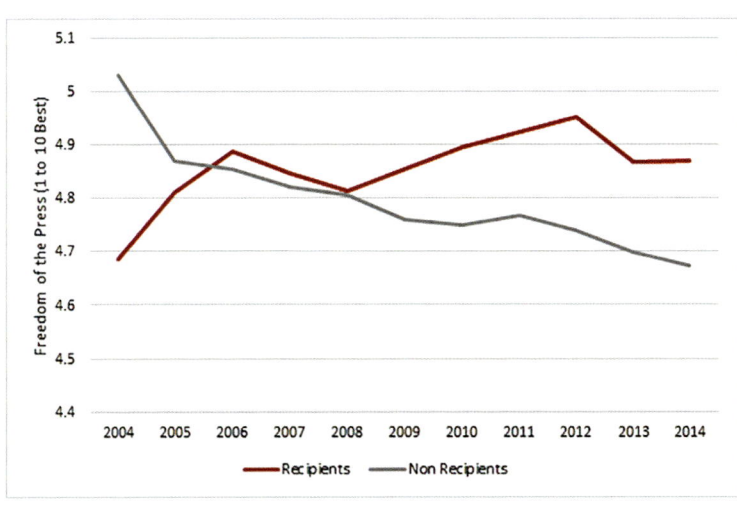

Sources: Freedom House – Freedom of the Press and OECD - QWIDS Official Development Aid. (Recipients N= +30, Non-Recipients N=+89)

Figure 18. Average trends in trading across borders and total ODA.

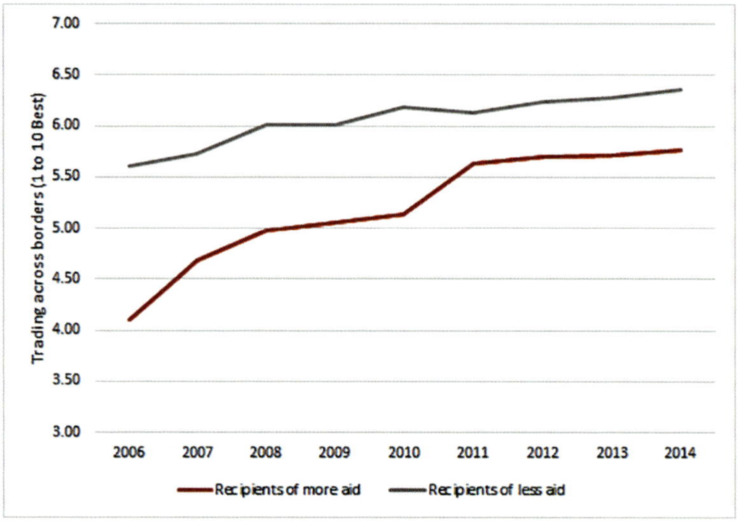

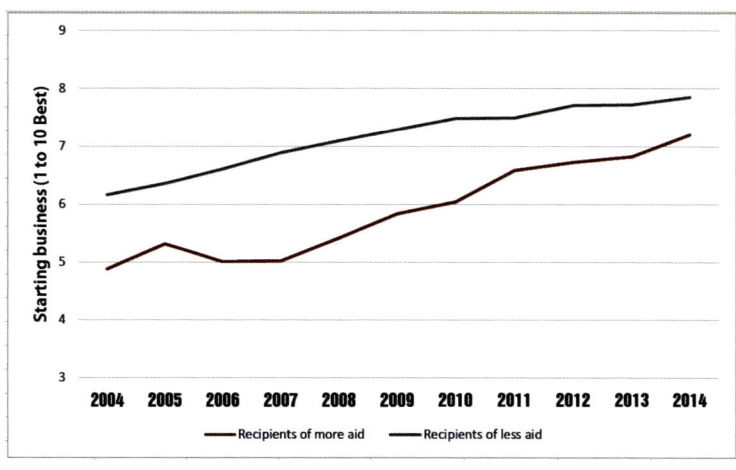

Sources: Doing Business Survey and OECD - QWIDS Official Development Aid

Figure 19. Average trends on starting business and total ODA.

Sources: Doing Business Survey and OECD - QWIDS Official Development Aid

Figures 16 to 19 show some selected components of the IPI across the two groups of aid recipients, below or above the mean. As aid recipients declined on average on both major constraints (legal independence of the judiciary) and normative (freedom of the press, where IPA and ODC countries are, in fact, regressing at alarming rates), and even at Broadband Subscriptions they drag behind less aid recipients (due to poorer original conditions), the resulting control of corruption cannot be expected to have made much progress. The little to be found is done on behalf of less political factors, such as red tape reduction and Internet connections expansion, which have been growing globally, but with no difference across aid groups. For judicial independence, only ODC seem to have progressed significantly. However, when checking for targeted aid's influence we find that countries receiving anticorruption aid finally do better on the average than those not receiving it on the perception of judicial independence and freedom of the press. **The focus on corruption in itself is positive, only the programmes seem not to impact corruption**.

Conclusions and policy options. What can and should the EU do?

EU total aid has led to an improvement of governance compared to bilateral aid from EU Member States, which has had no effect on governance for the large number of countries and the time interval studied here. EU targeted aid for good governance, however, failed to produce more improvement in control of corruption in aid recipients compared to non-aid recipients. By and large, even the positive effect of the total aid is so small that we do not have any success story, any country to have transitioned from institutionalised corruption to corruption is an exception in the past ten years. We find that many important determinants of control of corruption, which actually regressed in this interval, such as freedom of the press, are largely beyond EU control and are not even a target for EU aid, although the work of BBC Trust or other media-related development foundations provide some good models.

As chapters in the rest of this volume show, there is really no effective EU model working on the ground presently. Budget support conditionality has failed so far to create enough incentive, as other uncoordinated donors exist (see the Tanzania case); selected intermediates for targeted good governance work are not adequate and fail to create even modest developments (see the Egyptian case); strong repressive approaches put some people in jail but do not reduce corruption, risking instead to create anticorruption agencies which are not fully impartial and accountable (see the case of Romania); formal analyses in EU accession progress reports miss the political economy of a country and therefore the main story (the case of Turkey, where a state capture story has developed on EU watch entirely unreported, although it used classic capture means, such as control of economic rents); or by the time the lessons are learnt, the instruments are no longer adequate (Slovakia). Older cases, such as Spain, purposely included in this volume, shows that EU funds actually are themselves an important resource for corruption and fail to change local governance despite having other potentially beneficial effects.

The recommendations that we make to EU therefore are as follows:

Getting from a majority of corrupt transactions to a majority of clean ones requires long-term planning with the goal of building public integrity for the first time – a clear development goal- and not to punish deviation. In the same way that Millennium Development goals required coordination and common multi-year planning, the EU should take the initiative of bring all donors together for any serious plan to change governance. The joint planning of such efforts should start from sponsoring a diagnosis and some measurement by way of objective indicators, for instance, and continue through coordinated efforts to reduce resources and increase constraints. Such an approach also allows donors to diversify their efforts and avoid oversight, as some have strengths in civil society assistance, others in market development reforms, and others simply in spreading broadband. Finally, such a long-term plan (a basic departure point is how to improve on the six IPI components, for instance) has to be discussed with local civil society, journalists, mayors, reformers in government and anyone who can join a long-term coalition for change.

The process of assistance in itself should be an example of how governance should work. Aid recipients should qualify to receiving aid transfers (for instance in the case of budget support) by publishing all their calls for tenders and their results, which would allow for monitoring the percentage of transparent and competitive procurement from total or percentage of contracts going to one bidder. Why not make the full transparency of all aid recipients the main selection condition? Evolution or lack of evolution from one year to another could become feasible using such indicators. On top of this, using social accountability more decisively, for instance involving local pro-change groups in planning and audits of development aid projects, would also empower these groups and also set the example on how public spending should be monitored by local stakeholders.

References

Acemoglu, D. and Robinson, J. (2005). *Economic origins of dictatorship and democracy*. Cambridge: Cambridge University Press.

Acemoglu, D. and Robinson, J. (2012). *Why Nations Fail: The Origins of Power, Prosperity and Poverty*. New York: Crown Business.

Acemoglu, D. and Robinson, J. (2012). *Response to Fukuyama's Review* [blog] Available at: http://whynationsfail.com/blog/2012/4/30/response-to-fukuyamas-review.html

Dadašov, R. (2017). European Aid and Governance: Does the Source Matter? *The European Journal of Development Research*. R. Eur J Dev Res. doi:10.1057/ejdr.2016.16 pp 1–20.

Eisenstadt, S.N. and Roniger, L. (1984). *Patrons, Clients and Friends: Interpersonal Relations and the Structure of Trust in Society*. Cambridge: Cambridge University Press.

Fukuyama, F. (2012). Acemoglu and Robinson on Why Nations Fail. *American Interest* [online] Available at: http://www.the-american-interest.com/2012/03/26/acemoglu-and-robinson-on-why-nations-fail/

Fukuyama, F. (2014). *Political order and political decay*. New York: Farrar, Straus and Giroux.

Hofstede, G. (1999). Problems remain, but theories will change: The universal and the specific in 21st-century global management. *Organizational dynamics*, 28(1), pp. 34–44.

Husted, B. W. (1999). Wealth, culture, and corruption. *Journal of International Business Studies,* 3(2), pp. 339–59.

Hout, W. (2013). Normative power vs. political interest: EU aid selectivity beyond the European consensus on development, 2008–13. Paper presented at the European International Studies Associations 8th Pan-European Conference on International Relations, Warsaw, 18–21 September 2013.

Kaufman, D., Kraay, A. and Zoido-Lobatón, P. (1999). Aggregating Governance Indicators. World Bank Policy Research Working Paper No. 2195.

Kaufmann, D. and Vicente, P.C. (2011). Legal Corruption. *Economics and Politics*, 23, pp. 195–219.

Kersting, E. and C. Kilby (2014). Aid and democracy redux. *European Economic Review* 67: 125–143.

Klitgaard, R. (2014). *Addressing Corruption Together.* [online] Paris: OECD. Available at: https://www.oecd.org/dac/governance-peace/publications/FINAL%20Addressing%20corruption%20together.pdf

Mungiu-Pippidi, A. (2006). Corruption: Diagnosis and Treatment. *Journal of Democracy*, 17, pp. 86–99.

———. (2011). Contextual choices in fighting corruption: Lessons learned. *Norwegian Agency for Development Cooperation*.

———. (2015). *The Quest for Good governance: How Societies Develop Control of Corruption*. Cambridge: Cambridge University Press.

North, D., Wallis, J. and Weingast, B. (2009). *Violence and Social Orders: A Conceptual Framework for Interpreting Recorded Human History*. Cambridge: Cambridge University Press.

OECD. (2014). Query Wizsachd for International Development Statistics. Organisation for Economic Co-operation and Development. Paris: OECD.

Parsons, T. (1968). *The Structure of Social Action*. New York: Free Press.

———. (1997). *Introduction to Max Weber. The Theory of Social and Economic Organization*. New York: The Free Press.

Pritchett, L. and Woolcock, M. (2004). Solutions when the Solution is the Problem: Arraying the Disarray in Development. *World Development*, 32(2), pp. 191–212.

Treisman, D. (2007). What have we learned about the causes of corruption from ten years of cross-national empirical research?. *Annu. Rev. Polit. Sci.*, *10*, 211–244.

Uslaner, E. M. and Rothstein, B. (2016). The Historical Roots of Corruption: State Building, Economic Inequality, and Mass Education. *Comparative Politics*, 48(2), pp. 227–48.

Wallis, J. (1989). Towards a positive economic theory of institutional change. *Journal of Institutional and Theoretical Economics (JITE)/Zeitschrift für die gesamte Staatswissenschaft*, pp. 98–112.

Weber, Max. (1981). *General Economic History*. New Brunswick, NJ: Transaction Books (originally published in English in 1927).

World Bank. (2014a). World Governance Indicators. Washington: World Bank.

———. (2014b). World Development Indicators. Washington: World Bank.

Wright, J. and M. Winters. (2010). The politics of effective foreign aid. *Annual Review of Political Science*, 13: 61–80.

Appendix A

Table A: Glossary

Variable or Term	Description and Source
ACP	African, Caribbean, and Pacific Countries. (instrument)
ECA	Europe and Central Asia regional group
ENP	European Neighbourhood Partnership (instrument)
GNI	Gross National Income
HIC	High Income Countries (WB classification)[2]
IPA	Instrument for Pre-accession (instrument)
LAC	Latin America and Caribbean regional group
LIC	Low Income Countries (WB classification)
LMIC	Low Middle Income Countries (WB classification)
MADCT	More Advanced Developing Countries (WB classification)
MENA	Middle East and North Africa
ODA	Official Development Aid
ODC	Other Developing Countries (instrument)
SAsia	South Asia regional group
SSAfrica	Sub-Saharan Africa regional group
UMIC	Upper Middle Income Countries (WB classification)

Table B: Instrument Grouping

Instrument	Countries
African, Caribbean, and Pacific (ACP)	Angola, Barbados, Belize, Benin, Botswana, Burkina Faso, Burundi, Cabo Verde, Cameroon, Central African Republic, Chad, Comoros, Congo (Republic of), Côte d'Ivoire, Cuba, Djibouti, Dominican Republic, Equatorial Guinea, Eritrea, Ethiopia, Fiji, Gabon, Gambia, Ghana, Guinea, Guinea-Bissau, Guyana, Haiti, Jamaica, Kenya, Lesotho, Liberia, Madagascar, Malawi, Mali, Mauritania, Mauritius, Mozambique, Namibia, Niger, Nigeria, Papua New Guinea, Rwanda, Samoa, Senegal, Sierra Leone, Somalia, South Africa, South Sudan, Sudan, Suriname, Swaziland, Tanzania, Timor-Leste, Togo, Trinidad & Tobago, Uganda, Vanuatu, Zambia, Zimbabwe
European Neighbourhood Policy (ENP)	Algeria, Armenia, Azerbaijan, Belarus, Egypt, Georgia, Jordan, Lebanon, Libya, Moldova, Morocco, Syria, Tunisia, Ukraine, West Bank & Gaza Strip
Instrument for Pre-Accession Assistance (IPA)	Albania, Bosnia-Herzegovina, Macedonia FYRO, Kosovo, Montenegro, Serbia, Turkey
Other Developing Countries (ODC)	Afghanistan, Argentina, Bangladesh, Bhutan, Bolivia, Brazil, Cambodia, Chile, China PR, Colombia, Costa Rica, Korea DR, Ecuador, El Salvador, Guatemala, Honduras, India, Indonesia, Iran, Iraq, Kazakhstan, Kyrgyz Republic, Laos, Malaysia, Maldives, Mexico, Mongolia, Myanmar, Nepal, Nicaragua, Pakistan, Panama, Paraguay, Peru, Philippines, Sri Lanka, Tajikistan, Thailand, Turkmenistan, Uruguay, Uzbekistan, Venezuela, Vietnam, Yemen

Table C: Regional Grouping[13]

Instrument	Countries
East Asia and Pacific (EAP)	Cambodia, China PR, Korea DR, Fiji, Indonesia, Laos, Malaysia, Mongolia, Myanmar, Papua New Guinea, Philippines, Samoa, Thailand, Timor-Leste, Vanuatu
Europe and Central Asia (ECA)	Albania, Armenia, Azerbaijan, Belarus, Bosnia and Herzegovina, Macedonia FYR, Georgia, Kazakhstan, Kosovo, Kyrgyz Republic, Moldova, Montenegro, Serbia, Tajikistan, Turkey, Turkmenistan, Ukraine, Uzbekistan
Latin America and Caribbean (LAC)	Argentina, Barbados, Belize, Bolivia, Brazil, Chile, Colombia, Costa Rica, Cuba, Dominican Republic, Ecuador, El Salvador, Guatemala, Guyana, Haiti, Honduras, Jamaica, Mexico, Nicaragua, Panama, Paraguay, Peru, Suriname, Trinidad and Tobago, Uruguay, Venezuela
Middle East and North Africa (MENA)	Algeria, Djibouti, Egypt, Iran, Iraq, Jordan, Lebanon, Libya, Morocco, Syrian Arab Republic, Tunisia, West Bank and Gaza, Yemen
South Asia (SA)	Afghanistan, Bangladesh, Bhutan, India, Maldives, Nepal, Pakistan, Sri Lanka
Sub-Saharan Africa (SSA)	Angola, Benin, Botswana, Burkina Faso, Burundi, Cabo Verde, Cameroon, Central African Republic, Chad, Comoros, Congo Rep, Côte d'Ivoire, Congo DR, Equatorial Guinea, Eritrea, Ethiopia, Gabon, Gambia, Ghana, Guinea, Guinea-Bissau, Kenya, Lesotho, Liberia, Madagascar, Malawi, Mali, Mauritania, Mauritius, Mozambique, Namibia, Niger, Nigeria, Rwanda, Senegal, Sierra Leone, Somalia, South Africa, South Sudan, Sudan, Swaziland, Tanzania, Togo, Uganda, Zambia, Zimbabwe

---

[13] http://data.worldbank.org/country

1. EU Democracy Promotion, Conditionality and Judicial Autonomy

SIMONE DIETRICH[1]

Over the past two decades, the European Union has become a central actor in the promotion of democracy in its neighbourhood and across the world. Since the 1990s the EU has explicitly established democratic change as a central goal of its development cooperation. Of the many outcomes associated with democratic change, the EU has embraced the export of the rule of law as primary objective. This study investigates the effectiveness of EU efforts to strengthen rule of law. We evaluate the link between EU conditionality attached to economic aid flows and judicial autonomy and government behaviour towards the judiciary, alongside the EU's direct investment promoting these outcomes. Using a global sample of EU aid-receiving countries for the period from 1991 to 2010, we show that economic aid from the EU appears to increase judicial autonomy through the mechanism of judicial reforms. We also find that EU conditionality does not improve government compliance with higher court orders. Rather, it is associated with an increase in ad hoc attacks of courts. These findings have implications for how the EU allocates aid and pursues the promotion of the rule of law in developing countries.

Introduction

Since the end of the Cold War, a consensus in the international donor community argues that democracy and good governance is an integral part of development efforts. Over the last decades, donor focus on bringing about free and fair elections has shifted towards a more varied embrace of democratic norms, including democratic accountability, human rights, transparency and the rule of law (Elster and Slagstad 1993, Linz and Stepan 1996, Maravall and Przeworski 2003, Baylies and Szeftel 1997, O'Donnell 1998). Efforts to promote democratic deepening have emphasised the importance of the rule of law for democratic stability and consolidation (Carothers 1998, 4), with judicial reform assuming a central place in donor efforts to democratise the justice system (Wright, Dietrich and Ariotti 2017). Examples of judicial reforms include, for instance, the democratisation of the judicial selection processes by opening the size of the selection committee to a larger number of actors that get a vote in the appointment of judges to courts (Driscoll and Nelson 2012, 2015). The EU has been the most vocal and consistent donor in support of using foreign aid to engineer institutional change in the judiciary sector of countries in its neighbourhood but also around the world. Notably, the EU has formalised its commitment to democracy and governance promotion in various treaties, as evidenced in the Treaty of Maastricht (1992) and the EU's Common Foreign and Security Policy (Lavenex and Schimmelfennig 2011). And, using its foreign aid budget, the EU has sought to advance judicial reform primarily through political conditionality.[2]

---

[1] Senior Lecturer of Government, University of Essex, dietrich.simone@gmail.com
[2] More broadly, Lavenex and Schimmelfennig (2011) discuss the multiple mechanisms through which the EU promotes democracy and governance abroad

Political conditionality as a means of engineering institutional reform uses foreign aid flows as leverage. In return for aid, the EU requires countries to pursue institutional reforms and/or policy changes as explicitly set out in conditions attached to foreign aid (Lavenex and Schimmelfennig 2011, Dietrich and Wright 2015). Although the objectives of political conditionality vary, support among members of the EU is strongest and most consistent for promoting rule of law and state administrative capacity abroad.[3] Judicial reform consistently and prominently features in conditions attached to foreign aid, as judicial autonomy is a core founding principle in the EU's legal order.[4] Simultaneously the EU directly invests in judicial autonomy in developing countries through aid activities whose goal is to promote judicial reform and capacity. These direct investments often involve EU-based experts who provide technical assistance in the implementation of judicial aid projects. To date, however, little systematic evidence exists that shows that EU efforts in promoting institutional reform are successful. This chapter sheds light on EU efforts. Specifically, it examines how economic aid from the EU may influence judicial institutions and government behaviour vis- à-vis courts through conditions. We also examine how direct investment in the judiciary sector through specific aid projects influences the same outcomes. We are particularly interested in the efficacy of EU economic or judicial aid on judicial reform. This is because, once implemented, reforms are difficult to dismantle and should therefore be a "desirable" outcome from the donors' point of view.

Using a sample of 116 EU aid-eligible countries between 1991 and 2010 we find that EU conditionality can promote judicial reform in aid-receiving countries on average. However, it appears to lack the power to persuade incumbent governments to turn against courts when it is politically expedient for them. We also find that EU conditionality works better among recipient countries whose dependency on EU aid is higher.

EU conditionality, direct investment and judicial autonomy

Among foreign aid donors, the EU has become a particularly powerful force in development cooperation. Between 1990 and 2012, foreign aid coming out of the EU budget has increased more than two-fold. Historically, the EU has paid strong attention to developments in democracy and governance when dealing with countries in its neighbourhood (Mungiu-Pippidi 2012, Balknir and Aknur 2015). In particular, the EU has insisted on the autonomy, impartiality, and efficiency of the judiciary not only for candidate countries for accession but for its aid recipients around the world. For instance, in the 2008 Accession Partnership agreement with Croatia,[5] judicial reform was a priority, and continued to feature prominently in conditions attached to economic aid as well as in direct investment in the judicial sector through EU-funded projects.[6] Outside of the Eastern European accession context, the EU has also assumed global leadership in promoting judicial autonomy in Armenia and Georgia (Kostayan 2015, 141). In Ethiopia the EU has demanded improvements in judicial autonomy via aid conditionality and also serves as the biggest contributor to the Ethiopian judiciary: in the context of the Public Sector Capacity-Building Program (PSCAP 2005–2012), a multi-donor initiative, the EU supported activities to reform the justice system and has supported a training centre for judges and prosecutors (Del Biondo 2015). In Tunisia the EU has heavily invested in the modernisation of the judicial

---
[3] See Wetzel and Orbie (2015) for a discussion of the "out-put" oriented nature of EU democracy promotion
[4] See e.g., Sen (2012)
[5] Council of the European Union 2008, cited on p. 89
[6] For examples and in-depth discussion of judicial reform projects in Croatia see Balknir and Aknur (2015, 101)

system in recent years (Reynaert 2015, 157). These anecdotes serve to illustrate the prominence of the judiciary sector in the EU's democracy- and governance-promotion efforts.

Among the various tactics for promoting democracy and governance abroad, the EU's most frequently employed tactic is political conditionality. In intergovernmental negotiations, the EU uses economic resources in the form of development assistance as leverage to incentivise institutional reform. The argument behind this tactic focuses on the relationship between donor and aid- receiving governments. By specifying institutional reform outcomes or behavioural changes on the part of the government through conditions attached to foreign aid packages the EU leverages its economic prowess from the outside to encourage change within countries. It requires incumbent governments to adopt the requested reforms or policies as a prerequisite to receiving economic assistance from the EU. In addition to conditionality, the EU directly invests in the judicial sector through the mechanism of technical assistance. For instance, the EU's 'technical assistance for institutional strengthening of the ministry of justice' aims to improve key legal arrangements governing relations between the judiciary, the government, businesses and citizens. It also improves the efficiency, transparency and access to justice in Jordan, for example.

The focus on judicial reform in the EU's use of conditionality stems, in part, from its centrality in the EU's legal order. It also arises from the recognition that problematic judicial systems can be obstacles to good governance, democratic accountability, human rights and transparency. They can also be obstacles to a country's economic development. As a solid body of research shows, judicial autonomy is positively associated with economic growth.[7] The link between judicial autonomy and development matters insofar as aid-receiving governments view judicial autonomy as a means to promote development. If developing countries have at least some domestic incentive to promote judicial autonomy to improve the investment climate, we would expect EU efforts to be even more successful because domestic interests and political conditionality overlap, as has been argued by Schimmelfennig, Boerzel and other scholars.

However, the pursuit of judicial autonomy is a complex area for external policy intervention. Below we present three different empirical investigations that explore different outcomes associated with judicial autonomy and the circumstances in which EU conditionality is more likely to succeed in its goals: First, we investigate whether EU conditionality is associated with any improvements in the independence of courts from government interference across EU aid-receiving countries. Second, we examine the extent to which governments comply with court orders by assessing the government's implementation of court orders. Third, we investigate whether EU conditionality discourages governments from undertaking verbal attacks and purges of courts when it is politically expedient for them.

Data and analysis

The period of our sample (1991–2010) covers the first two decades after the end of the Cold War. During this period, the EU increasingly implemented political conditionality in an effort to promote democracy and good governance abroad. Further, the EU continually increased

---

[7] This association could be based on enhanced property rights protection of investment or lower transaction costs of capital investment, among others. See (Haggard and Tiede, 2011) for an excellent review of the literature evaluating judicial autonomy and economic growth and development.

economic assistance both within its neighbourhood and around the rest of the world. The sample includes 116 aid eligible countries with populations over 1 million (in 2009).[8]

Data on judicial autonomy. Drawing on the Varieties of Democracy (VDem) data set (Coppedge et al., 2016), we look at the efficacy of EU economic aid and judicial aid on judicial institutions and government behaviour towards the judiciary. To measure judicial institutions we use a linear combination of the judicial reform and review indicators to test our prediction about institutional reform; we call this variable *Institutions*. To model government behaviour towards the courts, we combine information from four variables that measure direct government treatment of the courts (attack, pack and purge the courts) and whether the government complies with court decisions. We call the latter variable *Behaviour*. Higher values of these two variables indicate better outcomes, meaning progress towards more autonomous judicial institutions and less government meddling in the operation of the courts, respectively. Combining information from all six raw variables from VDem (reform, review, attack, pack, purge and compliance) yields a final variable, which we call *Aggregate*. In the main reported set of models, we test separate equations for each of the three theoretically important variables: *Institutions*, *Behaviour*, and *Aggregate*.

Aid data. To assess the effects of EU aid, we examine both economic assistance and democracy aid. The former captures the conditionality argument. The latter is used to invest directly in the judicial sector (Wright, Dietrich and Ariotti 2017). We estimate the conditional correlation between economic assistance and judicial outcomes while accounting for the independent effect of democracy aid. We use foreign aid commitment data from AidData 2.1.[9] We aggregate foreign aid commitments by the EU at the recipient-country-year level, and stay at the highest level of aggregation, subsuming a range of different foreign aid sectors to be captured by EU aid flows, including aid for the social sector, economic infrastructure and services, domestic production, environment, commodity aid, debt relief and budget support. These categories comprise economic assistance. Democracy and governance aid (DGA) includes projects that directly target policy planning in areas such as fiscal and monetary policy, institutional capacity building and structural reform. DGA also finances tax assessment procedures, legal and judicial development as well as constitutional development. We measure EU foreign aid as the logged value of the lagged two-year moving average of constant dollar economic assistance.[10]

---

[8] The sample is derived from Geddes, Wright and Frantz (2014). We exclude all cases where the country is not classified as either a democracy or a dictatorship. Therefore, this excludes cases of state failure (e.g., Somalia after the fall of Siad Barre) and foreign occupation (e.g., Lebanon before the withdrawal of Syrian troops and Afghanistan and Iraq during U.S. occupation.

[9] Data downloaded from http://aiddata.org/aiddata-research-releases on 2.27.15

[10] EU Aid is: $\ln\left(\frac{EU\ A_{t-1} + EU\ A_{t-2}}{2}\right)$ where EUA is constant dollar EU economic aid commitments per capita. The moving average specification enables us to smooth over annual variation.

Figure 1

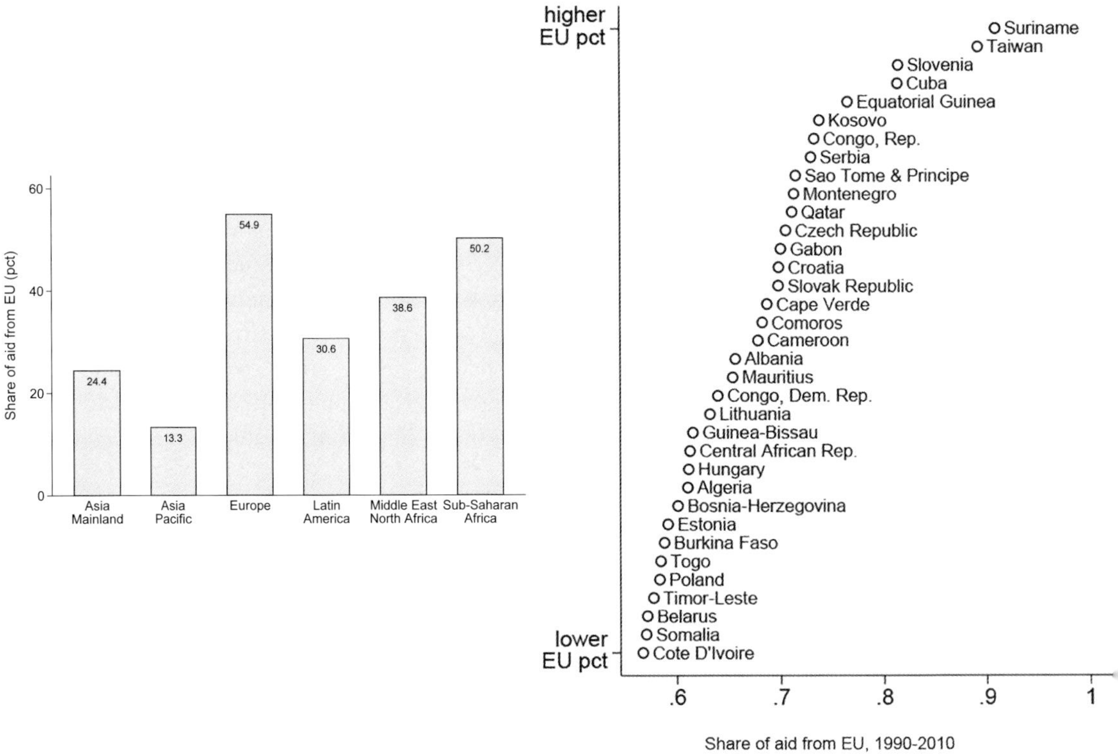

Share of aid from EU, 1990-2010

The left panel of Figure 1 shows the EU's share of total aid, by geographic region. More than half of the aid flowing to Europe and sub-Saharan Africa during this period comes from the EU, while less than a quarter of aid goes to Asian countries. The right panel shows the recipient countries with the highest share of aid from the EU. This list is comprised mostly of European countries and countries with strong colonial ties to France (e.g., Algeria, Côte d'Ivoire, Equatorial Guinea and Gabon) as well as countries where the US has few diplomatic ties (Cuba, Somalia), or where the EU provides security assistance rather than economic aid (Qatar, Taiwan).

Control variables

In the models reported below, we include a series of control variables. We use three control variables to account for domestic political conditions that may influence the judiciary in aid-receiving countries: a binary variable of *democracy* from Geddes, Wright and Frantz (2014); a variable measuring whether there has been a successful *coup* in the observation year or the prior year, from Powell (2012); and a variable that measures how long the current political regime has been in power, *duration*, from Geddes, Wright and Frantz (2014). Further, elections can influence the receipt of aid and perceptions of judicial institutions and the government's relationship with courts. We therefore include indicators of whether a multiparty executive election (*multi-party*) occurs in a particular election and whether the election was boycotted by the opposition (*boycott*).[11] Further, we account for the time since the last constitution (*legal system*) was written to capture the fact that aid poured into countries re-writing constitutions and holding first multiparty elections in the early 1990s. Finally, we control for foreign aid from other donor countries, *non-EU aid*. We view these variables as potentially confounding the relationship between EU foreign aid and judicial outcomes. To ensure that our selection of control variables is not driving our reported results, we offer evidence from a battery of tests that exclude control variables and include additional potential confounders, such as economic growth, GDP per capita and population size.

Estimation

We begin with a random effects linear model. Importantly, the cross-sectional unit is the regime-case from Geddes, Wright and Frantz (2014). This means that the disturbances across units stem from differences in particular regimes. In many countries, such as Botswana, a stable regime-case persists across the 20-year sample period and modelling the regime-case is no different than treating the unit as the country. In other countries, however, there can be distinct regime-cases at different points during the sample period. For example, when Kabila's rebels ousted the Mobutu regime in DRC-Congo (formerly Zaire) in 1997, a new regime took power. In 2005, mass protests toppled the Akayev regime in Kyrgyzstan, and a new government took its place. And in 1994, Rwandan Patriotic Front (RPF) rebels ousted an autocratic regime in power for nearly two decades. In these instances, each country has more than one regime during the sample period.

Modelling the regime-effect is important in this application because the outcome variables are based on expert judgment. Treating the regime-case as the appropriate cross-section unit allows the model to pick up systematic differences across regimes in expert evaluations, thus anchoring subjective assessments about judicial outcomes in regime-specific contexts. While we report estimates from random-effects models, we find similar results when using fixed effects. Further, the random-effects model estimates a coefficient for *Democracy*, which is subsumed in a regime-case fixed effect. The specification is:

$$J_{i,t} = \alpha_{j[i]} + \beta_1 EU\ Aid_{i,t-1:t-2} + \beta_3 X_{i,t-1} + \eta_t + \varepsilon_{i,t} \quad (1)$$

where $J_{i,t}$ is one of three judicial outcome variables (*Aggregate, Institutions, Behaviour*), *EU Aid*$_{i,-1:t-2}$ is the lagged two-year moving average of per capita EU aid, $X_{i,t-1}$ is a set of covariate (including EU democracy aid and non-EU economic assistance), and η_t are year fixed effects. $\varepsilon_{i,t}$ is an error term ($\varepsilon_{i,t} \sim N(0, \sigma^2)$) and $\alpha_{j[i]}$ are the random effects ($\alpha_{j[i]} \sim N(\mu_\alpha, \infty)$). Figures report errors clustered on the aid-receiving regime-case.

Results

Figure 2 shows the results from three separate models, each with a different outcome variable. The top estimate in each cluster, shown with bullets (•), is from a model that uses the combined measure of judicial outcomes, *Aggregate*, which subsumes both institutions and government behaviour measures. While the estimate for EU *Economic aid*, capturing EU conditionality, is positive (0.014), it is not statistically significant. Similarly, the estimate for EU

---

[11] These variables are drawn from NELDA.

Democracy aid, capturing direct investment in the judiciary, is small and statistically insignificant. Democracies and multiparty elections are associated with better aggregate judicial outcomes, while boycotted elections and coups are associated with worse outcomes. Finally, there is a positive correlation between non-EU economic aid and aggregate judicial outcomes.

Results from the *Institutions* model are shown with bullets (•). The estimate for EU *Economic aid* is positive (0.035) and statistically significant, while the estimate for EU *Democracy aid* is negative. The positive estimate for economic aid suggests that EU conditionality is associated with institutional reform in the judicial sector. The negative estimate for democracy aid suggests a negative association between direct investments in judicial reform, though the estimate is not statistically significant. Last, estimates for both types of EU aid are statistically insignificant in the *Behaviour* model, shown with plus signs (+).

The result linking EU economic assistance to better judicial institutions in recipient countries is fairly robust. We consistently find a positive and statistically significant estimate for this variable when we: model fixed effects (0.030); drop control variables; add control variables (GDP per capita, population size and economic growth); or model the time trend in various ways (period effects, non-linear trend, decade effect). Further, the estimate remains positive and significant when we control for *Behaviour* (0.033), which ensures that the estimated effect is not due to different types of judicial outcomes being positively correlated with one another. Finally, replication files show the *Institutions* finding is mostly due to judicial reform (0.053), not judicial review (0.028).

Of course, empirical work on aid and judicial autonomy faces concerns of possible endogeneity bias because donors may send more aid to countries that have greater levels of judicial autonomy. For example, the EU's strategy may be to increase aid to recipient governments they believe are most likely to implement judicial reform. This would mean that the empirical pattern linking aid to judicial autonomy is the result of strategic selection and not the result of buying political reform.

Figure 2

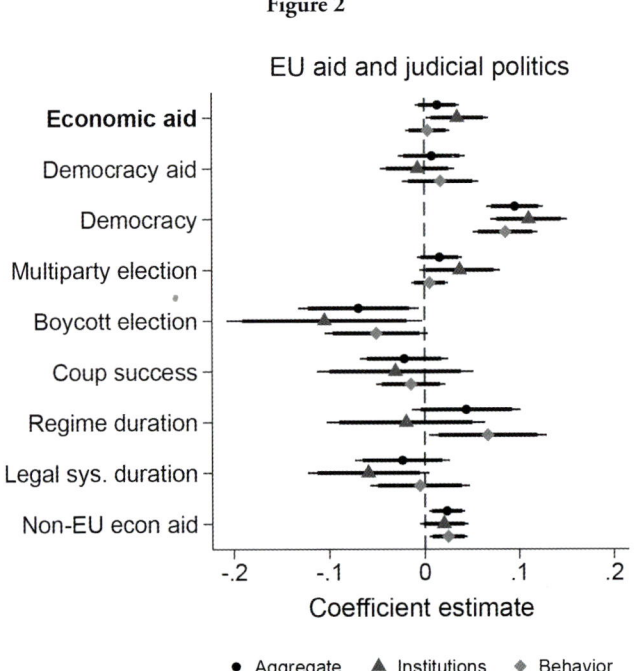

EU aid and judicial politics

While we have taken initial steps to mitigate against possible endogeneity bias in this paper we are unable to rule it out completely. However, in a related paper (Wright, Dietrich and Ariotti, 2017), we employ information about unemployment in donor countries to capture variation in economic aid. This approach relies on previous findings in the literature that difficult economic times in donor countries lead to decreases in foreign aid commitments. We find that foreign aid promotes judicial reform but is not systematically associated with changes in government behaviour toward courts.

Leverage

Results in the last section indicate that EU economic assistance is positively correlated with better judicial institutions but not improved government behaviour towards the judiciary. We believe that this differential effect of aid on the two judicial outcomes results, in part, from the fact that some outcomes are easier to monitor for donors. For instance, institutional changes are relatively easy to monitor and verify, as they are often publicly discussed in parliaments and reported by the media. Governmental behaviour towards the judiciary, on the other hand, is more difficult to monitor. For example, incumbent governments may undermine judicial autonomy by ordering politically expedient ad hoc attacks on courts. Such attacks are more difficult to monitor systematically and likely more difficult to verify. Further, we find that the statistical association between EU aid and judicial institutions runs through economic assistance and not democracy aid. Because the former does not directly fund activities related to the judiciary but the latter often does, the findings are more consistent with the conditionality mechanism than the investment mechanism.

We then turn to examine how the positive effect of EU economic aid on judicial reform varies by how much leverage the EU has over the aid-receiving country. If EU leverage over the recipient is greater we would expect the effects of EU economic aid to be stronger than when leverage is less. To measure leverage, we employ information on each recipient country's geographic distance from Europe, level of economic development and economic size.[12] These variables measure two concepts related to donor leverage over the recipient. Geographic proximity captures both a determinant of bilateral trade, namely distance, as well as the leverage that stems from being in the same region. To further capture the close proximity of European countries that are either current EU members or prospective members (excluding Russia), we log the (inverse) distance variable twice to increase the distance weight for European countries. This latter feature captures the special migration and investment connections between EU donors and governments in this region. Second, the size of the economic market ($ln(GDP)$) and relative economic development ($GDP\ pc$) are proxies for governments' vulnerability to external economic pressure: governments in countries with larger markets and higher wealth should be less vulnerable to external economic pressure in the form of aid conditionality (Levitsky and Way n.d.).

Note that this conceptualisation of leverage does not include the extent to which recipients are dependent on EU aid *relative to other Western aid*. Thus information about strategic competition between Western donors that recipients might use to subvert compliance with aid conditions is not used to measure leverage, at least as conceptualised here. We believe this is an

---

[12] The leverage variable is calculated as the inverse of GDP per capita multiplied by logged distance from Brussels (Belgium) and logged economic size This formula weights GDP per capita more than distance and economic size.

accurate assumption because substantial evidence suggests that Western donors, including EU donors, increasingly coordinate aid-related activities within recipient countries, thus undercutting the potential for recipient governments to use competition between Western donors as a wedge to avoid complying with aid conditions.

Figure 3

Figure 3 shows the average level of leverage for each recipient country in the sample, ordered from highest leverage in the left plot to lowest leverage in the right plot. Poor countries with small economies are over-represented in the high-medium leverage plot, along with smaller and poorer European countries, such as Albania, Armenia and Moldova. Oil-rich countries in the Middle East and North Africa as well as most of Latin America and the middle-income countries of East

Asia are in the medium-low leverage plot on the right. Wealthier sub-Saharan African countries, such as Botswana, Namibia and South Africa, also have low leverage levels.

Figure 4

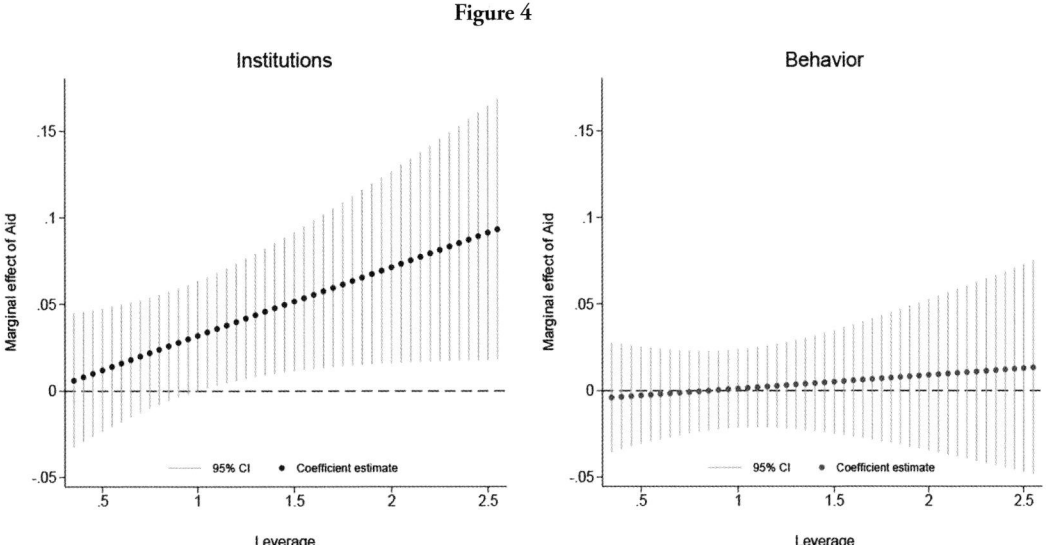

The left panel of Figure 4 shows the result from a test of the leverage idea for *Institutions*. Recall that the average correlation – or estimated marginal effect – across all levels of leverage (from the test reported in Figure 2) is 0.035. At low levels of leverage, roughly 0.5 on the horizontal axis, the estimated marginal effect is 0.011 and not statistically significant. However, at the median level of leverage (1.2), the estimated effect is 0.041 and statistically significant, while at high leverage (2.4) the estimate is 0.089. Thus the estimated marginal effect of EU economic assistance on judicial institutions is increasing when the leverage donors have over recipients is high, at least according to this measure. The right plot shows the results from the *Behaviour* model. The estimated effect is close to zero and not statistically significant at any level of leverage, suggesting that the effect of EU conditionality on government behaviour towards courts is not conditional on the leverage of the donor.

Conclusion

Consistent with other research, this study confirms that EU foreign aid can play a role in shaping institutions in other countries. We show that economic aid from the EU is positively associated, at a statistically significant level, with judicial reform. The mechanism of EU influence on the judiciary is one of political conditionality, with donor governments exerting pressure on recipient governments to promote autonomy of courts via institutional reform. On the other hand, the EU's direct investment in the judiciary via democracy-promotion projects is not associated with systematic increases in judicial autonomy.

As we would expect, our results show that political conditionality is more successful when donors hold more leverage in aid-receiving countries. Across all EU aid-receiving countries we find that donors demands for greater judicial autonomy are more likely to be implemented when the leverage of donors on the recipient government is great, as is the case when alternative resources are relatively low. However, our results also suggest that EU economic aid is positively but not systematically associated with greater levels of compliance with court decisions by incumbent governments. This suggests that incumbent governments will act outside of expectations set out by EU conditionality when it is politically expedient. This finding is consistent with research by Wright, Dietrich and Ariotti (2017) which shows that, during election periods with uncertainty about the outcome of the election, incumbent governments will attempt purges and attacks on courts to strengthen their position. The findings also show that greater leverage of the EU over the recipient government does not translate into improved government behaviour. Even at high levels of leverage, EU economic aid fails to translate into systematic improvements according to our measures of government compliance with court orders or behaviour towards courts.

While the fate of a country's judiciary sector ultimately lies in the hands of its own citizens, this study shows that the EU still has substantive influence in bringing about judicial reform, especially when recipient government access to resources is constrained. Yet, the EU's influence appears to be more limited in ensuring that recipient governments act consistently with judicial autonomy principles when it comes to compliance towards courts. After all, an autonomous judiciary provides checks on the recipient government and may at times be threatening to the government's political survival. The effect is that, no matter the aid circumstances, recipient governments generally do maintain some interest in exerting control over the judiciary.

References

Balknir, Canan and Muge Aknur. (2015). Comparing Country Cases: Output-Oriented EU Democracy Promotion. *The Substance of EU Democracy Promotion: Concepts and Cases*, eds. Anne Wetzel and Jan Orbie. London: Palgrave Macmillan.

Baylies, Carolyn and Morris Szeftel. (1997). The 1996 Zambian elections: Still awaiting democratic consolidation. *Review of African Political Economy* 24(71):113–128.

Carothers, Thomas. (1998). The Rule of Law Revival. *Foreign Affairs*.

Coppedge, Michael, et al. (2016). V-Dem [Country- Year/Country-Date] Dataset v6. *Varieties of Democracy (V-Dem) Project*.

Del Biondo, Karen. (2015) Comparing Country Cases: Output-Oriented EU Democracy Promotion. *The Substance of EU Democracy Promotion: Concepts and Cases*, eds. Anne Wetzel and Jan Orbie. London: Palgrave Macmillan.

Dietrich Simone and Joseph Wright. (2015) Foreign Aid Allocation tactics and Democratic Change in Africa. *Journal of Politics*, 77(1):216–234.

Driscoll, Amanda and Michael J. Nelson. (2012). The 2011 judicial elections in Bolivia. *Electoral Studies*, 31(3):628–632.

———. (2015). Judicial Selection and the Democratization of Justice: Lessons from the Bolivian Judicial Elections. Journal of Law and Courts, 3(1):115–148.

Elster, Jon and Run Slagstad (1993). *Constitutionalism and Democracy*. Cambridge: Cambridge University Press.

Geddes, Barbara, Joseph Wright and Erica Frantz. (2014). Autocratic Breakdown and Regime Transitions: A New Data Set. *Perspectives on Politics*, 12(2):313–331.

Haggard, Stephan and Lydia Tiede. (2011). The Rule of Law and Economic Growth: Where are We?" *World Development*, 39(5):673–685.

Kostayan, Hrant. (2015). Comparing Country Cases: Output-Oriented EU Democracy Promotion. *The Substance of EU Democracy Promotion: Concepts and Cases*, eds. Anne Wetzel and Jan Orbie. London: Palgrave Macmillan.

Lavenex, Sandra and Frank Schimmelfennig. (2011). EU Democracy Promotion in the Neighborhood: From Leverage to Governance. *Democratization*, 18(4):885–909.

Levitsky, Steven and Lucan Way. (Forthcoming). *Comparative Politics*.

Linz, Juan J. and Alfred Stepan. (1996). *Problems of Democratic Transition and Consolidation: Southern Europe, South America, and Post-Communist Europe*. Baltimore: The Johns Hopkins University.
Maravall, Jose Maria and Adam Przeworski. (2003). *Courts and Power in Latin America and Africa*. Cambridge: Cambridge University Press.
Mungiu-Pippidi, Alina. (2012). The Transformative Power of Europe Revisited. *Journal of Democracy,* 25(1):20–32.
O'Donnell, Guillermo. (1998). Challenges and Opportunities of Judicial Independence Research." *Journal of Democracy,* 9(3):112–126.
Powell, Jonathan M. (2012). Determinants of the Attempting and Outcome of Coups d'´etat. *Journal of Conflict Resolution,* 56(6):1017–1040.
Reynaert, Vicky. (2015). Comparing Country Cases: Output-Oriented EU Democrac Promotion. In *The Substance of EU Democracy Promotion: Concepts and Cases*, ed. Anne Wetzel and Jan Orbie. London: Palgrave Macmillan.
Sen ,Mahmut. (2012). The Rule of Law Conditionality of the European Union and Developments in Turkish Judiciary. *Law and Justice Review,* 3(4):81–136.
Wright, Joseph, Simone Dietrich and Margarete Ariotti. (2017). *Foreign Aid and Judicial Autonomy*. Unpublished manuscript.

2. Spain: Roads to Good Governance? How EU Structural Funds Impact Governance across Regions

ELISKA DRAPALOVA[1]

The Southern European countries and regions have received a substantial help from the European Union to rebuild their infrastructure, modernise their productive sector, and help to develop adequate human resources. However, the economic crisis uncovered many unresolved structural problems. This chapter deals with the Spanish case, particularly with the regional variation in use and control of EU funds. Cumulatively, Spain has received a significant share of the funds since it joined the European Union. Yet, the corruption scandals point to the possibility that the funds did not have only positive effects, but were a source of "cheap" and uncontrolled money ready to be used in the corrupt network to purchase favours or to buy support from voters and businessmen.

Introduction

The Southern European countries and regions have received a substantial help from the European Regional Development Fund to rebuild their infrastructure, modernise their productive sector, and to develop adequate human resources. However, the global and the euro crisis have compromised the picture of successful cohesion and good governance within Europe. It has slowly emerged that too much cash from the structural funds has been funnelled into infrastructure construction and that too little was used to improve administrative capacity and quality of government. A large amount of mismanagement and corruption scandals that emerged in SE countries showed that the controls that EU offered were not sufficient to prevent mismanagement and waste in some cases (Quesada, Jiménez-Sánchez and Villoria 2013).

This chapter aims to evaluate the impact of European Structural and Investment funds (ESI) on the Spanish regional governance using the framework developed by Alina Mungiu-Pippidi (2013, 2015). This framework analyses the confluence between the resources available for corruption versus the legal and societal controls that would constrain them. I argue that the EU funds increased the resources for corruption disproportionally without matching them with control mechanisms and administrative capacity. The problem seems to be that EU funds relied on the complex administrative control process, the maximisation of the absorption rate, and on the presumption that high capacity and rule of law are in place equally across but also within Member States. As a result, funds might favour the emergence of increased opportunities for corruption in regions with low administrative capacity and controls.

The rest of the chapter is structured as follows. In section one, I introduce the outcome indicators and compare regional performance. In section two, I describe the theory and the third section applies the resources versus constraints framework and discusses their effect on the governance characteristics. The last section presents my conclusions.

---

[1] Hertie School of Governance, Drapalova@hertie-school.org

Spain

Cumulatively, Spain is one of the highest recipients of EU regional funds. Spain has received more than EUR 13.696 billion since it joined the European Union in 1986 (1.27% of Spanish GNP) (European Commission 2016). Yet, the enormous socio-economic progress that Spain has made was recently compromised by a series of corruption scandals that involved EU funds. In early 2016, the European Commission requested clarifications to the regional government of Valencia whether EU money was involved in a large regional corruption scheme (*elMundo* 2016). Shortly before, the EU had stopped the absorption of funds to Andalusia because of a large corruption scandal that uncovered a scheme to embezzle ESF money for requalification courses (*País* 2016). These scandals point to the possibility that the funds did not have only a positive effect, but were a source of "cheap" and uncontrolled money ready to be used in the corrupt networks to purchase favours and support from voters and businessmen.

While all the money was pouring in over the last 25 years, Worldwide Governance Indicators and Corruption Perception Index scores on regulatory quality and corruption have remained unchanged or even have decreased (See figure 1). According to the Worldwide Governance Indicators (Kaufman et al. 2013), Spain (significantly) regressed in the Control of Corruption dimension in the period 1996–2015 (figure 1). Transparency International's Corruption Perception Index reveals a similar dynamic, as Spanish corruption improves between 1996 and 2000 (probably with the EU pressure before the single currency adoption), then stagnates and decreases in 2001, despite the Spanish economic boom.

Figure 1: The evolution of corruption in Spain, summary of indicators

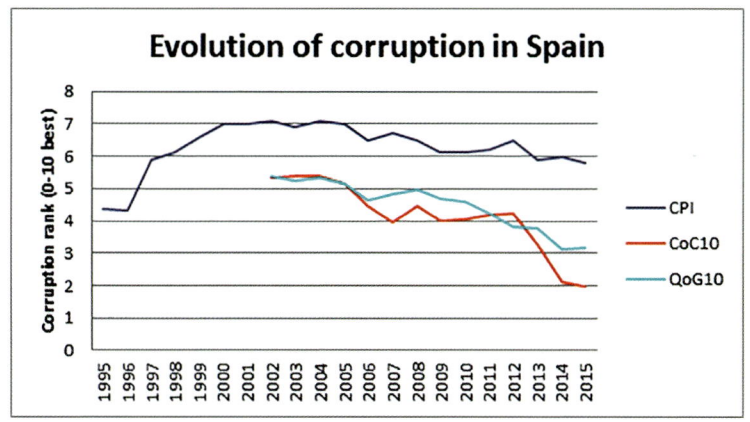

Source: CPI (TI), CoC (WGI) and EQI (QoG)

This deterioration of governance culminated in mass street protests in 2011 that denounced soaring levels of political corruption. 88% of Spanish population considers corruption as widespread across all levels and institutions and 72% says that government is not effective in curbing corruption (European Commission and DG Home Affairs 2014). The survey of enterprises conveys similar results, showing that 77% of Spaniards believe corruption and connections seem to be driving profit more than market competition and innovation does (Villoria and Jiménez 2016).

The pattern, however, varies considerably at the regional level. Spain is a decentralised country; the autonomous regions account for around 35% of total general government expenditure and have legislative power in the areas set out in their statutory legislation, such as health, education and social policies. As far as good governance performance is concerned, Spain is among the five EU Member States with the largest intra-country variation (Charron and Lapuente 2013). Similarly, the components of the Index of Public Integrity[2] (Mungiu-Pippidi and Dadašov 2016), adapted by the author to the regional level, show large regional differences in corruption, transparency, business regulation, administrative effectiveness and tribunal performance (see table 1).

Regarding transparency, the difference is almost 35 points in the various scores between the most transparent Basque country (100 points) and Madrid (65 points) or Murcia (79 points) (scale ranges from 0 to 100 where 0 is least transparent and 100 the most). In regional budgets and procurement transparency, the variation is even larger. While Catalonia or Basque country reaches full transparency (100 points), Andalusia and Madrid hardly reach 53 points in the last assessment in 2014.[3] The administrative burden also differs between regions. According to subnational indicators of Ease of Doing Business by the World Bank in 2013, to start a business in Cantabria takes 7 procedures, in Galicia or Navarre it is 10 and 12 steps respectively. Even dealing with property registration does not take the same amount of time: while in Madrid and La Rioja this simple procedure takes 13 days, in Galicia and Balearic Islands one has to wait 21 days. Finally, the time to process a building permit (the most reported area for corruption) takes 100 days (10 procedures) in La Rioja, while in Galicia one must wait 295 days and undertake 17 procedures. Similarly, in Aragon, it takes 250 days and 12 procedures.

---

[2] The IPI components are: administrative burden, judicial independence, trade openness, budget transparency, e-citizenship and freedom of the press. The freedom of the press component is not considered here. The press freedom scores for Spain are already high. Spain ranks 28 from 133 countries.

[3] Similarly, the number of politicians that are prosecuted for corruption shows a large variation. While Rioja or Navarra did not have reports of corruption, Andalusia or Valencia reported 144 and 76 politicians prosecuted in the last years (elMundo 2014).

Table 1. Summary of indicators of the Index of Public Integrity (adapted to regional level)

Region	Judicial Performance			Administrative burden			Transparency		E-citizenship	Trade openness
	Annul.	Congestion	Pending rate	Admin. Burden	Construction procedures	Construction permit time	Transparency Procurement	Transparency index	Internet % (2012)	Export %GNP (2014)
Spain	10	28	28	7	13	205	.	.	23.62	.
Galicia	7	31	30	10	17	297.5	64.7	90	23.16	33.81
Asturias	9	24	24	9	12	114	52.9	66.3	28.02	17.38
Cantabria	0	22	22	7	12	161	23.5	95	26.83	19.24
Basque Country	15	23	24	10	14	173	17.6	97.5	27.98	33.30
Navarre	25	17	17	12	12	145	58.8	91.3	23.38	46.35
La Rioja	0	35	35	9	11	101	47.1	97.5	23.50	21.43
Aragon	0	20	20	10	12	250	41.2	75	23.92	31.27
Madrid	13	26	27	7	13	205	70.6	72.5	26.54	13.85
Castile León	6	25	25	10	12	133	41.2	90	21.58	27.64
Castile -La Mancha	15	39	37	10	11	153	35.3	58.8	20.14	15.90
Extremadura	0	25	23	9	10	147	52.9	87.5	16.11	9.78
Catalonia	18	26	27	10	15	153.5	58.8	78.8	23.63	31.19
Valencia	12	32	32	9	11	121	29.4	63.8	22.56	28.11
Balearic Islands	0	27	28	9	14	203	41.2	83.8	28.82	4.04
Andalusia	4	27	28	7	13	162	82.4	92.5	20.82	17.22
Murcia	12	38	37	10	12	247	82.4	55	21.16	33.22
Canary Islands	30	25	26	10	11	142	29.4	63.8	30.07	5.76

Source: own elaboration with the data from Transparency international, Ease of Doing Business, CGPJ 2015Table 1. Summary of indicators of the Index of Public Integrity (adapted to regional level)

Moreover, the data show a similar variation in performance of regional tribunals. Due to unavailability of judicial independence indicators at the regional level, I substituted these with alternative measures of judicial performance using the pending and elevation rates which are the standard measures of quality of judiciary used by the Spanish Ministry of Justice. While one has to wait for a sentence on average 30 months in Galicia and 38 in Castile La Mancha, it is only 17 months in Navarre and 23 months in Basque Country. Similarly, the elevation rate of regional tribunals varies greatly. The elevation rate of tribunals in Cantabria or Castile-Leon is 11 and 13, while in Baleares or Madrid reach 28 and 33 points (Consejo General de Poder Judicial 2015).

Combining the total amount of funds received in the 2007-2013 period with the quality of government (EQI2013) indicator, we see (Figure 2) those regions that were receiving larger stock of money are those with worse quality of government. Taken together, the data suggest that the regional funds do not seem to help to improve governance in the least developed regions. *What does limit the impact of EU funds on the quality of government in Spanish regions?* I focus on this question in the next sections.

Figure 2: Relation between Regional quality of government (EQI2013) and EU funds (billions of Euros), OLS regression

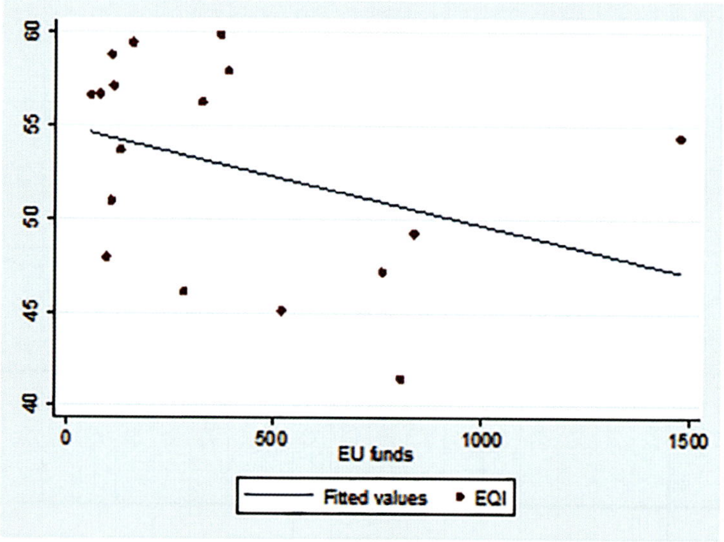

Theory and literature

In the years 2014–2020, the EU envisages the enhancement of quality of institutions and administrative capacity as one of the keystones for European cohesion (Dijkstra 2013). For the pursuit of this objective, the European Commission has implemented anticorruption reports, reforms of procurement and administrative capacity. Using its leverage and conditionality rule, especially during the accession period, the EU has promoted a large number of institutional reforms and guidelines that led to alignment in administrative rules and laws (Meyer-Sahling 2011). Yet, the unequal implementation of these rules and laws across and within countries casts doubts on the effectiveness of this approach (Mungiu-Pipidi 2007).

At the regional level, the bulk of literature on the EU regional funds has proliferated considerably, as has the budget dedicated to these funds. Research to date has looked mostly at the effects of structural funds allocation in delivering economic cohesion, measured as GDP convergence (Becker, Egger and von Ehrlich 2010, Tosun 2014) and at the determinants of the regional distribution of funds depending on government ideology, number of veto players or government quality (Charron 2016). However, apart from few studies (Dimulescu, Pop and Doroftei 2013, Fazekas et al. 2014), very little work has been done and the literature remains divided on whether and how regional funds can contribute to good governance.

EU representatives argue that funds are responsible for successfully narrowing the gap between countries and that additional monitoring and planning mechanisms provide enough guarantees to minimise the opportunities for mismanagement and corruption. Nevertheless, Fazekas et al. (2014) indicate that EU funding considerably increases corruption risk in procurement in countries that they have studied. It happens by "making a large number of funds available for rent extraction and by failing to implement sufficient controls of corruption to counterbalance this source of resources" ibid., 71). Yet, this effect is not uniform across regions. Therefore, we have to ask what components are responsible for more or less effective control of corruption.

Control of corruption refers to "society's capacity to constrain corrupt behaviour in order to enforce the norm of individual integrity in administration and politics to prevent state capture by particular interests, and thus promote the social welfare" (Mungiu-Pippidi 2015). Control of corruption is an equilibrium reached when opportunities for corruption are checked by constraints imposed by the state and the society. In this model, the resources for corruption includes both material resources and discretionary power, such as privileged access of reduced groups of actors, intentionally poor regulation or its excess and lack of transparency. Alina Mungiu-Pippidi (2015) distinguishes two types of restrictions. On the one hand, we have the dissuasive legal measures administered by the state, effective autonomous judicial power and audit institutions that are capable of enforcing legislation that deal with conflicts of interest, and the application of a clear separation of public and private spheres. On the other hand, normative dissuasive measures include both the existence of social norms that promote government impartiality as well as societal monitoring through the active role of the media and civil society.

This framework is suitable to assess the impact of the EU funds on subnational governance as it could be easily adapted to the regional level. Especially in federal countries, regions enjoy the autonomy that enables them to create different governance configurations. Secondly, although several institutions such as tribunals are administrated centrally, the regional approach can elucidate the gap between *de jure* and *de facto* performance. Finally, each region has slightly different approach regarding how to organise the administration of the EU funds.

Analysis of resources and constraints

This chapter maps the evolution of resources and institutional and societal controls in Spanish regions. I argue that the funds increased disproportionally the resources for corruption without effective implementation of control mechanisms. The unconstrained resources, along with the lack of consideration of different regional administrative capacities and governance conditions increased the opportunities for corruption.

Regional policy is implemented through three main funds: the European Regional Development Fund (ERDF), the Cohesion Fund (CF) and the European Social Fund (ESF). Additionally, the European Agricultural Fund for Rural Development (EAFRD) and the European Maritime and Fisheries Fund (EMFF) make up altogether the Structural Funds and European Investment Funds (Becker, Egger and von Ehrlich 2010). The institutionalisation of European cohesion policy was given impetus in the late 1980s in the context of the accession of poorer Mediterranean countries – Greece (1982), Spain and Portugal (1986) – and an ambitious drive to adopt the single market. The type, the sector and the amount of funding were targeted depending on the socio-economic conditions of each region. For Objective 1 (lagging regions), eligibility was based on regions having an average GDP per capita of less than 75% of the Community average. Cohesion Fund (CF) was intended for countries whose per capita GDP is below 90% of the EU average. The eligibility of Objective 2 and 5b regions (industrial areas in decline and rural areas) were selected on the basis of unemployment rates and percentage of industrial and agriculture employment and income (Bodenstein and Kemmerling 2012, 3). In 2000–2006, eleven Spanish regions were classified as Objective 1: Galicia, Asturias, Castile-Leon, Castile-La Mancha, Extremadura, Valencia, Andalusia, Region of Murcia, Ceuta, Melilla and Canarias. Since then, however, just four of the regions (Galicia, Castile-La Mancha, Extremadura and Andalusia) remained in that category in 2007–2013 and only one (Extremadura) in 2014–2020.

Resources for corruption

The regional funds, due to the "additionality principle", constitute by definition extra source of assets. Although ESI funds are not comparable in amount or in purpose to Official Development Assistance, the ERDF and Cohesion Fund available for the 2007–2013 period amounted to EUR 26.6 billion, equivalent to 0.4% of GDP and around 7% of government capital expenditure. Funding allocated to Convergence regions was nearly three times greater than that going to Competitiveness and Employment ones, equivalent to an average of EUR 163 per capita per year over the period (European Commission 2016, 10). Especially during the economic crisis, the EU funds were frequently the principal component for continuation of regional investment. The purpose of the funds varies according to the EU targets, the relative development of regions' and Member States' strategies. In the Spanish case, the central government has given a high priority to the development of economic infrastructure.

After a close look at indicators from the first section, we observe mixed evidence on the relation between higher resources availability and corruption. We see that, although most regions with a low quality of government are also those with the most resources available for misappropriation, some wealthier regions that perform well on the EQI index have also high resource availability. Regarding transparency, Murcia, Andalusia, Galicia and Valencia are among the least transparent regions (especially the financial transparency component) and they also received a greater amount of EU funds. The administrative burden, frequently measured by the number of procedures that businesses and citizens face, shows that Galicia and Murcia are regions where new businesses and citizens have to undergo a greater number of steps, higher payments and longer waiting time. Nevertheless, some traditionally well-governed regions – Basque Country and La Rioja – also have low score on transparency (17.6 and 47) and high administrative burden (10 and 9 procedures).

Another component of resources that increases the potential for corruption, the power discretion, also seems to influence the effect of funds on the government quality. Most of the regions with low performance are governed historically by one dominant party. Andalusia and Extremadura are strongholds of the Spanish Socialist Workers' Party (PSOE); while Galicia, Murcia and Valencia are governed by the People's Party (PP), although previously these were governed by the PSOE with again ample majorities. The lack of competition and alternation contributed to clientelism, the politicisation of public administration and to the discretionary power of narrow political elite over the distribution and role of EU funds in their respective regions. These strong regional political actors, known as *caciques*, have gained influence with political decentralisation and control over distribution of EU funds (Bukowski, Piattoni and Smyrl 2003). Spain has many of these "personal" political projects co-financed by the EU. Perhaps the most notorious is the unused airport in Castellón in Valencia, which was promoted by regional politician and *cacique* Carlos Fabra and paid for by the EU (*elDiario* 2015), the airport in Murcia or the Palma Arena velodrome in Balearic Islands (*lainformacion* 2013).

The shared implementation between subnational bodies and civil society was left to the discretion of Member States and regions (Cazorla Perez 1995, European Commission 1995). Its application and quality, thus, depended on domestic administrative traditions and regional settings. Altogether, the rivalry between central government and regions with growing powers, the relative weakness of local governments and civil society in some regions have impinged upon the application of partnership. Given their discretion, every region had a different arrangement that ranged from fairly open, participative and institutionalised process in Catalonia (with the association of municipalities, associations and unions participating in decision and management) to informal and regional-government-led process in Aragon or Valencia (Aja 2001).

Finally, the purpose of the funds contributed indirectly to higher corruption risks. Especially in the early stages and in the poorest regions, funds were invested in large infrastructure projects, urban renovation and other discretionary investments that are associated with larger corruption risks (Aguilera and Naredo 2009). This risk was high due to strong political incentives, the high political visibility of projects, and business pressure in public procurement. Regions classified under Objective 2 had a different situation in which the funds were to go to non-discretionary investment projects, such as research in innovation and education. Although the EU stipulates how funds should be spent, the stipulations tend to be rather vague, giving freedom to Member States to diverge from the original purpose. In Galicia, journals reported the clientelistic and partisan use of regional funds for road construction for pork-barrel projects by regional political leaders (C. M. Dudek 2005). Carolyn Dudek found that "party affiliation and personal connections mattered for the distribution of EU funded projects as municipalities and associations that were ideologically close to the ruling party received more funds (ibid., p. 127)". She argues that funds were used to perpetuate clientelistic networks and relations that siphoned off EU funds for partisan purposes (C. M. Dudek 2003, 123).

The role of restrictions

European funds increased considerably the pool of resources available for investment and redistribution but also for mismanagement. However, it may be that at the same time the EU funds were complemented with strict controls and constraints over these resources. Legal and societal constraints indeed seem to be the crucial component in the puzzle. Regions with a low quality of government and high corruption have consistently high availability of resources but also the lowest constraints. On the contrary, the regions that score high on the quality of government index also have the highest constraints, especially on the social accountability indicator.

(a) Legal and institutional controls

The evaluation and control mechanisms of funds only grew more important with the volume of resources poured into regional convergence (Bachtler and Mendez 2007). As the result, the EU has devised a complex and detailed audit system of fund tracking, ex-ante evaluations and early warning systems combined with national and sub-national audits. On paper, the EU control system indeed seems bullet proof, however, findings by Fazekas et al. (2014) show that the risk of EU funds being misplaced is higher than for the national funds – even despite this detailed screening process.

One of the reasons behind the low effectiveness of the EU control system is its decentralisation, which especially complicates ex-ante accountability. The EU audit office has devolved much of the oversight responsibility to the Member States and regions. These, however, tend to implement a highly diverse system of control with various levels of quality that frequently overlap and contribute to the ineffectiveness of audit mechanisms (Dellmuth 2011). The Spanish central government implements separate mechanisms for an audit of European and national funds. These are combined with the regional controls and committees. Consequently, the management of funds has created additional bodies and procedures that were difficult to assess (Milio 2010).

The effectiveness of audit institutions (ex-post controls) is limited while the regional tribunals' performance varies largely among regions. The national audit tribunal is understaffed and overburdened. Its controls are generally ex-post and are focused only on the correct application of rules without searching for or preventing fraud. Regional tribunals perform well in regions like Navarre, Cantabria or Basque Country, while their capacity (pending rate) and performance (annulment rate) are much lower in those regions that manage most of the funds like Galicia, Extremadura, Murcia or Castile-La Mancha (Table 1).

Moreover, Spain lacks lobby regulation and comprehensive legislation against conflict of interest among politicians (TI 2014). Only Catalonia has created an antifraud office. Politicisation of administration further decreases the effectiveness of institutional controls. In Galicia, Andalusia and Valencia the politicisation of administration is considered to be high (Jordana, Mota and Noferini 2012, Mota and Noferini 2010). In other regions, like Basque Country, these tendencies were limited. Unlike other regions, the Basque Country has its *Instituto Vasco de Adminstración Pública* (Basque Institute of Public Administration), which is responsible for the recruitment and formation and overview of Basque civil servants.

(b) The societal accountability

Although the EU recommends that regions involve civil society and economic actors in the drafting of the regional strategies and operational programmes. However, as already mentioned it is in full discretion of the regions. Their involvement and the openness of the process are low and vary across the territory.

Spain was a centralised and semi-authoritarian country until 1975. Due to its authoritarian past, Spanish civil society is considered weak and more politicised in relation to most other Western European countries (Verge 2012). Despite the general popular outcry against corruption (according to 2014 Special Eurobarometer on corruption, 84% believe that bribery and connections are the easiest were to obtain public services), civil society's role in monitoring EU funds and regional implementation of European programmes is almost non-existent (Jimenez and Villoria 2014). At least until 2011, there were very few civil society organisations engaged in the fight against corruption or dedicated to monitoring public spending. Institutionalised civil society organisations are few and poorly organised; consequently, they have little impact and limited influence. Attending to the number of NGOs per thousand inhabitants and by the autonomous community, we find that Castillas, Rioja, Aragon and Navarra are the regions that present the highest values of this indicator. On the other hand, the autonomous communities with smaller values are Madrid, Baleares and Valencia (Pérez-Grueso, Servós and Abadía 2007, 84).

According to recent research, the strength of civil society and spread of the Internet in regions are correlated positively with the quality of government (Mungiu-Pippidi and Dadašov

2016). According to the data on Spanish regional Internet subscription, Spain has low Internet penetration. On average, only 23% of the population had Internet access as of 2012. In accordance with previous indicators, this average value hides an interesting variation among regions. Once more, stronger and more connected citizens are concentrated in the historical communities of Catalonia and Basque Country where Internet subscription reaches 28%. On the opposite end, we can find Extremadura with only 16% and Andalusia with 20%.

This chapter has aimed to evaluate the role of European Structural and Cohesion Funds and their impact on governance in the various Spanish regions. From the exploratory empirical analysis, it seems that despite EU membership the quality of governance varies considerably within countries. Indeed, the numerous corruption scandals in regional government and the empirical evidence show that EU funds, despite the control mechanisms, seem not to improve regional institutions but rather increase the temptation for rent seeking. I have argued that the way funds were distributed (increased discretionary power of politicians versus open participatory processes) and to which purpose they were committed (infrastructure and large investment projects as opposed to projects dedicated to education and SMEs) has augmented the resources for corruption. This increase in resources was not matched with effective control by the Commission, by regional government and by societal accountability from civil society. Moreover, the shared management between the EU and Member States, together with the complexity and frequent reforms of supervisory mechanisms, added a burden to regions with low administrative capacity and further limited the control capacity of these regions. This contributed to variations of governance quality between different regions.

Within the last three years, quite a few new laws and regulations intended to fight and prevent corruption and fraud have come into force in Spain. Although it is important to create effective institutional deterrents for corrupt behaviour, legal constraints alone are not likely to work without societal support. Civil society monitoring and stakeholder engagement is weak and regions with more problems with corruption are the same regions with low transparency, low political participation and low Internet connectivity. To end on a brighter note, after 2011, Spanish civil society has been showing signs of mobilisation and a stronger will to oversee public funds and to participate in political decisions. Many new civil society activities (like open data and budgetary control of local governments) and new political parties with anticorruption platforms give hope for more control of political wrongdoing.

References

Aguilera, Federico, and Jose Manuel Naredo. (2009). *Economía, Poder Y Megaproyectos*. Economía Y Naturaleza. Teguise: Fundación Cesar Manrique.

Aja, Eliseo. (2001). Spain: Nations, Nationalities and Regions. In: *Subnational Democracy in the EU: Challenges and Opportunities*, edited by J. Loughlin. Oxford: Oxford University Press.

Bachtler, John, and Carlos Mendez. (2007). Who Governs EU Cohesion Policy? Deconstructing the Reforms of the Structural Funds. *JCMS: Journal of Common Market Studies*, 45 (3): 535–64..

Becker, Sascha O., Peter H. Egger and Maximilian von Ehrlich. (2010). Going NUTS: The Effect of EU Structural Funds on Regional Performance. *Journal of Public Economics*, 94 (9–10): 578–90.

Bodenstein, Thilo and Achim Kemmerling. (2012). Ripples in a Rising Tide: Why Some EU Regions Receive More Structural Funds than Others. SSRN Scholarly Paper ID 2006413. Rochester, NY: Social Science Research Network. Available at https://papers.ssrn.com/abstract=2006413

Bukowski, Jeanie J, Simona Piattoni and Marc E Smyrl, eds. (2003). *Between Europeanization and Local Societies: The Space for Territorial Governance*. Governance in Europe. Lanham, Md: Rowman & Littlefield.

Cazorla Perez, J. (1995). El Clientelism de Partido En La Espana de Hoy: Una Disfunccion de La Democracia. *Revista de Estudios Políticos*, 28: 114–32.

Charron, Nicholas. (2016). Explaining the Allocation of Regional Structural Funds: The Conditional Effect of Governance and Self-Rule. *European Union Politics*, 17 (4): 638–659.

Charron, Nicholas, and Víctor Lapuente. 2013. Why Do Some Regions in Europe Have a Higher Quality of Government? *The Journal of Politics,* 75 (3): 567–82.
Consejo General de Poder Judicial. (2015). Justice Data 2011–15. Madrid: Consejo General de Poder Judicial.
Dellmuth, Lisa Maria. (2011). The Cash Divide: The Allocation of European Union Regional Grants." *Journal of European Public Policy,* 18 (7): 1016–33.
Dijkstra, Lewis. (2013). A Focus on the European Union and the Sub-National Dimension of QoG. In *Quality of Government and Corruption from European Perspective. A Comparative Study of Good Government in EU Regions,* edited by Nicholas Charron, Victor Lapuente and Bo Rothstein. Cheltenham, UK: Edward Elgar. pp. 3–16.
Dimulescu, Valentina, Raluca Pop and Irina Madalina Doroftei. (2013). Risks of Corruption and the Management of EU Funds in Romania. *Romanian Journal of Political Science,* 13 (1): 101.
Dudek, Carolyn Marie. (2005). *EU Accession and Spanish Regional Development: Winners and Losers.* P.I.E.-Peter Lang.
———. (2003). Creation of a Bureaucratic Style: Spanish Regions and EU Structural Funds. In *Between Europeization and Local Societies: The Space for Territorial Governance.* Boston: Rownam and Littlefield Publishers. pp. 111–132.
elDiario. (2015). Europa Investiga Supuestas Irregularidades En La Concesión Del Aeropuerto de Castellón. *Eldiario.es.* Available at http://www.eldiario.es/cv/aeropuerto-de-castellon/Europa-investiga-irregularidades-Aeropuerto-Castellon_0_429407692.html
elMundo. (2014). El Mapa de La Corrupción En España. *ELMUNDO.* November 3. Available at http://www.elmundo.es/grafico/espana/2014/11/03/5453d2e6268e3e8d7f8b456c.html.
———. (2016). Bruselas Pregunta Si La Corrupción En Valencia Afecta a Fondos Europeos. *ELMUNDO,* March 9. Available at http://www.elmundo.es/comunidad-valenciana/2016/03/09/56e0728946163fdf4e8b45a0.html
European Commission. (1995). The Implementation of the Reform of the Structural Funds in 1993. Fifth Annual Report COM(95). Brussels.
———. (2016). EUROPA - Spain. Text. *European Union Website, the Official EU Website - European Commission.* Available at https://europa.eu/european-union/about-eu/countries/member-countries/spain_en.
———. (2016). Ex Post Evaluation of Cohesion Policy Programmes 2007-2013, Focusing on the European Regional Development Fund (ERDF) and the Cohesion Fund (CF). Brussels: European Commission.
European Commission and DG Home Affairs. (2014). Corruption (Special Eurobarometer 397).
Fazekas, Mihály, Jana Chvalkovka, Jiri Suhrovec, Istvan János Tóth and Lawrence P. King. 2014. Are EU Funds a Corruption Risk? The Impact of EU Funds on Grand Corruption in Central and Eastern Europe. In *Controlling Corruption in Europe,* edited by Alina Mungiu Pippidi. Berlin: Barbara Budrich Publishers.
Jimenez, Fernando and Manuel Villoria. (2014). Corruption Perception and Collective Action: The Case of Spain. In *Corruption in Contemporary World: Theory, Practice and Hotspots.* Maryland: Lexington Books. pp. 197–222.
Jordana, Jacint, Fabiola Mota and Andrea Noferini. (2012). The Role of Social Capital within Policy Networks: Evidence from EU Cohesion Policy in Spain. *International Review of Administrative Sciences,* 78 (4): 642–64.
lainformacion. (2013). El 'Top Ten' de La Corrupción En España. *Lainformacion,* March 26. Available at http://www.lainformacion.com/espana/el-top-ten-de-la-corrupcion-en-espana_Aj9BB2UIz0cdeFmE2liB93/
Meyer-Sahling, Jan-Hinrik. (2011). The Durability of EU Civil Service Policy in Central and Eastern Europe after Accession. *Governance,* 24 (2): 231–60.
Milio, Simona. (2010). *From Policy to Implementation in the European Union : The Challenge of a Multi-Level Governance System.* London, New York: Tauris Academic Studies.
Mota, Fabiola, and Andrea Noferini. (2010). Evidence Form Structural Funds Implementation in Two Spanish Regions. In *From Policy to Implementation in the European Union : The Challenge of a Multi-Level Governance System,* edited by Simona Milio, London, New York: Tauris Academic Studies. pp 125–149.
Mungiu-Pippidi, Alina. (2007). EU Accession Is Not End of History. *Journal of Democracy* 18 (4).
———. (2013). *Controlling Corruption in Europe. The ANTICORRP Report.* Opladen: Barbara Budrich Publishers.
———. (2015). *The Quest for Good Governance.* Cambridge: Cambridge University Press.
Mungiu-Pippidi, Alina and Ramin Dadašov. 2016. Measuring Control of Corruption by a New Index of Public Integrity. *European Journal on Criminal Policy and Research,* 22 (3): 415–38.

País, Ediciones El. (2016). La UE congeló 468 millones para Andalucía al detectar irregularidades." March 14. Available at http://politica.elpais.com/politica/2016/03/14/actualidad/1457977551_725016.html

Pérez-Grueso, Ana José Bellostas, Chaime Marcuello Servós and José Mariano Moneva Abadía. (2007). *Capital social y organizaciones no lucrativas en España: el caso de las ONGD*. Fundacion BBVA.

Quesada, Mónica García, Fernando Jiménez-Sánchez and Manuel Villoria. (2013). Building Local Integrity Systems in Southern Europe: The Case of Urban Local Corruption in Spain. *International Review of Administrative Sciences,* 79 (4): 618–37.

Transparency International Spain. (2014). Una Evaluación Del Lobby En España: Análisis Y Propuestas.

———. (2015). Indice de Transparencia de Ayuntamientos. Transparency Intenational Spain.

Tosun, Jale. (2014). Absorption of Regional Funds: A Comparative Analysis. *Journal of Common Market Studies* 52 (2): 371–87.

Verge, Tània. (2012). Party Strategies towards Civil Society in New Democracies The Spanish Case. *Party Politics,* 18 (1): 45–60.

Villoria, Manuel, and Fernando Jiménez. (2016). Exploring Citizens' Perceptions of Political Finance and Political Corruption: Lifting the Lid on Legal Corruption in Spain. In *Corruption and Government Legitimacy. A 21st Century Perspective,* edited by J. Mendilow and I. Peleg. Maryland: Lexington Books. pp. 93–120.

3. Slovakia: The Impact of EU Good Governance Aid 2007–2013

MIROSLAV BEBLAVÝ[1], EMÍLIA SIČÁKOVÁ-BEBLAVÁ[2]

This chapter looks at the European financial assistance provided to Slovakia during the period 2007–2013. The main research question is whether EU good governance aid (with focus on the 2007–2013 period) has measurably contributed to improvement in Slovak governance. The chapter consists of three parts. The first is devoted to the overview of governance regime in Slovakia and defines the research questions and methodology. The second part concerns the findings on EU financial assistance and good governance. The final part provides discussion and conclusions.

Slovakia's governance regime

Many scholars and organisations (prominently the World Bank, UNDP and OECD) devote their capacity to the study of *governance*; however, there is hardly a universally accepted definition of this concept (Weiss, 2000). Alina Mungiu-Pippidi defines governance as: "the set of formal and informal institutions that determine who gets what in a given country – in other words, how public goods are allocated" (2014). She forecasts that governance is difficult to change, as "governance orders reproduce fundamental patterns of social organisation and power distribution in a society, and thus tend to be stable once they reach a certain equilibrium. They are hard to transform even by means of a change of political regime" (ibid.). For Slovakia, the evolution of good governance can be shown using the World Bank Control of Corruption indicator CoC[3] (see figure 1). Slovakia registered some steep progress during EU accession years, climbing nearly to the upper third of best governed countries, then entered a slower, but mostly constant decline, losing most of the gains of the previous fifteen years. Mungiu-Pippidi (ibid.) thus puts Slovakia to the group of the borderline countries borderline cases scoring around 5 – between competitive particularism – where elections are competitive, but victors tend to spoil public resources as a rule – and a regime based on universalism and good governance. The evidence collected by Transparency International Slovakia supports this, showing that only the education sector, the tax administration and the customs office improved significantly in the interval 1999–2012, while central and local government, the judiciary and the police were not perceived to improve (Sičáková-Beblavá and Šípoš 2015). Furthermore, the mechanism of political corruption related to financing of political parties versus public procurement contracts awards or public jobs has endured. Although formal rules on financing of political parties have been changed by several governments since 1998, their implementation is a challenge to bring a real change in the existing equilibrium. Although it varies across the ruling governments and particular ministries, the personnel in the public administration is recruited also on political grounds, without a prop-

---

[1] Senior Research Fellow at CEPS, Brussels, miroslav.beblavy@ceps.eu
[2] Assoc. Prof., Comenius University, Faculty of Social and Economic Sciences, Institute of Public Policy, emilia.beblava@fses.uniba.sk
[3] The WB indicator captures perceptions of the extent to which public power is exercised for private gain, including both petty and grand forms of corruption, as well as "capture" of the state by elites and private interests. The governance score scales from -2.5 to 2.5: the higher the better.

erly structured and meritocratic selection procedure (Beblavý – Sičáková-Beblavá, 2011). That is reflected in the varying government favouritism in Slovakia (figure 1).

Figure 1. Control of corruption pre- and post-accession in Slovakia

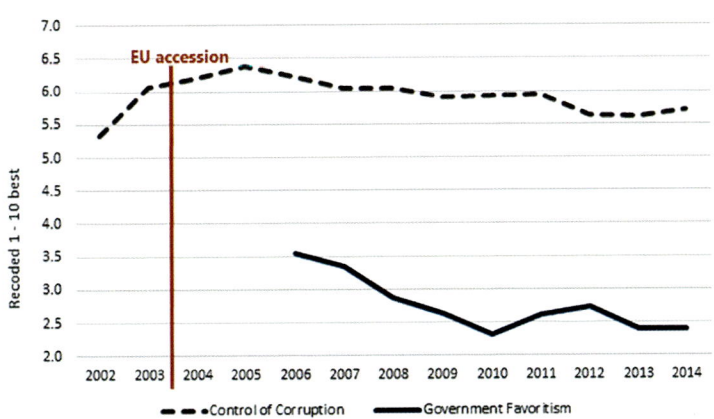

Source: World Bank, Worldwide Governance indicator: Control of Corruption [Percentile rank indicates the country's rank among all countries covered by the aggregate indicator, with 0 corresponding to the lowest rank and 100 to the highest.] *http://databank.worldbank.org/data/reports.aspx?source=worldwide-governance-indicators*; World Economic Forum Global Competiveness indicator: Government Favoritism [1 = favouritism to a great extent; 7 = no favouritism at all], *http://reports.weforum.org/global-competitiveness-report-2015–2016/appendix-a-measurement-of-key-concepts-and-preliminary-index-structure/*

The role of EU

In this paper we look at the European financial assistance provided to Slovakia during the period 2007–2013. The main research question is whether EU good governance aid (with focus on the 2007–2013 period) has measurably contributed to improvement in Slovak governance. To answer this, we examine EU financial assistance during the 2007–2013 period in its broader context by comparing this period with earlier and later ones.

We complement the macro-analysis with a micro-view and analyse in detail EU financial assistance to good governance to Slovakia in 2007–2013 at the level of projects. Since there is no data available concerning details of project implementation and evaluation, we collect data about project themes and size. In addition to financial data, we conducted several interviews with country authorities that are responsible for EU funds management as well as with local EU representatives. We look at both channels of EU funding: Structural Funds managed by national authorities and other types of funding (directly allocated by the European Commission, Norwegian funding provided in the context of its EEA membership).

Four distinct periods exist in the EU's approach to Slovakia's governance:
• The pre-accession period (1999–2004)
• Immediate post-accession period (2004–2006)
• The 2007–2013 period
• The 2014–2020 period

The reason for this division is that it corresponds to very different means of EU financial assistance to Slovakia. Before the accession, there were pre-accession funds, much smaller in size and also much more controlled by the European Commission. The immediate post-accession period witnessed Slovakia starting to utilise regular Structural Funds in a heavily truncated three-year part of the seven-year EU budgetary cycle (2000–2006). The volume of funding then increased massively during the 2007–2013 cycle and increased additionally during the 2014–2020 period, which has just begun.

It is worth noting that, due to the so-called n+2 rule, implementation of each cycle lasts for two additional years (2004–2006 cycle actually lasted until 2008, 2007–2013 until 2015). At the same time, actual spending in Slovakia started about two to three years late in the 2007–2013 and 2014–2020 cycles. This means that the different periods are, to some extent, arbitrary and in practice overlapping.

Starting with the pre-accession period, there is no research looking at good governance in Slovakia during this period from the perspective of EU funding impact. We will therefore refer to research on corruption control. Beblavý and Sičáková-Beblavá (2014) show that before 1999, the European Union's influence on corruption was close to zero, and between 1999 and 2004, its influence was strong and positive. European Commission tackled these issues through the EC Regular Reports that created the imperative "to do something" stronger. the procurement, state aid and competition *acquis* were transformed into the domestic law prior to accession. The political conditionality of accession meant both the exclusion of the political parties most prone to corruption from the government and pressure to introduce and implement a formal anticorruption policy. Reforms were also supported by technical assistance and the transfer of EU rules concerning competition, state aid and procurement into Slovak legislation, including the creation and strengthening of national regulators (ibid.). At the same time, EU influence was limited in areas where structural reforms would have been needed to curb corruption, and thus the overall effect of policy conditionality and technical assistance was minor. The increasing flows of pre-accession aid and their gradual decentralisation to domestic authorities, on the other hand, meant an increased risk of corruption. Overall, we can conclude that prior to 2004 the EU had a strong, positive influence on corruption, with the most positive influence related to the exclusion of corruption-prone parties from the government (ibid.).

As to the immediate post-accession developments (2004–2006), this period seems to be more ambiguous, but despite an apparent worsening of corruption after 2004, a transformation rather than a loss of European Union influence occurred (ibid.).

Accession changed the situation significantly. Conditionality was lost both in terms of government composition and in policy areas, which was manifested in the increasing acceptability of Vladimír Mečiar and Jan Slota as government partners and in a reduced emphasis on anticorruption policies amongst all mainstream parties. Anticorruption technical assistance, which was part of the pre-accession funding, was also gradually wound down. The sharply increasing aid flows began to dominate the EU influence on corruption in Slovakia, with a major negative influence due to their discretionary nature and the decentralisation of management to national government authorities. On the other hand, accession meant that the European Commission and the European Court of Justice finally had the possibility to intervene directly in the areas of competition, state aid and procurement, thereby strengthening the impact of EU rules (ibid.).

During the **2007–2013** and **2014–2020 periods**, governance has been a major preoccupation of the EU with regard to Slovakia. The country-specific recommendations, which have been, since 2011, issued annually by the European Council based on the proposal by the European Commission are illustrative in this respect. During the 2011–2014 period, governance-related civil society recommendations (CSR) constituted around half of all recommendations. This drops off sharply in 2015 and 2016, when only one recommendation out of three to four is governance-related. This would lead one to conclude that governance became a less pressing issue for the European Council and the European Commission with regard to Slovakia.

However, if we do an analysis of actual text of the CSRs, a much more nuanced picture emerges. The reason for fall-off in the number of governance-related recommendations is the disappearance of sectorial governance-related recommendations. During the 2011–2014 period, the Council and the Commission consistently pushed Slovakia to improve capacity of its public employment services and fiscal administration and (during 2013 and 2014) to improve governance of its energy sector. Since 2015, the number of CSRs has dropped sharply and the governance-related recommendations focused solely on the cross-cutting issues. At the same time, the level of detail and specificity of these recommendations crystallised over time in areas of civil service and public procurement, though developments have proven uneven. For the civil service as such, there was no recommendation in 2011 and only a general injunction to "strengthen the quality of the public service" in 2012 (CSR 2012). The next year, there was a very extensive recommendation to "[t]ake measures, including by amending the Act on Civil Service, to strengthen the independence of the public service. Improve the management of human resources in public administration. Step up efforts to strengthen analytical capacities in key ministries, also with a view to improving the absorption of EU funds" (CSR 2013). In 2014, this recommendation was nearly completely retained, before disappearing in 2015 and reappearing in 2016 as "[i]mprove the transparency, quality and effectiveness of human resources management in public administration, in particular by adopting a new civil service act" (CSR 2015, 2016).

A similar development can be seen with regard to public procurement, the second most extensive area in the cross-cutting recommendations. In 2011, the EU recommended that Slovakia "ensure the implementation of planned measures aimed at a more effective application of public procurement rules". The follow year, the emphasis was to "strengthen the role of the Public Procurement office as an independent body". Then the theme disappeared in 2013 and reappeared with a 2014 recommendation to "step up efforts to improve the efficiency of public procurement" (CSR 2014). Then, in 2015 and 2016, the recommendations became more specific by suggesting Slovakia "increase competition in public tenders and improve supervisory mechanisms in public procurement" (CSR 2015) and "consolidate governance, reinforce the shift from price only to quality-based competition and improve the prosecution of illicit practices in public procurement" (CSR 2016).

For the third element of cross-cutting issues – the judicial sector – there has been no clear development. While it appeared in every year but one – 2015 –, it remained at a general level of exhortation to improve efficiency of the system.

It is worth remembering that the programming for the 2007–2013 period was generally done during the 2005–2007 period. It reflected a growing interest – post-enlargement – in building administrative capacity, with 1.1% of European Social Fund (ESF) aid dedicated to administrative capacity building, which is about EUR 3.7 billion (EC 2014a). In Slovakia strengthening administrative capacity (as a proxy for good governance) was part of the ESF operational programme Employment and Social Inclusion. During this period, the EU did not apply any conditionality on Slovakia to improve good governance.

The 2014–2020 period brought significant change in both prioritisation of good governance and pressure to have it integrated in the programming of Structural Funds. To ensure that Cohesion Policy is better linked to the European Semester and the wider EU economic governance, programmes have to be consistent with National Reform Programmes and should address the relevant challenges identified through the relevant Country Specific Recommendations in the European Semester. In order to contribute to the Union's strategy for smart, sustainable and inclusive growth and to the fund-specific missions, the General Regulation introduces 11 thematic objectives on which the funds should focus their support.

Specifically with regard to institutional capacity building by ESF, it is worth noting that reform of public administrations is a key priority for the successful implementation of the Europe 2020 Strategy. The importance of the issue has been recently explained by the Directorate General for Employment, Social Affairs and Inclusion (DG EMPL) itself as follows: "The quality of public administration is important for economic competitiveness and societal well-being (…). The quality of public administration has a direct impact on the economic environment and is thus crucial to stimulating productivity, competitiveness and growth. Apart from its key role as an economic regulator, the public sector also stands out as a service provider and employer. It accounts for more than 25% of total employment and a significant share of economic activity in the EU28 Member States. Additionally, an efficient and productive public sector can be a strong driver of economic growth through its support for and governance of the private sector" (European Commission 2014b).

The Annual Growth Survey 2013, the Economic Adjustment Programmes and other frameworks of Financial Assistance in EU Member States highlighted the need for Member States to increase the efficiency and effectiveness of public services, as well as the transparency and quality of public administration and the judiciary.

For the 2014–2020 period, "enhancing institutional capacity of public authorities and stakeholders and an efficient public administration" is included as a separate thematic objective (Thematic Objective 11 or "TO11") in the Common Provisions Regulation for the 2014–2020 programming period.[4] While both the ESF and ERDF should contribute to this TO11, their role is quite different. ERDF has a narrow scope of either supporting ESF TO11 interventions with infrastructure or in focusing on the ERDF implementation per se.

On the contrary, in the ESF case, the effectiveness and efficiency of public administration is crucial in order to achieve the results in all other TOs. Institutional capacity is thus not just a narrow, technical question of upgrading civil servants' skills; it relates to how public authorities define their scope, how they interact with businesses and citizens, and how they deliver services to these groups. Institutional capacity and efficiency of public administration and stakeholders is therefore a horizontal element. This notion is substantiated by the fact that TO11 is not directly related to any of the Europe 2020 headline targets; it is a condition sine qua non.

Under the EU pressure, Slovakia also created a specific Operational Programme called the Efficient Public Administration for the TO11, which allocates EUR 335 million. The EU also created a mechanism of "ex-ante conditionality" for Structural Funds whereby release of Structural Funds is conditional on Member States achieving specific policy benchmarks related to their challenges as identified by the Commission. For Slovakia, a new Civil Service Act and five other benchmarks are an ex-ante conditionality for accessing the funds, translating the above-mentioned country specific recommendation into much more powerful leverage over the Structural Funds.

Results and discussion

What impact has this EU approach had on good governance in Slovakia at the macro-level?

No evaluation from the perspective of good governance has been done by the Slovak authorities. European Commission provides its evaluation in its report called ESF Main Achievements 2007–2013: ESF Expert Evaluation Network Final synthesis report: Main ESF achievements, 2007-2013: "Despite the ESF strongly promoting innovation and innovative approaches to enhance the design, management and implementation of policies and action, the role effects of the ESF in Slovakia have been very limited. The mechanisms for facilitating innovation and mainstreaming of innovation under the ESF are under-developed. Consequently, knowledge and experience from projects with innovative elements are not being ef-

---

[4] REGULATION (EU) No 1303/2013 OF THE EUROPEAN PARLIAMENT AND OF THE COUNCIL, 17th December 2013, *Laying down common provisions on the European Regional Development Fund, the European Social Fund, the Cohesion Fund, the European Agricultural Fund for Rural Development and the European Maritime and Fisheries Fund and laying down general provisions on the European Regional Development Fund, the European Social Fund, the Cohesion Fund and the European Maritime and Fisheries Fund and repealing Council Regulation (EC) No 1083/2006*, [2013], L 347/320, Art. 9.

fectively utilised" (European Commission, 2014a). Therefore, from a macro point of view, the 2007–2013 period represents one in which the EU as a whole paid less attention to good governance, which either worsened significantly or did not change much depending on the indicator. In terms of the big picture, compared to the earlier period, the EU did not do much and it does not appear to have had measurable impact.

We examine in more detail EU funding: Structural Funds managed by national authorities and other types of funding (directly allocated by the European Commission, Norwegian funding provided in the context of its EEA membership).

Most of the financial assistance to Slovakia is provided through the first channel, where the national authorities and the European Commission have to agree on programmes constrained by the legal framework of Cohesion policy. The actual allocation of European funds is then decided upon and administered by Slovak authorities.

Good governance and capacity building were recognised issues when the 2007–2013 period programming was taking place, but it did not have the special status it later acquired in the 2014–2020 period. For Slovakia, strengthening administrative capacity (as a proxy for good governance) was part of the ESF Operational Programme Employment and Social Inclusion and 3 of its priorities (Výročná správa (2014)):

- 3.3. Capacity Building and Improving of Public Administration in the Bratislava Region
- 4.1. Improving of Services Provided by Public Administration and Non-profit Organisations
- 4.2. Introduction of quality management systems into the public administration and for NGOs in the area of employment policy and social policy

This structure reflects the fact that the Bratislava region was the only region in Slovakia to exceed the GDP per capita threshold that denied it much of the Cohesion Funding. Therefore, the ESF programmes were split into priorities for Bratislava and for the rest of the country. This presented a challenge for nationwide good governance projects implemented by institutions predominantly located in the capital. The solution was that the interventions were funded jointly by "Bratislava" and "the rest of Slovakia" priorities provided they concerned national institutions located in the capital and had a nationwide impact. We can therefore frequently observe a combination of priorities 3.3 and 4.1.

This scope of priorities provides for various types of projects to be implemented by the Slovak public administration to support good governance:

- to strengthen skills of the public administration through trainings/education
- and/or to improve processes in the particular public institutions, focus on management
- and/or develop and implement policies for strengthening good governance in the Slovak public administration.

Table 1. Overview of concrete allocations to good governance up to December 2014

ESF Priorities:	Allocated by EU (EUR)	Calls (national projects vs open calls)	Number of projects allocated by Slovak authorities
3.3.	4,021,063.00	27/0	29
4.1.	66,842,518.00	32/3	198
4.2.	772,541.00	1/0	0
Total		60/3	

Source: Výročná správa o vykonávaní operačného program Zamestnanosť a sociálna inklúzia za rok 2014. Ministerstvo práce sociálnych vecí a rodiny SR. *https://www.employment.gov.sk/files/slovensky/esf/op-zasi/vyrocna-sprava/vs-op-zasi-2014.pdf*

The much narrower approach to good governance used in Slovakia in this period is exhibited by the specific amounts allocated by EU for the given area, the amounts of EU funds used (see table 1) in the given period as well as the overview of concrete national projects (table 2): Improvement was expected for mostly trainings, education and communication skills. Smaller amounts were devoted to processes and quality management. In relation to the project on quality management (4.2.), it is important to stress that this programme received the smallest allocation of all good governance programmes and in 2011 a part of the funds was reallocated to different priorities. No project for development of good governance policies of the Slovak public administration has been supported by ESF in the given period. From the perspective of the projects' main foci, it is important to mention that the focus of the projects within the priority 3.3. and 4.1. changed slightly over time; however, only in 2014 (formally after closing this facility) were the projects focusing on analytical skills (e.g., in the case of the Ministry of Finance) supported. The impact of this kind of capacity building can not be perceived/measured in 2016 yet.

Table 2. Focus of the national projects

Area	Priority	Alloc. year	Institution/ Focus	Sum (EUR)
Training	4.1, 3.3.	2009	Supreme Audit Office / education	2.532,938.34 317,543.70
	4.1.	2009	Confederation of Trade Unions / education	894,632
	4.1. 3.3.	2009	Customs Office / education, trainings	2.346,272.15 294,142.16
	4.1. 3.3.	2009	Tax Office / education	4,011,472.00 502,900.00
	4.1. 3.3.	2012	Ministry of Finance / education	20,901.09 166,720.91
	4.1. 3.3.	2012	Association of the Slovak Towns / Capacity Building of local governments, primarily training	1,696,317.44 212,660.10
	4.1. 3.3.	2012	Government Office / improving qualification of the staff	331,749.49 41,590.00
	4.1. 3.3.	2014	Supreme Audit Office / education of the staff at the SAO	222,015.19 27,833.14
	4.1, 3.3.	2014	All government institutions / improving language skills for EU Presidency	1,485,842.28 186,273.72
	4.1. 3.3.	2013	Ministry of Social Affairs / increasing qualification of the staff	30,082.17 239,955.23
	4.1. 3.3.	2009	Ustredie práce a rodiny / education of the staff	6,849,940.24 1,208,812.98
	4.1, 3.3.	2012	National Labour Inspectorate / education, trainings	245,313.12 30,753.86
	4.1.	2010	Ministry of Health / education, trainings, communication standards	1,817.353.40
	4.1.	2010	Ministry of Interior / education	3,473,593.40
	4.1.	2014	Constitutional Court in Slovakia / education	362,518.36
	4.1.	2014	Prison Authority / education	117,766.70

Training and process reengineering	4.1. 3.3.	2014	Ministry of Interior / processes at client centres, education, trainings, analytical capacity	4,014,108.69 503,231.72
	4.1. 3.3.	2014	Ministry of Interior / processes building, information systems, education/trainings	689,093.68 86,390.11
	4.1.	2010 - 2013	Banska Bystrica Regional Government / trainings and processes improvement	2,615,001.78
Trainings and analytical skills building	4.1. 3.3.	2014	Ministry of Finance / strengthening analytical skills	67,697.52 540,000.00
	4.1. 3.3.	2010	Centre of Education, Ministry of Social Affairs / education, analytical skills	5,708,766.53 715,684.34

Source: Výročná správa o vykonávaní operačného program Zamestnanosť a sociálna inklúzia za rok 2014. Ministerstvo práce sociálnych vecí a rodiny SR. *https://www.employment.gov.sk/files/slovensky/esf/op-zasi/vyrocna-sprava/vs-op-zasi-2014.pdf*

As for the process, mostly so-called national projects (see table 3) with **low competition for project**s and ideas were used by ESF. This approach more or less related to direct allocation of funds to the public institutions.

Inconsistency in the timing of project allocation and funds management can be identified as well. The ESF programme started since 2007, but the first calls for priority 3.3. were announced in 2010; for priority 4.1. only one call in 2009 was opened; and for priority 4.2. the first calls were announced in 2010. Most of the calls and projects were allocated in 2014 with implementation in following years. The impact of these projects therefore cannot be recorded/measured yet.

The second channel of support for good governance is financial assistance that bypasses national authorities. In this paper, we analyse funding provided by the European Commission directly to Slovak non-governmental organisations. Additionally, one could also analyse funding provided by the Norwegian government in the context of its payments for EEA membership. However, we could not find comprehensive data, and there is also the issue of whether the Norwegian funds are actually part of EU good governance aid conceptually.

Although there are several NGOs in Slovakia that operate in good governance area, only two of them were able to receive the EU funds (see table 3). It is mostly Transparency International Slovakia that leverages its chances through its international network and a team of experts operating in Brussels.

Table 3: The overview of the projects allocated to the Slovak NGOs directly by (2007–2013)

Name of the project	Donor	Year	Amount allocated (EURO)	Beneficiary institution in Slovakia
European National Integrity Systems Project	EC Directorate General for Home Affairs	2010 - 2012	68,773	TI Slovakia through TI-S
Strengthening the role of the local and regional government watchdogs	EC Directorate General for Justice, Freedom and Security	2006 – 2007?	50,000	TI Slovakia
Integrity of public procurement – set of trainings	EC OLAF	2010	9,700	TI Slovakia

Integrity of public procurement – set of trainings	EC OLAF	2009	10,797	TI Slovakia
Enhancing whistleblower protection	EC Directorate General for Justice, Freedom and Security	2009–2010	30,751	TI Slovakia through TI-S
Public Interest Protection and Implementation Kit: Contribution of Civil Society to Good Governance in Enlarged Europe (JLS/2005/NGO/005)	EC Directorate General for Justice, Freedom and Security	2007	107,525	Via Iuris
The risks of systematic political corruption in the management of EU funds and state-owned enterprises in the Czech Republic, Slovakia and Poland	EC Directorate General for Home Affairs	2012–2014	22,000	Slovak Governance Institute
Total			294,546	

Source: www.transparency.sk, www.governance.sk, www.viaiusris.sk

The data allow for two following observations at least. First, the amount of EU financial assistance allocated to the Slovak NGOs directly by Commission to foster good governance is much lower than EU assistance through ESF programs. Second, the difference lies in the focus of the projects – they were expected to have horizontal effects across the public sector.

As the financial framework 2007–2013 represented the first major EU investment in new Member States and is the only one to have since concluded (on the 31st December, 2015), we focus on it for our evaluation. We conclude that in the 2007–2013 period the EU as a whole paid less attention to good governance in programming its financial aid than in the subsequent period – and this also applied to Slovakia. While Brussels was highly concerned with good governance in Slovakia – at least since 2011 –, EU institutions did not have effective instruments at their disposal to impose conditionality, which they could use to push the issue to the forefront (country-specific recommendations did not have much impact, as the repetition of similar recommendations year by year demonstrates). The good governance situation in Slovakia during this period either worsened significantly or did not change much depending on the indicator. By and large, compared to an earlier period, the EU did not do much on governance and it does not appear to have had a measurable impact.

The microanalysis brought additional explanations, showing that related Structural Fund projects were mainly staff training projects for specific institutions without an overarching strategy or link to other changes in the functioning of public administration. A small percentage of the funds was provided directly by the Commission to NGOs. These projects were much more horizontal in nature and focused on good governance issues, but they amounted to such a small volume that they could not have had major impact.

In other words, the investment made during the 2007–2013 period was small, so it should not come as a surprise that positive outcomes are hard to find. Neither is it surprising that no significant impact could be detected using the data available. However, a process of learning by EU institutions and of upgrading the policy framework and the level of funding for the 2014–2020 period is also noticeable. This might actually be the most significant legacy of the 2007–2013 period, whose effects will be observed in the following years.

References

Alesina, Alberto, and Beatrice Weder. *Do corrupt governments receive less foreign aid?*. No. w7108. National bureau of economic research, 1999.

Beblavý, Miroslav and Emília Sičáková-Beblavá. (2011). Koaličná zmluva či zákon? Právna úprava a realita politicko-administratívnych vzťahov na Slovensku [Coalition Treaty or Law? Legislation and Reality of Politico-Administrative Relations in Slovakia].

———. (2014). The Changing Faces of Europeanisation: How Did the European Union Influence Corruption in Slovakia Before and After Accession?. *Europe-Asia Studies,* 66.4: 536–556.

European Commission. (2014a). ESF Expert Evaluation Network: ESF Main Achievements 2007–2013. file:///Users/emiliabeblava/Downloads/esf_final_synthesis_report_2014_en-1%20(2).pdf

———. (2014b). Promoting good governance – European Social Fund thematic paper. Directorate-General for Employment, Social Affairs and Inclusion, Unit E1, January 2014, p. 4.

Grabbe, H. (2003) 'The Process of EU Accession: What Will It Bring to South East Europe?', available at: http://www.wiiw.ac.at/balkan/files/GDN_EU_Grabbe_EUaccessionprocess.pdf, accessed 18 June 2013. Grabbe, H. (2003) 'The Process of EU Accession: What Will It Bring to South East Europe?', available at: http://www.wiiw.ac.at/balkan/files/GDN_EU_Grabbe_EUaccessionprocess.pdf, accessed 18 June 2013.Mungiu-Pippidi, Alina. (2014). The Transformative Power of Europe Revisited. *Journal of Democracy,* 25.1:20–32.

Sičáková-Beblavá, Emília – Šípoš, Gabriel. (2015). Korupcia a protikorupčná politika na Slovensku. In: Šoltés, Peter – Voros, Lászlo et. al: "Korupcia". *Historický* ústav *SAV.* Bratislava: 464–519.

Weiss, Thomas G. (2000). Governance, good governance and global governance: conceptual and actual challenges. *Third world quarterly,* 21.5: 795–814.

Ministerstvo práce sociálnych vecí a rodiny SR (2014). Výročná správa o vykonávaní operačného program Zamestnanosť a sociálna inklúzia za rok. https://www.employment.gov.sk/files/slovensky/esf/op-zasi/vyrocna-sprava/vs-op-zasi-2014.pdf

4. Romania: Europeanisation of Good Governance Where and why does it fail, and what can be done about it?

MARTIN MENDELSKI[1]

What impact does the European Union (EU) have on the development of good governance in Romania? Does EU conditionality facilitate or hinder the transition towards good governance? This brief policy-oriented chapter argues that the EU's promotion of good governance in Romania leads to some selective progress but, overall, to the persistence of bad governance. In particular, the paper shows that Romania's process of Europeanisation has resulted in 1. some progress across three dimensions of governance (*substantive legality, capacity* and *efficiency/effectiveness*) but 2. regress in three others (*formal legality, impartiality and coherence*). In other words, reforms generate more substantive laws that are adapted to international/European standards (best practices), but at the same time the new laws become instable, incoherent (contradictory), hardly enforced and less general. In addition, reforms improve capacity (inputs) and partly efficiency (outputs) or effectiveness (outcomes) but undermine the procedural and structural aspects of government quality (impartiality, coherence), for instance through increased politicisation and fragmentation of the state structures. Overall, the analysis suggests that there is no transition towards good governance in Romania, despite selective progress.

What is good governance?

Good governance is conceived as a multi-dimensional concept that relates to the legal, judicial, prosecutorial and administrative quality in a state, and in particular to 1. the existence of stable, coherent, general and enforced laws that are embedded in universal good governance standards, 2. capable, efficient, independent, accountable and non-fragmented state structures that are able to deliver public goods effectively and 3. implement and prioritise coherent policies. Governance consists of two main qualities and six distinct dimensions (see appendix, figure 1). In particular I distinguish between *de jure* good governance (quality of laws), which consists of 1. formal legality and 2. substantive legality, and *de facto* good governance (quality of state structures/government), which consists of four additional dimensions 3. capacity, 4. impartiality, 5. efficiency/effectiveness and 6. coherence (see Mendelski 2015; 2016b).

De jure good governance reflects the quality of formal rules and the way in which these rules are created and enforced. It can be assessed both in terms of formal legality, that is, the technical or formal quality of laws, and in terms of substantive legality, for instance, whether laws are good laws, whether they promote certain values such as justice and fairness, and which are reflected in international best practices of good governance (e.g., United Nations Convention against Corruption). D*e facto* good governance, on the other hand, reflects the quality of the government – in particular the impartial, efficient, coherent adoption and enforcement of rules, policies and reforms by state structures (e.g., legislative, judiciary, administration, etc.). Particularly important is the presence of well-coordinated, coherent and integrated (autonomous) state units, structures and policies (OECD 1997). Incoherence, in contrast, is associated with fragmentation, overlap, duplication and detrimental competition within state structures (Mendelski 2013; 2016b).

---

[1] Max Planck Institute for the Study of Societies, Cologne, mendelski@mpifg.de

Finally, all six dimensions of governance are interdependent. In order to create good governance, reformers must seek to improve all six dimensions in a balanced way. Achieving progress in one dimension and regressing in others does not necessarily enhance governance. For instance, aligning domestic legislation with international standards will not establish the rule of law if the new laws and regulations become unstable, incoherent or are not enforced. Similarly, creating efficient but not sufficiently impartial prosecutorial and judicial structures (and vice versa) will not necessarily improve the rule of law. Adapting to best practices through institutional transplantation without assuring coherence of state structures will undermine good governance. The next section shows that the EU (together with its domestic reformers) had precisely such an uneven effect across the six dimensions of governance. While substantive legality, capacity and efficiency improved, reforms undermined formal legality, impartiality and coherence.

Where does the Europeanisation of good governance fail?

Substantive legality: Considerable improvement

The first part of figure 1 presents the main a good governance treaty ratification indicator, which measures the development of the substantive legality, and in particular Romania's embeddedness in international good governance treaties. The indicator exhibits considerable progress. In a relatively short period of time (2001–2004) Romania's leaders signed and ratified all five major good governance conventions. In addition, several *de jure* provisions to strengthen judicial independence, anti-corruption and integrity were introduced. This intensified alignment of domestic legislation with European and international standards can be attributed to EU conditionality, which generated incentives for domestic reformers (e.g., Adrian Nastase) who were eager to gain legitimacy abroad and to obtain access to resources (EU funds, IMF credits, etc.). Romanian elites thus were able to fulfil most obligations imposed by external conditionality. However, while the *de jure* alignment with international standards was fairly easy and rapid, the same cannot be said for the second dimension of *de jure* good governance (formal legality), which experienced regress.

Figure 1. Good governance treaty ratification

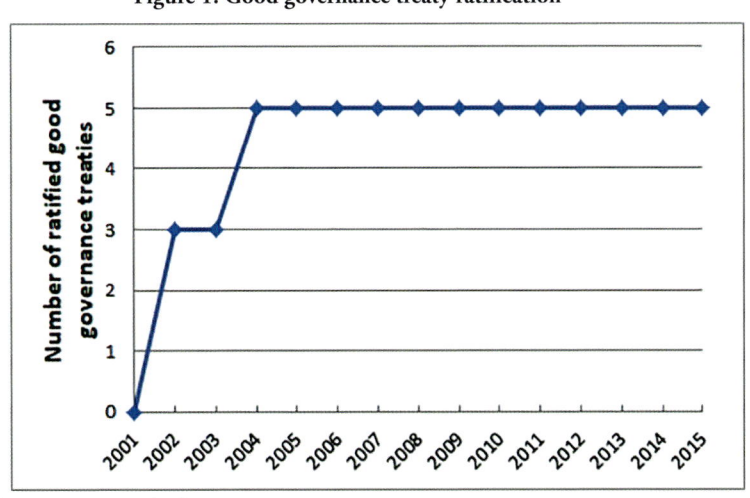

Sources: United Nations; Council of Europe.
Notes: This indicator consists of the proportion of the five more important anti-corruption conventions ratified by Romania (1. United Nations Convention against Corruption, 2. CoE Civil Law Convention on Corruption, 3. CoE Criminal Law Convention on Corruption, 4. CoE Additional Protocol to the Criminal Law Convention on Corruption, 5. Convention on Laundering, Search, Seizure and Confiscation of the Proceeds from Crime.

Formal legality: Pathological development

Figure 2 presents data to measure *legislative output and instability*, as reflected in the number of laws adopted yearly in the parliament.[2] Between 1995 and 2001 the number of adopted laws (legislative output) grew considerably in Romania, i.e., from 135 to 782 adopted laws per year. The "legislative explosion" occurred between 2000 and 2001 when the legislative output more than tripled and gradually declined afterwards. It also seems that the stability of legislation deteriorated during the pre- and post-accession period to the EU. This was particularly the case in the area of justice and anticorruption. Law no. 92/1992 on the organisation of the judiciary was modified 21 times between 1997 and 2005. Law no. 304/2004 on the judicial organisation was amended 26 times between 2004 and 2013. Other frequently amended laws concerned the competencies of the Superior Council of Magistracy and relevant prosecutorial and administrative structures (e.g., DNA, DIICOT and ANI legislation). The legislative growth and instability was reflected in growing number of emergency ordinances, which increased from 13 to 290 (between 1996 and 2000) and of presidential decrees, which rose from 13 to 1063 (between 1996 and 2002). Accelerated (i.e., fast-track) legislative procedures during the pre-accession process to the EU were mis(used) in many accession or candidate countries (e.g., Poland, Slovakia, Czechia, Croatia, Serbia, etc.), but comparative data on legislative output indicates that this reform pathology (of Europeanisation) was especially grave in Romania (see Mendelski 2014). How can this deterioration of formal legality be explained?

According to my interviews with several legal experts and judges, legal inflation/instability was directly or indirectly linked to Romania's EU integration process. EU demands for legal approximation and reforms (which were often accompanied by coercive pressure from the World Bank and the IMF) account for a considerable percentage (approx. 30%) of the rising legislative output. In addition, Romania's anticorruption, judicial and legal reforms were accompanied by intensified political struggles between liberal change agents and reform opponents (Mendelski 2012), which resulted in a vicious cycle of reform counter-reform, increased politicisation and the mis(use) of law as a political weapon. In sum, EU-driven reforms had an uneven effect. On the one hand, domestic laws were aligned with international/European laws and standards. On the other hand, laws became more instable, incoherent and less enforced (Mendelski 2014, 2015, 2016).

---

[2] The legislative growth indicator can be seen as a proxy indicator for legislative instability because many new laws have been introduced through amendments of the legal framework.

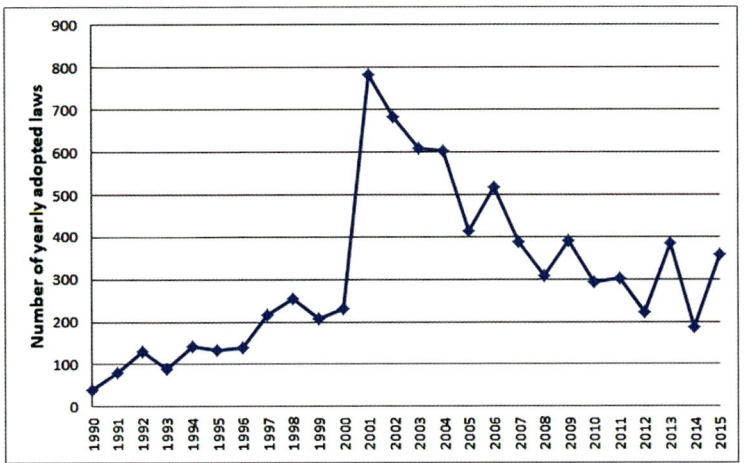

Figure 2. Legislative output

Source: Database of the Legislative Council, http://www.clr.ro/rep_dil_2002/rep.aspx.

Capacity: Considerable progress

Figure 3 presents the main indicator (judicial budget p.c.) to measure (judicial) capacity. The indicator shows that the budget of the Romanian judicial system grew considerably (from 7.8 to 35.0 EUR, p.c.). Improved (judicial) *capacity* has been the outcome of higher salaries, increased computerisation and infrastructural reforms (e.g. investment in court building), creation of new state structures (DNA, DIICOT, ANI), which more than often resulted from demands and support by the EU and international donors (and in particular USAID, Council of Europe). The progress on this indictor suggests an overall beneficial potential impact of EU-driven reforms. Surely, alternative explanations added to this positive trend, such as beneficial domestic economic conditions until 2008 (interrupted only briefly by the international financial crisis).

Figure 3. Judicial capacity

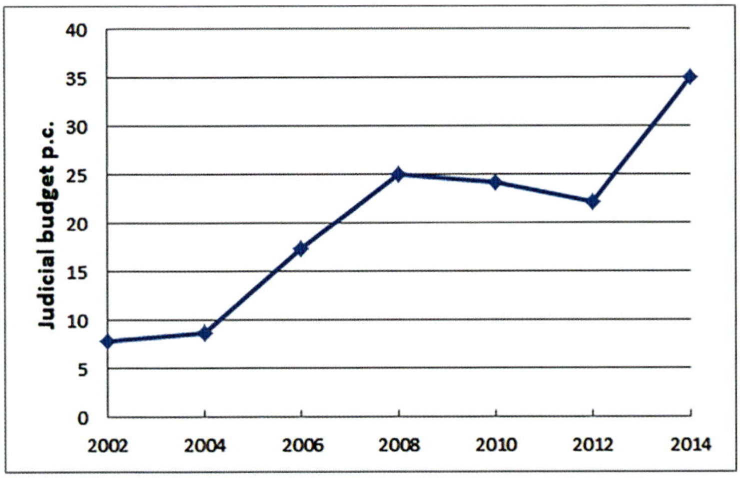

Source: CEPEJ. See http://www.coe.int/cepej.

Impartiality: Only judicial independence, the rest of the state lags behind

Figure 4 gives an overview of several impartiality indicators for the period between 2002 and 2014. In contrast to the progress of judicial capacity, the three indicators of impartiality did not experience a similar positive trend. The indicators *Favoritism in decisions making* (-0.4) and *Diversion of public funds* (-0.2) experienced some decline. The *judicial independence* indicator improved (+0.9), but experienced a fluctuating trend and remains at a median level. Progress can be most probably attributed to the EU's insistence on judicial self-organisation through judicial councils and the general trend towards judicialisation. Fluctuation of the indicator suggests that the judiciary has not been able to avoid politicisation by the executive despite the strengthening of legal safeguards and the empowering of the Superior Council of Magistracy. Overall, the three indicators of impartiality indicate that despite selective progress, EU-driven reforms have not been able to achieve transformative change at this dimension.

Figure 4. Selected indicators of impartiality

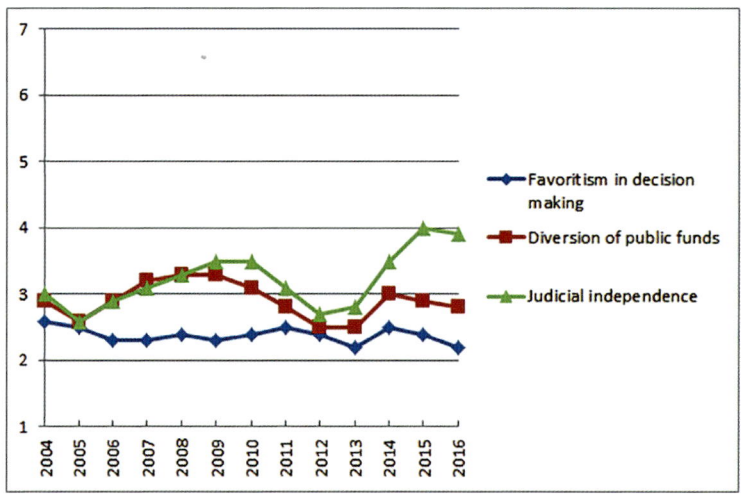

Source: World Economic Forum's Executive Opinion Survey (WEFEOS);
Notes: Scale from 1 (worst) to 7 (best).

Coherence: Towards increased fragmentation

Figure 5 offers an overview of several agency and process-related indicators of coherence. First, the *elite factionalisation* indicator by the Fund for Peace shows a decline (-1.4), suggesting the domestic elites in Romania became more divided over reforms and policies. Second, the BTI *party system* indicator regressed from 8.0 to 7.0 between 2004 and 2014, suggesting that the party system in Romania became more fragmented polarised and instable. Third, the BTI *policy coordination indicator*, which measures the ability of the government to coordinate conflicting policy objectives, shows a fluctuating and declining development (-2.0) between 2004 and 2014. Lack of potential policy coordination is also reflected in the fragmentation of the executive branch, which consists of 22 ministries. The executive has also experienced constant tensions between the president and the prime minister. In addition, structural incoherence/heterogeneity is reflected in the fragmented nature of governance which has been reinforced by the introduction of "islands or enclaves of excellence" (e.g., 1. Anti-Corruption Directorate, DNA, 2. National Integrity Agency, ANI, 3. Organised Crime and Terrorism Department,

DIICOT) that undermine the coherence of the prosecutorial (administrative) system. This process of fragmentation began already in the 1990s, with the transplantation of several autonomous organs from abroad (e.g., Ombudsman, Superior Council of Magistrates, Constitutional Court, Central Bank, regulatory agencies etc.). The problem here is not autonomy or pluralism (of different units) *per se*, but the lack of unity (corporate ethos, unitary judicial and political decisions), cooperation and coordination of activities between the different government structures (state agencies, within ministries, judicial structures etc.), which results more than often in fragmentation, frictions, quarrels over competency and inefficiency of the governance system. Overall, the trends in the coherence indicators point to continuing divisions between political elites, fragmentation of state structures and the lack of policy coordination.

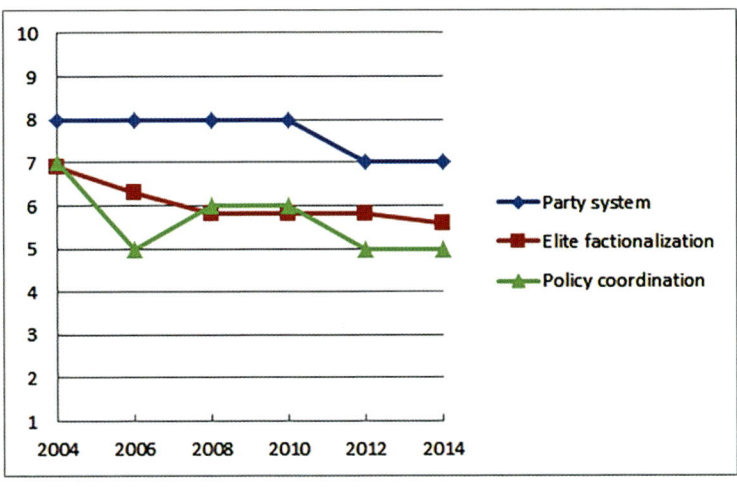

Figure 5. Selected indicators of coherence

Sources: Bertelsmann Transformation Index (BTI).
Notes: Scale:1 (worst) to 10 (best)

Efficiency-effectiveness: Selective progress within broad stagnation

Figure 6 presents one indicator of government efficiency and two indicators of government effectiveness. The indicator of *wastefulness of government spending*, which measures how efficiently the government spends public revenue, experienced a small decrease from 2.9 to 2.5. Two indicators of the government's effective provision of public goods show mixed development. While the *quality of overall infrastructure* improved by +1.1, the *quality of the educational system* declined by -1.4. Overall, no clear tendency can be identified and more indicators would be needed to assess the impact of reforms in the public sector. The mixed development at the efficiency/effectiveness dimension can be attributed to a mixture of improved economic conditions (until 2009), EU and international donor conditionality.

Figure 6. Selected indicators for efficiency/effectiveness

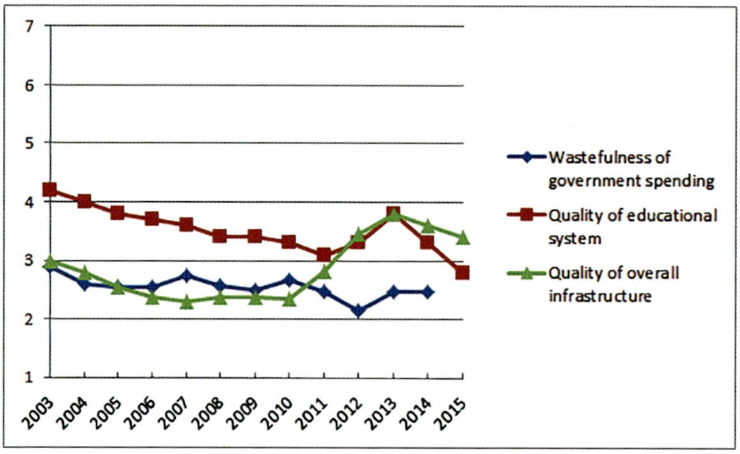

Sources: World Economic Forum's Executive Opinion Survey (WEFEOS)
Notes: Scale:1 (worst) - 7 (best)

Overall, good governance developed unevenly across its six dimensions, suggesting a differential/uneven impact of the EU-driven reforms in Romania. With regard to the *de jure* good governance, while laws became more similar to European and international standards, they became at the same time less stable. As regards the *de facto* good governance, capacity was considerably improved but this was not always reflected in indicators of impartiality, coherence, and efficiency/effectiveness which mainly stagnated or declined. Thus, EU conditionality did not lead to transformative change in most dimensions of good governance. The reasons for this unexpected lack of progress are explored in the next section.

What prevents Europeanisation of governance?

Why did EU-driven good governance reforms not result in more transformative progress and even in deterioration in several key dimensions of good governance? This section identifies three fundamental problems of EU conditionality (Europeanisation), which explain why well-intended reforms do not lead to the establishment of good governance.

The problem of valuing quantity over quality

The first fundamental problem of Europeanisation is reflected in the EU's quantitative approach to good governance promotion, which follows essentially a "the more the better" mindset. The EU's approach emphasises reforms that stress quantitative outcomes (more laws, more resources, more convictions, more arrests, etc.) over the quality of reform processes and procedures (i.e., how laws, arrests or convictions are made). The EU's approach can be criticised for creating distorted quantitative incentives for reformers by stressing quantitative "track records" to evaluate progress, such as the number of prosecuted high-level corruption cases, regular indictments of senior politicians and civil servants, number of projects, number of assets frozen and recovered, number of convictions (number of corruption cases brought to conclusion), number of laws adopted/amended, number of conflict of interests detected, number of judges and prosecutors trained, number of best practices successfully exchanged and applied, number of working groups established, etc. These indicators to measure progress have been reflected in the EU's progress reports, several twinning projects, and the main reform good governance strategies.[3]

However, by relying on a "more is better" approach, the EU (together with domestic actors) has produced and reinforced legal pathologies which have undermined the rule of law and good governance in general. The demand for more transplanted laws and adaptation to international standards has improved the substantive legality but at the time has fostered legal inflation and instability. The demand for more regulations has increased discrepancy between formal rules and informal practice (see Slapin 2015). The call for more judicial independence has resulted in more independent but less accountable judicial councils, anticorruption structures and courts (Transparency International 2012; Mendelski 2016a). The demand for a "solid track records" in fighting high-level corruption cases has increased the number of convictions (efficiency), but it has also undermined the procedural quality of anti-corruption policies (Mendelski 2016a). The demand for more judicial capacity has created expensive information and court administration systems (based on Western technology and software), which are expensive to maintain and rely on continuous foreign assistance. Finally, more material resources (in the form of EU funds) have resulted in more opportunities to engage in corruption and rent seeking (Mungiu-Pippidi 2014). Overall, the EU's quantitative approach with its perverse incentives has produced or reinforced several legal and political pathologies, which have undermined crucial aspects of good governance.

The EU's partisan empowerment and evaluation of change agents

The second fundamental problem reflects the EU's selective and partisan empowerment and support of selected, reformist, "liberal" change agents (associated with the National Liberal Party or "PNL"), to the detriment of so-called "illiberal" reform opponents (associated with the Social Democratic Party or "PSD"). Partisan empowerment was for instance visible when the EU selectively supported reformist political change agents (e.g., Monica Macovei, Traian Basescu and Klaus Iohannis) and key actors in newly created or empowered state structures (e.g., DNA, ANI, DIICOT, CSM, Constitutional Court). Most of these autonomous enclaves were created under the pressure of EU conditionality during the pre-accession process and were initially weak but from 2005 onwards considerably empowered. But why should selective empowerment of reformist change agents be detrimental for the development of good governance? Eventually change agents would propel required reforms and achieve desired outcomes (e.g., judicial and prosecutorial independence, checks on politicians, integrity, reduction of corruption and organised crime). This is wishful thinking, however. The partisan support of reformers is a double-edged sword. It may result in some formal changes but at the same time reduce external accountability over them, potentially leading to the accumulation and misuse of power.

The sobering reality is that both political change agents and reform opponents are embedded in the same environment of bad governance (i.e., legal and political instability, state fragmentation, informality, politicisation, clientelism, lack of effective oversight, etc.) from which they can hardly escape (only if they leave the country). Thus, change agents often lack the

---

[3] For instance, annex no. 5 to Romania's anticorruption strategy (2016–2020) mentions mainly quantitative indicators to measure reform progress, among others: 1. number of persons which were dismissed due to potential conflicts of interest, 2. number of complaints received from third parties regarding conflict of interests, 3. number of indictments / convictions regarding conflicts of interest, 4. number of public meetings 5. number of complaints received regarding the breach of legal provisions, 6. number of complaints filed in the court 7. numbers of sanctions imposed by the courts.

appropriate incentives, norms and skills to conduct reforms in a non-politicised, impartial and inclusive way. In a situation of *detrimental political competition* between elites – both pro- and anti-reform political elites –, instead of respecting the rule of law, may (mis)use the law and the judicial system as a weapon against each other. In Romania, different competing factions (i.e., both change agents and reform opponents) have repeatedly instrumentalised the law, resorted to informal practices and secret deals, which undermined the separation of powers, transgressed their competencies and politicised the reform process (Mendelski 2012, 2015, 2016b). However, despite these structural deficiencies, the EU has selectively supported the liberal-reformist camp in Romania, thus giving them in many instances a free hand (discretion) in conducting reforms without the necessary restrictions. The partisan empowering of change agents thus resulted in new possibilities to accumulate and abuse power. Once reform opponents from the PSD came to power, they tried to launch a protective counter-movement by weakening oversight structures (e.g., at ANI, DNA, Constitutional Court, the CSM) through emergency ordinances or replacing their heads/members with their own protégés. The result of these political power struggles have been recurrent vicious cycles of reform and counter-reform with detrimental effects for the rule of law and good governance (in particular for legal stability, state coherence and the creation of impersonal, impartial and accountable state structures) (Mendelski 2015).

Biased evaluation of progress in good governance

The third fundamental problem of EU conditionality is reflected in biased evaluation of good governance (and particularly the rule of law). The EU's lack of a coherent and objective monitoring and evaluation methodology of the rule of law and anti-corruption policies (see Dimitrov et al. 2014; Toneva-Metodieva 2014), which I have termed elsewhere the "EU's rule of law evaluation deficit" (Mendelski 2016a), opens doors for ad-hoc approaches, leeway, partisanship and double standards. The EU's assessment deficit has been reflected in several problematic issues (see Mendelski 2016a):

1. Politicised progress reports (e.g., European Commission 2012) contained positive information about change agents and include negative assessments of reform opponents.[4] Especially, the newly created and empowered state structures (e.g. DNA, ANI, High Court of Cassation and Justice, CSM, Constitutional Court etc.) have been repeatedly praised and evaluated positively when they were stuffed with reformist "change agents", but negatively assessed when they were under control of reform-opposing "veto players".
2. One-sided, harmful rhetoric by members of EU institutions during "inter-institutional conflicts" in Romania: Here can be mentioned the exaggerated "rule of law crisis" and "coup d'etat rhetoric" by leading representatives of the EU during the Romanian constitutional crisis from 2012. By invoking the concept of the rule of law to support change agents, the EU risks transforming this core fundamental value into a politicised and instrumental buzzword, rather than strengthening it as an impartial principle and constraint valid for *all* actors.
3. A reactive "problem-based approach" which relies on the ringing of "alarm bells" by Western-financed NGOs and a well-connected legal, liberal epistemic expert community, which however avoids ringing the alarm bells in the case of liberal, reformist governments.
4. One-sided reliance on liberal advisors and experts that have a liberal-constitutionalist perspective which emphasises only selective aspects of the rule of law (e.g., independence

---

[4] <http://<www.nineoclock.ro/the-report%E2%80%99s-dangerous-omissions>. See letter by former president Constantinescu to the European Commission: <http://<www.nineoclock.ro/former-president-emil-constantinescu-writes-to-ec-president-jose-manuel-barroso/>.

of Constitutional Courts and judicial councils) to the detriment of accountability of these bodies and a systemic assessment of the rule of law as a socially, politically and historically embedded concept.

Why should this lack of objective evaluation be a bad thing? One main argument is that the selective and inconsistent evaluation methodology of EU conditionality cannot function as an impartial external accountability mechanism and can no longer discipline change agents. In fact the EU risks becoming an accomplice who turns a blind eye to the transgressions of change agents within newly created state structures which themselves may become 1. politicised, captured or controlled by influential and dominant politicians, transnational coalitions or informal and hidden networks, or 2. that these autonomous state structures become so independent and powerful that they are no longer accountable to the law, democratic oversight and public scrutiny.

Romania is an unfortunate example where the newly created network of autonomous structures (controlled by externally-empowered change agents) turned into unaccountable, instrumentalised and politicised "state enclaves" (see Transparency International 2012). In the course of reform, many of the new structures became autonomous but unaccountable and dis-embedded. The EU, together with US representatives, parts of the "liberal" civil society (including reformist journalists), have continued to support and evaluate their "islands of excellence" in a positive way, despite increasing evidence of deficient functioning, such as: 1. non-transparent and personalised stuff selection procedures in key judicial and anti-corruption structures (e.g., through interviews, arranged voting, bargains between elites) which have undermined the principle of merit-based selection; and 2. a deficient fight against corruption, which includes abuse of fundamental rights and procedural aspects (e.g., misuse of wire-tapping, disrespect for immunity of judges, problematic pre-trial detention, non-transparent selection methodology of cases), allegations of fabricated/invented files and deals with prosecutors, reported pressure and intimidation of judges by DNA prosecutors, inconsistent notion of the "abuse in office", potential hidden influence by informal networks and secret service structures and a focus on perverse, quantitative indicators (track records), which undermine procedural quality (see Mendelski 2016a; Clark 2016). By turning a blind eye on the transgressions of reformist, "anticorruption fighters", the EU (together with several partisan Western diplomats/politicians) has reduced external and domestic accountability over them, therefore undermining the procedural and democratic functioning of anti-corruption policy in Romania.

Concsion: What can be done about it?

Does the EU enhance or undermine good governance in Romania? This study suggests that EU-driven reforms improve some aspects of governance (1. substantive legality, 2. capacity) but undermine several other ones (3. formal legality, 4. impartiality, 5. coherence and partially also 6. efficiency/effectiveness). Overall, the analysis suggests that there is no transition towards good governance in Romania, despite selective progress. This sobering result is reflected in the deficient functioning of autonomous but unconstrained accountability structures (e.g., DNA, ANI, CSM) that do not function in an impartial, impersonal, transparent and accountable way. Reform failure can be attributed (among other factors) to EU conditionality (CVM), which develops into a pathological form when applied in an institutional context of bad governance (particularism). What can be done to improve external promotion of good governance in Romania and beyond?

First, the EU should refrain from partisan empowerment of reformist, liberal change agents, particularly when they instrumentalise the law, disrespect procedural aspects and human rights and misuse their prerogatives to fight competitors. The EU's empowerment strategies are probably helpful to push reforms and to attain certain geopolitical goals, but they also undermine the establishment of the rule of law (and good governance). Rather than focusing on a small group of selected liberal change agents, the EU should reward elites and movements who have gained domestic legitimacy, foster domestic consensus and unity and regard the law as a necessary constraint rather than a tool. By supporting a small minority of delegitimised and abusive change agents, the EU may further reinforce the polarisation of the Romanian polity and society.

Second, EU conditionality should be re-focused from quantitative outcomes towards qualitative processes. In particular, the EU should not link conditionality to specific reform outcomes or benchmarks (e.g., bringing war criminals before the court, increasing the number of high-level corruption cases, adoption of specific laws or one-size-fits-all solutions). Rather, the EU should link conditionality to the reform process itself, which underlies these outcomes This process-related and qualitative approach should pay attention to formal legality, coherence of state structures and interdependencies between dimensions of governance.

Third, the EU needs to improve the currently flawed and inconsistent methodology of governance (rule of law) evaluation, which opens the doors to bias and double standards. An enhanced approach requires a more objective, qualitative and multiplicative methodology, which would pay attention to reform and policy processes. In addition, the EU's (CVM) progress reports should contain more detailed references and all relevant sources of information in a large appendix (e.g., containing original screening reports by experts, documented interviews, opinions of the respective government and opposition) More objectivity and validity through triangulation and transparency of the evaluation methodology could help to diminish the "EU's evaluation deficit" and the pathological effects it generates.

References

Clark, D. (2016). *Fighting Corruption with Con Tricks: Romania's Assault on the Rule of Law*. The Henry Jackson Society. http://henryjacksonsociety.org/wp-content/uploads/2017/01/Romania-paper.pdf

Mendelski, M. (2009). The Impact of the European Union on Governance Reforms in Post-Communist Europe: A Comparison between First and Second-Wave Candidates. *Romanian Journal of Political Science* 9(2): 42–64.

———. (2012). EU-Driven Judicial Reforms in Romania: A Success Story? *East European Politics* 28(1): 23–42.

———. (2013). They Have Failed Again! Donor-driven Promotion of the Rule of Law in Serbia. *Südost-Europa: Zeitschrift für Politik und Gesellschaft* 61(1): 79–113.

———. (2015). The EU's pathological power: The failure of external rule of law promotion in South Eastern Europe. *Southeastern Europe* 39 (3): 318–346

———. (2016a). Europeanisetion and the Rule of Law: Towards a Pathological Turn", *Southeastern Europe* 40 (3): 346–384.

———. (2016b). The EU's rule of law promotion in post-Soviet Europe: what explains the divergence between Baltic States and EaP countries? *Eastern Journal of European Studies* 7(2): 107–140.

Mungiu-Pippidi, A. (2014). The Transformative Power of Europe Revisited. *Journal of Democracy* 25(1): 20–32.

OECD. (1997). The OECD Report on Regulatory Reform: Synthesis Report. OECD Publishing.

Slapin, J. B. (2015). How European Union membership can undermine the rule of law in emerging democracies. *West European Politics*, *38*(3), 627–648.

Toneva-Metodieva, L. (2014). Beyond the Carrots and Sticks Paradigm: Rethinking the Cooperation and Verification Mechanism Experience of Bulgaria and Romania. *Perspectives on European Politics and Society* 15(4): 534–551.

Transparency International. (2012). *National Integrity System Assessment Romania*.

5. Turkey: The Paradoxical Effects of EU Accession

DIGDEM SOYALTIN[1]

Rather than achieving good governance in Turkey, the formal institutional change promoted by the EU has failed to eliminate the informal institutions of clientelism and patronage. Instead, the ruling party has been instrumental in using anticorruption measures to gain more control over state structures and replace old patronage structures with new ones, all the while enlarging on some neoliberal reforms in the economy. Recent deteriorations of press freedom and judiciary independence have also weighted down on control of corruption.

The origins of EU's anticorruption policy in Turkey

Corruption has been a pervasive problem in Turkey for many years. Yet, a decisive anticorruption policy was formulated only after the EU and other external donors started to challenge the problem of corruption more prominently in the aftermath of the 2001 financial crisis. Facing increasing pressure, the incumbent government mostly formed by the Justice and Development Party (Turkish acronym, "AKP") responded to the EU's demands for change and expanded the legal framework with regard to fight against corruption. The conditional incentives of the EU membership process, which became more credible when Turkey received the EU candidacy status at the Helsinki Summit in 1999, had a considerable impact on the adoption of domestic anticorruption reforms. Given the impressive number of reforms adopted to comply with the EU's rules, Turkey was considered "a textbook example" of the EU's transformative power (Kirişçi 2011). Yet, the EU accession process lost momentum after 2006 in terms of pushing Turkish government to comply with the EU rules (Noutcheva and Düzgit 2012).

Combating corruption is an integral part of the EU's enlargement policy (Vachudova 2009, pp. 49–50). The legal and administrative changes required by the EU's ambitious reform agenda incur adaptation costs for target governments. Domestic change becomes more likely when the EU's conditional incentives are credible enough to compensate the costs of adaptation (Börzel and Risse 2003). As shown in the Central and Eastern European countries (CEEs), membership conditionality, as the strategy of reinforcement by reward, have enabled the EU to induce governments to comply with its conditions and adopt certain policies (Schimmelfennig and Sedelmeier 2005) to fight against corruption. Another instrument used by the EU to support the CEECs in their transition to democracy and good governance was financial and technical assistance. Especially provided the financial assistance by the Instrument for Pre-accession Assistance (IPA) was actively linked to the fulfilment of certain democratic criteria, thus creating further stimulus for the massive reforms (Smith 2004). EU assistance was also geared towards enhancing capacity of state institutions along with strengthening of media and civil society, which was thought in turn to be able to pressure the government for further change (Börzel and Pamuk 2012). In this regard, the free media, strong civil society and active citizens can put constraints on those who have opportunities to spoil public resources (Mungiu-Pippidi 2015).

Since the civil society is traditionally too weak in Turkey to put domestic pressure on its government, the reform process of sensitive issues, including the fight against corruption,

---

[1] Assistant Professor Istanbul Kemerburgaz University, Turkey, didemsoyaltin@gmail.com

was primarily driven by the credible incentive structure of the EU (Düzgit and Çarkoğlu 2004, Müftüler-Baç 2005). Moreover, the capacity-building programmes of the EU provided technical and financial assistance for the anticorruption agencies that are necessary to facilitate reform.

Corruption has been a long-standing problem for Turkey (Baran 2000). Although the scope and form of corruption has evolved over the years, the patronage networks that had historically been part of Turkish society dating back to the Ottoman Empire largely sustained and enabled certain groups of individuals to have access to resources and appropriate gains throughout Turkey's modern history (Buğra 1994). The drastic increase in the use of particularistic politics throughout the 1980s and 1990s disproportionately benefited capital groups with close relations and affiliations with high-level representatives of the government and weakened the regulatory capacities of the existing state bureaucracy and judiciary (Güneş-Ayata 2010). Coupled with ineffective civil society organisations and poor media environment, the weak governance structure further promoted institutionalisation of complex networks of mutual dependence and favour trading (Heper 1973, Kalaycıoğlu 2005). Yet, the absence of independent strong anticorruption controllers left too much discretion to the executive and gave rise to favouritism, eventually leading to corrupt practices that went unreported or investigated for many years.[2]

Until the early 2000s, prior to the launch of the reforms as part of the EU accession process, corruption did not used to be considered an urgent problem by Turkish politicians (Şarlak and Bali 2008). However, corruption was listed as one of the most serious and acute problems in several surveys of the public at that time (Adaman, Çarkoğlu and Şenatalar 2001). Experts also placed Turkey among the group of countries perceived as the most corrupt in Europe. In the Corruption Perception Index (CPI) published by Transparency International (TI) Turkey never scored more than 3.8, and generally fluctuated around a figure of 3 in the late 1990s and in the beginning of the 2000s (Yaşar 2005).

Given the high level of corruption, the EU has paid greater attention to fighting corruption in Turkey (Adaman 2011, Doig 2012, Ulusoy 2014). After the EU granted Turkey candidacy status in 1999, the European Commission consistently stated that corruption had been a very serious and widespread problem in Turkey. In this context, EU officials strongly supported the implementation of the structural economic reform programmes agreed upon with the IMF and the World Bank (European Commission 2003, p. 125) and induced Turkish authorities to take more specific legal and institutional measures with regard to strengthening governance and fighting corruption. Accordingly, Turkey had been obliged to develop management and financial control systems, ensure transparency in public procurement and political funding, and support capacity building for law enforcement and judicial authorities, as well as civil society organisations and media.[3]

Conditionality unleashed

The conditional incentives provided by the EU have been a main driver of the anticorruption reforms in Turkey. In the aftermath of the 2001 crisis, the EU has played a substantial role in the formulation of the anticorruption reforms that were enshrined in various national action plans.[4] Turkey's reform efforts, combined with its desire to join the EU, went a significant way towards satisfying the conditions for the start of accession negotiations in 2005 (Uğur

---

[2] Interview with a former member of Parliamentary Investigation Committee on Causes of Corruption, June 2012, Istanbul

[3] This list is derived from Accession Partnership documents of 2003, 2006 and 2008.

[4] Interview with a former member of Parliamentary Investigation Committee on Causes of Corruption, June 2012, Ankara

2010). However, the EU's ability to push government into compliance with EU rules in the wake of deteriorating Turkey-EU relations, which have been in a downward spiral since 2006 (Noutcheva and Düzgit 2012, p.68).

The EU has largely relied on strategy of promoting reforms through positive incentives in Turkey. Yet, the EU's monitoring tools (accession partnerships, peer based reviews and the progress reports) do not indicate the benchmarks employed to assess the level of progress and implementation, therefore they remain rather inefficient (Börzel and Pamuk,2012, p.84; Szarek-Mason 2010, p.30). This, in turn, empowered Turkish politicians in their accusations of the EU's double standards[5] and gave more space for political actors to selectively implement the EU demands (see Spendzharova and Vachudova 2012).

Besides conditional incentives, the EU provided financial support aimed at strengthening the capacity of state agencies to cope with the reform agenda. Under IPA, Turkey received EUR 4.87 billion, an average of EUR 608 million per year between 2007 and 2013. The EU allocation for Turkey under IPA-II for the 2014–20 periods is planned to be EUR 4.45 billion (European Commission 2014). Together with the funds provided under the Turkey Pre-Accession Assistance until 2006, the IPA funds make Turkey the largest recipient of EU aid with over EUR 13 billion (EU Ministry 2014).

Moreover, EU supports capacity building in framework of various projects co-founded by other external donors. There are relatively few international donors that are active with grant support in Turkey, while some of them receive EU grants to implement pre-accession assistance in their fields of expertise (European Commission 2014). Together with the Council of Europe, the EU is implementing projects specifically aimed at the Turkish judiciary and anticorruption agencies. Since 2007, 14 projects were completed in the judicial sector, which combined amounted to more than EUR 70 million.[6] In recent years, the Turkish judiciary system has benefitted from higher salaries, increased technical infrastructure and investment in court buildings (CEPEJ 2011).

The legal, financial, technical and cognitive support provided by the EU accession process also empowered civil society actors and increased their visibility in Turkey (Diez *et.al.* 2005). Furthermore, the EU also urged Turkish authorities to include civil society in the policy-making process. Yet, in processes of preparation of laws, government programmes and plans, successive Turkish governments have acted unwilling to reflect views of the civil actors which are not co-opted into the clientele system. Only the Union of Chambers and Commodity Exchanges of Turkey (TOBB), known for its close ties with the government, was invited to take part in the anticorruption ministerial commission.[7] Mostly controlled or channelled by the state, Turkish civil society is far from being able to push reforms in the country or being a strong monitoring actor pursuing the public interest (TUSEV 2014). Similarly, big business, with its growing control over the media sector,[8] has particularistic ties with politicians and benefits from government's reform-adverse decisions, especially in the procurement and tendering policies (Emek and Acar 2015).

---

[5] "Recep Tayyip Erdogan accuses EU of double standards", Telegraph, 07.06.2013, in: http://www.telegraph.co.uk/news/worldnews/europe/turkey/10106816/Turkey-protests-Recep-Tayyip-Erdogan-accuses-EU-of-double-standards.html

[6] Interview with Council of Europe, Ankara office, April 2016, Ankara

[7] Interview with Economic Policy Research Foundation of Turkey (*Türkiye Ekonomi Politikaları Araştırma Vakfı, TEPAV*), May 2012, Ankara

[8] Sözeri and Güney (2011) argue that media in Turkey has become a tool of manipulation for big capital groups to gain political and economic benefits in their relationships with the Turkish government.

In sum, the main driver of anticorruption reforms in the post-2006 period has not been EU conditionality nor has it been domestic pushback from civil actors and business; rather the AKP government's political preferences lead the charge (Yilmaz and Soyaltin 2014). The AKP government immediately declared combatting corruption to be one of its three policy priorities[9] after winning a landslide victory in the 2002 elections. A year after the elections, the new government established a parliamentary investigation committee and adopted proposals to open investigations into corruption allegations against a former prime minister as well as several other ministers of the previous government (Bertelsman Stiftung 2006, p. 23). The government's ambitious anticorruption agenda also resulted in the development of a robust legal framework upgrading corruption to a serious crime (see Ömürgönülşen 2009).

Review of reforms

The anticorruption policy in Turkey is mostly intended to create legal instruments through national action plans. The most comprehensive step towards fighting corruption has been the action plan to promote transparency and enhance good governance in the public sector in 2002.[10] In the same year, a parliamentary investigation committee was established and started investigations into a number of public-sector improprieties. In line with the committee's 1200-page report (!), an Emergency Action Plan was issued with a special section on corruption, listing necessary anticorruption measures. The follow-up actions were taken with the introduction of a new strategy for enhancing transparency and strengthening the fight against corruption in 2010. In line with the national anticorruption plans, a substantive number of legal reforms have been introduced over the last two decades (Macauley 2015, Ömürgönülşen 2009, TESEV 2014). The alignment of domestic legislation with European and international standards was rather unproblematic and fast.

Next to legal measures, the government took steps to strengthen the institutional capacity of law enforcement agencies with regard to fighting corruption. As mentioned by scholars and international observers, Turkish bureaucracy is well equipped with institutional mechanisms to fight corruption (Acar and Emek 2009, SIGMA 2015). Yet, their autonomy and capacities to do so vary greatly (Soyaltin 2017).

All in all, however, the legal measures put in place by the AKP have hardly changed the level of corruption in the country. This outcome is at least partly due to decoupling of formal institutions and behavioural practices (Ömürgönülşen and Doig 2012). The legal change with regard to combatting corruption has also been selective (Börzel, Soyaltin and Yilmaz 2015, p.224). The ruling AKP gave special priority to the fight against petty corruption permeating the public sector while high-level corruption has been mostly left untouched[11] This selective approach has helped the party to consolidate its power by intervening in government institutions and neutralizing the power of their political opponents – and thus undermined the overall governance quality.

Given the electoral majoritarian system in Turkey, authority and power are largely concentrated in the government, whose preferences determine the direction and extent of domestic political change. Meanwhile civil society organisations and the media cannot exert systematic pressure on government. This is, to a great extent, related to the paternalistic mode of governance

---

[9] The other two were fight against poverty and restrictions (in Turkish *3Y kurali: Yoksulluk, Yolsuzluk, Yasaklar*), available online at: http://m.akparti.org.tr/site/haberler/basbakan-Erdoğanin-2014-butce-gorusmeleri-konusmasinin-tam-metni/56600#1

[10] Interview with a former member of Parliamentary Investigation Committee on Causes of Corruption, Istanbul, June 2012.

[11] Interviews with Turkey project team, ANTICORRP Project, April 2012, Ankara

and centralised bureaucratic machinery inherited from the Ottoman Empire and its efforts to restrict modernisation (Heper 1985). This patrimonial structure has remained unchallenged for many years (Kayaycıoğlu 2001). The AKP government claims to have eliminated patrimonial governance structures and informal practices by promoting good governance principles, yet it accommodated them in new forms (Özel 2014). Furthermore, the AKP has won four consecutive parliamentary elections and effectively established a single party government over the last decade (Öniş 2015). The electoral dominance of the AKP government further reinforced the authority and power of the executive. The government cabinet has been stacked with loyal allies of President Erdogan, including his son-in-law, who was named energy minister.

Like for other major policies, the AKP government centralised its control in the fight against corruption. Since 2009, a ministerial anticorruption commission has been charged with the drafting and enforcement of anticorruption policies, while the Prime Ministry Inspection Board became the coordinating body for national anticorruption strategy, providing secretarial and technical support to the ministerial anticorruption commission. Similarly, the Ethics Council for Public Servants and Board of Review of Access to Information, established with the aim to promote transparency and accountability in the promotion of public services, were actually physically located under the Prime Minister's office. Moreover, the EU's programmes for technical assistance and twinning projects largely focused on capacity building of the executive central state agencies. On the other hand, major areas that affect the implementation of anticorruption measures, such as the external auditing mechanism, public procurement regime, corruption investigations by state prosecutors and the office of Ombudsman have become subjected to political interventions (Soyaltin 2017). Furthermore, civic participation and public oversight have been largely ignored in the formulation and implementation of anticorruption plans.

In addition to its dominance in the government and state bureaucracy, the party gained control of a large portion of the economy over the years. Turkey has gone through a radical restructuring in line with the neoliberal economic programme, supported by the IMF and EU. The remarkable fiscal consolidation and structural reforms improved macro-financial stability and led to uninterrupted strong growth and economic catching-up until the second half of 2008 (Öniş 2009). In the same period, Turkey became the world's seventeenth economy with a GDP of USD 800 billion (World Bank 2015a).

The fight against corruption has become an integral part of the AKP government's liberal economic programme. The then President Erdoğan highlighted the economic achievements of the preceding decade as a result of strict monetary policies and anticorruption reforms.[12] The adoption of egulatory reforms streamlined business registration, cut red tape and boosted Turkey's success in attracting large scale of foreign direct investment after 2001 (Anti-Corruption Research Centre 2012, Bertelsmann Stiftung 2010). This general success in the economy also allowed the AKP government to invest heavily in public services, which in turn contributed to the party's electoral success. The party increased its percentage of the vote at each succeeding election (Öniş 2015).

Furthermore, party's unprecedented access to state and private resources provided space for discretionary involvement in the process of capital accumulation and created new opportunities for patronage and interpersonal forms. The companies with close relations and affiliations to high-level representatives of the government were awarded with lucrative contracts and have turned into giant conglomerates in the recent years (Buğra and Savaşkan 2014, p. 89; Özal 2014, p. 186). Since 2008, "17 out of 72 PPP contracts, including a multibillion-euro third airport in Istanbul and some other major transport and energy projects, were awarded to eight

---

[12] Prime Minister Erdoğan's Speech, 2011 Election Campaign, 5 June, Istanbul Prime Minister Erdoğan's Speech, 2011 Election Campaign, 4 June 2011, Izmir

companies, which control 82 percent of the market" (Emek and Acar 2015, p. 91). Disproportionately benefiting its own constituency, AKP's politico-business strategies accommodated the particularistic power relations in new forms.

Finally, the AKP government instrumentalised the fight corruption to strengthen state apparatus and to replace the power structures established by the Fethullah Gülen, whose followers have allegedly occupied positions in the police and the judiciary. When a massive corruption scandal erupted in December 2013, the then Prime Minister Erdoğan purged thousands of police officers and hundreds of prosecutors. It is argued that these attempts aimed at cleansing the judiciary and the police from followers of the so-called Gülenists (Transparency International 2016, p.84).

The government's reactions to the corruption probe was followed by an amendment on the law on High Council of Judges and Prosecutors, the legally independent self-governance body of the judiciary, to transfer many critical powers of the Plenary of the Council to the Minister of Justice. The government also restricted the scope of investigations by state prosecutors. The purge in the public sector, especially in the judiciary, has continued in the aftermath of the July 2016 coup attempt, which was organised by a small faction of the military believed to have ties to the *Hizmet* movement.[13]

The unlawful government interference in the judiciary was coupled with increasing restrictions on freedom of the press, which has steadily deteriorated from 2010 onwards and took a steep decline following the 2013 corruption probe (GRECO 2016; Transparency International 2016). The AKP government used corruption allegations to promote its control over media and to prevent news coverage critical of its politics (Freedom of House 2014). While a huge number of journalists and writers have been arrested and prosecuted in recent years, the placement of several outlets under government trusteeship has resulted in dozens of dismissals and changes in the outlets' editorial lines. Coupled with lack of legal framework guaranteeing transparency of media ownership, increasing political intervention and self-censorship has significantly damaged the press freedom in Turkey.

Precisely such elements are dropping the country's rank on public integrity below EU Member States, even recent ones like Croatia, as well as below EU accession countries like Serbia and Macedonia. It currently outranks only much poorer Albania in the public integrity index with 6.19 out of 10 possible points, coming in 52nd from 105 countries. Turkey does well only on trade-related red tape and e-citizenship, a component measuring Internet and Facebook empowerment, but lags behind the average of its income rank group on judicial independence and freedom of the press, the two elements which have been recently deteriorating.

Table 1. Turkey's public integrity deconstructed

Components	Component score	World rank	Regional rank	Income group rank
Judicial independence	3.96	78/105	6/12	18/28
Administrative burden	8.46	39/105	7/12	7/28
Trade openness	7.04	59/105	4/12	17/28
Budget transparency	8.07	32/105	5/12	10/28
E-citizenship	6.02	44/105	3/12	9/28
Freedom of the press	3.57	79/105	7/12	21/28

Source: www.integrity-index.org

---

[13] Named after the US-based Islamic cleric Fethullah Gülen, Gülen movement -known in Turkey as Hizmet, or service – is a religious and social movement whose followers have allegedly occupied positions in the police and the judiciary. The movement runs schools around the world, including in Turkic former Soviet Republics, Muslim countries such as Pakistan and Western nations including Romania and the US

What went wrong? A hybrid governance context

Given the steady decline in media freedom and judicial independence, it can hardly be said that the EU catalysed governance improvements in the intended fashion. Apart from the ease of starting a business, which has slightly improved due to reduction of red tape for economic activity, the major indicators of governance have been backsliding considerably (figure 1). This outcome reflects the certain degree of blending that occurs between the formal institutions and norms of market liberalisation with the particularistic modes of governance in Turkey (Özel 2014). Yet, more importantly, it is this hybrid context that empowers certain groups of individuals in the system and enables them to appropriate gains, while formal institutions are infused with the particularistic politics of the rulers (Soyaltin 2016). Thus, it could be argued that the EU reform process promoted bad governance in Turkey, since the incumbent elites exploited anticorruption policies to change existing power structures in the state institutions and instead consolidate their own power. The consolidation of power around the executive prevents other institutions, such as the legislature, judiciary, audit agencies, ombudsman and media, to perform their duties in effectively participating in anticorruption measures while disrupting the checks and balances in the state structure (Esen and Gümüşçü 2016, Özbudun 2014). Recent developments in the country have raised further concerns with regard to the separation of powers and system of checks and balances. In April 2017, a national referendum was voted in favour of replacing the parliamentary system with the executive presidency long sought by incumbent Erdogan. Time will tell how the new system will take shape and influence Turkish democracy.

Figure 1. Governance indicators for Turkey 2007–2014

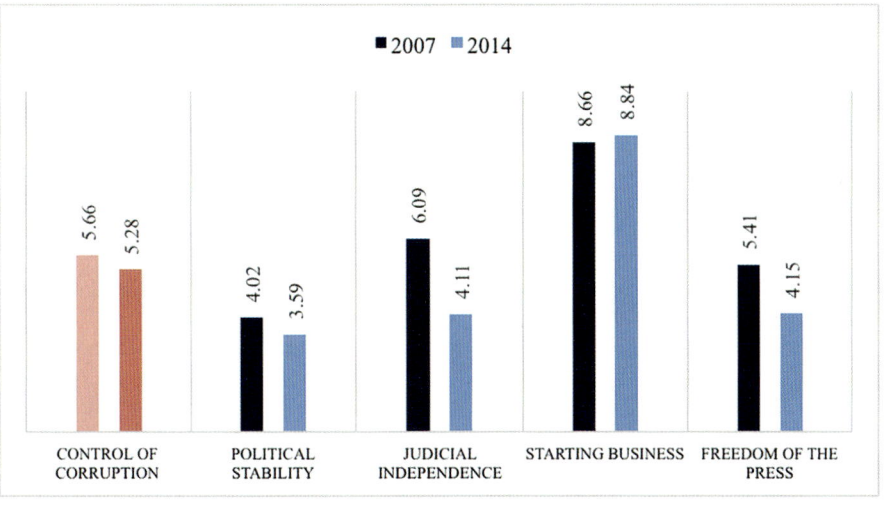

Available data has been standardised to a scale from 1 (worst) to 10 (best).
Sources: World Bank (2016), World Bank (2016a), Freedom House (2016)

In conclusion, the EU's demands for improving governance increased significantly for Turkey after the 1999 Helsinki Council granted candidacy status to Turkey. Given the high level of corruption and increasing pressure for adaptation, incumbent authorities introduced a rather impressive amount of reforms to fight corruption. Apart from exerting pressure on the government through its political conditionality, the EU provided substantial amount of financial and technical assistance to Turkey to improve the capacities of anticorruption institutions. However, the

EU and its fading conditionality have not managed to improve control of corruption in Turkey. Instead, the EU accession process empowered incumbent elites, who have used the corruption-fight agenda to consolidate their own power and change existing institutional structures. As observed since summer 2016, this restructuring of power is still going on, and its impact on control of corruption in Turkey is more a source of concern than of optimism at this stage.

References

Acar, M. and Emek, U (2009). Preventing Corruption in Turkey: Issues, Institutions, Instruments. In *Preventing Corruption in Asia: Institutional Design and Political Capacity*, edited by T. Gong and S. K. Ma, 164-188. London: Routledge.

Adaman, F. (2011). Is Corruption a Drawback to Turkey's Accession to the European Union? *South European Society and Politics,* 16(2), 309–321.

Adaman, F., A. Carkoglu & B. Senatalar (2001). Corruption in Turkey, Results of Diagnostic Household Survey. TESEV (The Economic and Social Studies Foundation of Turkey).

Ademmer, E. and Börzel, T. A. (2013). Migration, Energy and Good Governance in the EU's Eastern Neighbourhood. *Europe Asia Studies*, 64(4), 581–608.

Anti-Corruption Research Centre (2012). *U4 Expert Answer Overview of Corruption and Anti-corruption in Turkey*, January, Bergen.

Baran, Z. (2000). Corruption: The Turkish Challenge, *Journal of International Affairs,* 54(1), 127–46.

Bertelsmann Stiftung. (2006). BTI 2006: Turkey Country Report.

———. (2010). BTI 2010: Turkey Country Report.

Börzel, T.A. and Risse, T. (2003). Conceptualising the Domestic Impact of Europe. In *The Politics of Europeanisation,* edited by K. Featherstone and C. Radaelli, 57–82, Oxford: Oxford University Press.

Börzel, T., Soyaltin, D. and Yilmaz, G. (2015). Same Same or different? Accession Europeanization in Central Eastern Europe and Turkey Compared. In *Handbook of Europeanization of Turkey: Policies, Politics and Polity*, edited by A. Tekin and A. Güney, 217–234. New York, NY: Routledge.

Börzel, T. A. & Pamuk, Y. (2012). Pathologies of Europeanization: Fighting Corruption in the Southern Caucasus, *West European Politics,* 35(1), 79–97.

Börzel, T. A. & van Hüllen, V. (2014). External State-Building and Why Norms Matter. The European Union's Fight against Corruption in the Southern Caucasus. *SFB-Governance Working Paper Series*, no. 59, Collaborative Research Center (SFB) 700, Berlin.

Buğra, A. (1994). *State and Business in Modern Turkey: A Comparative Study.* Albany, NY: State: University of New York Press.

CEPEJ (2011). Scheme for Evaluating Judicial Systems: Turkey, available at: http://www.coe.int/t/dghl/cooperation/cepej/evaluation/2012/Turkey_en.pdf

Diez, T., Agnantopoulos, A. and Kaliber, A. (2005). Turkey, Europeanization and Civil Society. *South European Society and Politics,* 10(1), 1–15.

Doig, A. (2012). Asking the right questions? Addressing corruption and EU accession: The case study of Turkey, *Journal of Financial Crime* 17(1), 9–21.

Düzgit Aydın, S. and Çarkoğlu, A. (2009). Reforms for a Consolidated Democracy: Turkey. In *International Actors, Democratization Rule of Law: Anchoring Democracy?* Edited by L. Morlino and A. Magen, pp. 120–156. UACES Contemporary European Studies, New York: Routledge.

Emek, U. and M. Acar. (2015). Public Procurement in Infrastructure: The Case of Turkey. In Government Favouritism in Europe, edited by Alina Mungiu-Pippidi, 84-96, Opladen: Barbara Budrich Publishers.

Esen, B. and Gümüşçü, Ş. (2016). Rising competitive authoritarianism in Turkey. *Third World Quarterly.* DOI: 10.1080/01436597.2015.1135732

European Commission. (2003). On a comprehensive EU policy against corruption, COM(2003) 317 final, Brussels.

———. (2003a). Turkey 2003 Regular Report, SEC (2003) 1426, Brussels.

———. (2014). DG Enlargement, Guidelines Indicative Strategy Paper for Turkey, 2014-2020, available at: http://www.ab.gov.tr/files/isp_turkey_2014_2020.pdf

Freedom House. (2016). Freedom of Press, Turkey country Report, available at: https://freedomhouse.org/report/freedom-press/2016/turkey

Group of States against Corruption (GRECO) (2016). Fourth Evaluation Report, Strasbourg: Council of Europe, 2016, available at: http://www.coe.int/t/dghl/monitoring/greco/evaluations/round4/Eval%20IV/GrecoEval4Rep(2015)3_Turkey_EN.pdf

Güneş-Ayata, A. (1994). Roots and Trends of Clientelism in Turkey. In *Democracy, Clientelism, and Civil Society*, eds. Luis Roniger and Ayse Güneş-Ayata, 49–63. Boulder: Lynne Rienner

Heper, M. (1985). *The State Tradition in Turkey*. Walkington: Eathen Press.

Kalaycıoğlu, E. (2001). Turkish Democracy: Patronage versus Governance. *Turkish Studies,* 2(1), 54–70.

Kirişci, K. (2011). Reforming Turkey's Asylum Policy: Is it Europeanization, UNHCR-ization or ECHR-ization? , KFG Conference on "Faraway, So Close? Reaching beyond the Pro/Contra Controversy on Turkey's EU Accession," 2–4 June, Istanbul, Turkey.

Macauley, R. (2015). Fighting Corruption: Incriminations, GRECO Evaluation report, Council of Europe, Strasbourg.

Mungiu-Pippidi, A. (2016). The Quest for Good Governance: Learning from Virtuous Circles. *Journal of Democracy*, 27 (1), 95–109.

Müftüler-Baç, M. (2005). Turkey's Political Reforms and the Impact of the European Union. *South European Society and Politic,* 10(2), 17–31.

Noutcheva, G. and Aydın Düzgit, S. (2012). Lost in Europeanisation? The Western Balkans and Turkey, *West European Politics*, 35(1), 59–78.

Ömürgönülsen, U. and A. Doig (2012). Why the Gap? Turkey, EU Accession, Corruption and Culture. *Turkish Studies,* 13(1), 7–25.

———. (2009). Ethics for the Prevention of Corruption in Turkey (TYEC), System Studies Report, Council of Europe.

Öniş, Z. (2009). Beyond the 2001 financial crisis: The political economy of the new phase of neo-liberal restructuring in Turkey. *Review of International Political Economy*, 16(3), 409–432.

———. (2015). Monopolising the Centre: The AKP and the Uncertain Path of Turkish Democracy, *The International Spectator*, 50(2), 22–41.

Özbudun, E. (2014). AKP at the Crossroads: Erdoğan's Majoritarian Drift, *South European Society and Politics*, 19(2), 155–167.

Özel, I. (2014). Emerging on an illiberal path: the Turkish variety of Capitalism. In *The BRICs and Emerging Economies in Comparative Perspective Political economy, liberalisation and institutional change,* edited by Uwe Becker, 163–182. London and NY: Routledge.

Sarlak, Z. and Bali, B (2008). Corruption in Turkey: Why Cannot an Urgent Problem Be a Main Concern? Crime and Culture, University of Konstanz.

Schimmelfennig, Frank and Sedelmeier, Ulrich. (Eds.) (2005). *The Europeanization of Central and Eastern Europe,* Ithaca, NY: Cornell University Press.

Smith, K. (2004). *The making of EU foreign policy: The case of Eastern Europe*. Basingstoke: Palgrave Macmillan.

Soyaltin, D. (2016). Transformation of corporate governance in Turkey: Eliminating or accommodating corruption? In *Stare Capture, Political Risks and International Business: Cases from Black Sea Region*, edited by H. Meissner and J. Leitner, 137–155, Oxon: Routledge.

———. (2017). Public Sector Reforms to Fight Corruption in Turkey: A Case of Failed Europeanisation? *Turkish Studies*, (forthcoming).

Sözeri, C. and Güney, Z. (2011). "The Political Economy of the Media: A Sectoral Analysis", Democratization Program, TESEV Publications, Istanbul.

Support for Improvement in Governance and Management (SIGMA). (2015). The principles of Public Administration, Monitoring report for Turkey, Paris: OECD Publishing.

Szarek-Mason, P. (2010). *The European Union's Fight Against Corruption: The Evolving Policy Towards Member States and Candidate Countries*, Cambridge University Press: Cambridge.

Third Sector Foundation of Turkey (TUSEV). (2014). Civil Society Monitoring Report, Istanbul.

Transparency International. (2016). The National Integrity System Assessment Turkey, Istanbul.

———. (2015). Corruptions Perceptions Index. available at: http://www.transparency.org/research/cpi/overview

Turkish Economic and Social Studies Foundation (TESEV). (2014). Corruption Assessment Report Turkey Istanbul: TESEV Publications.

Uğur, M. (2010). Open-Ended Membership Prospect and Commitment Credibility: Explaining the Deadlock in EU–Turkey Accession Negotiations *Journal of Common Market Studies*, 48(4), 967–991.

Ulusoy, K. (2014). Turkey's fight against corruption: A critical assessment, global Europe in Turkey' *Commentary* 19.

Vachudova, M. A. (2009). Corruption and Compliance in the EU's Post-Communist Members and Candidates. *Journal of Common Market Studies,* 47(1), 43–62.

World Bank. (2015). Worldwide Governance Indicators.

———. (2015a). Turkey-Country partnership strategy for the period 2012–2015.

———. (2016). Doing Business Data, available at: http://www.doingbusiness.org/data

———. (2016a). Political Stability Index, available at: http://info.worldbank.org/governance/wgi/index.aspx#report

Yaşar, M. M. (2005). A Complex Systems Model For Understanding the Causes of Corruption: Case Study-Turkey, PhD Dissertation, University of North Texas.

Yılmaz, G., and D. Soyaltın. (2014). Zooming into the 'Domestic' in Europeanization: Promotion of Fight against Corruption and Minority Rights in Turkey. *Journal of Balkan and Near Eastern Studies, 16(1),* 11–29.

6. Egypt: The Failed Transition

JUSTINE LOUIS[1]

Egypt's 2011 revolution seemed to have created a great improvement on the *constraints* side to corrupt governance, but this was offset by Egypt's underperformance in freedom of the press and judiciary independence. Under President al-Sisi, laws expanding corruption *resources*, particularly in the field of public procurement, and curbing *constraints* on corruption have thus proliferated with the result of even poorer control of corruption. The EU has had little impact on strengthening *constraints* on corruption, but Sector Budget Support (SBS) potentially contributed to increasing *resources*. There is no immediate perspective for Egypt to enter into some real transformation process away from a form of governance based on particularism.

Particularism rules

Over the 30-year rule of President Hosni Mubarak, Egypt's institutions and state services deteriorated into a highly personalist system of rule that was dominated by clientelism and patronage. Access to both the political and economic systems was progressively limited to the president's coterie. In Egypt, *particularism* has been the norm rather than the exception for many years and survived even after the 2011 revolution.

Relying heavily on the State Security Agency, the president maximised internal security expenditure at the expense of the military, which was given increased financial autonomy in exchange (Soliman 2012). Mubarak's "you are either with me or against me" governing style meant that, in practice, the president had the arbitrary power to remove or nominate anyone he pleased and even transferred the authority of independent institutions to the executive (Osman 2011). Through the use of electoral manipulation tactics the regime's well-oiled election-rigging machine, Mubarak strengthened his ruling National Democratic Party's (NDP) control over parliament as a way to secure his re-election and tighten his grip on state institutions (Lesch 2012, Fahmy 2012). In the last parliamentary elections before Mubarak's fall, the NDP won over 90% of the seats, a number that contributed to the political disillusionment that fuelled the revolution.

The two waves of privatisation of the early 1990s and again in the 2000s further eroded the state's autonomy and substantively increased resources for corruption, resulting in widespread state capture that helped trigger the 2011 uprising. The first wave took place at the beginning of the 1990s and the second in the early part of this century, when a new generation of technocrats led by Hosni Mubarak's youngest son, Gamal, took over the financial and human resources of the aging NDP (Soliman 2012). The rise of the business elite and its infiltration into the political system culminated in the 2004 appointment of a neoliberal government headed by Ahmed Nazif, where all the ministers in charge of economic portfolios were either business tycoons or relatives of wealthy businessmen close to the Mubaraks (Fahmy 2012). Mubarak's last decade in power, characterised by unprecedented levels of corruption and nepotism – together with the outrageously fraudulent 2010 parliamentary elections –, led to his demise. The

---

[1] American University Cairo, justinelouis@aucegypt.edu

success of the popular uprising rested on the army, which had grown incredibly wary of the neoliberal technocrats threatening the independent economic military complex, ultimately siding with the protesters (Ashour 2015, 16).

The immediate post-revolution period was marked by constant political instability. The first relatively fair and democratic parliamentary and presidential elections were held in 2011 and 2012. In both cases the Muslim Brotherhood (MB) won the elections, and in both cases the MB failed to stay in power. After a series of controversial political decisions that stirred up massive popular discontent, General Abdel Fattah Al-Sisi deposed the first civilian president Mohamed Morsi in the July 2013 popularly backed coup d'état. Al-Sisi won the following presidential elections after Adly Mansour's interim presidential term. Currently, the country is undergoing an authoritarian reversion with the regime gradually suppressing any *normative constraints*.

Evolution of Egypt's anticorruption legal and institutional framework

The control of corruption model has to be understood as equilibrium between *constraints/deterrents* (legal and normative) on corruption and *resources/opportunities* for corruption (power discretion and material resources) (Mungiu-Pippidi et al. 2011).

Table 1. Evolution of integrity components in time for Egypt (2004–2014):

Year	RESOURCES			CONSTRAINTS			
	EB SB (0–100 best)	EB Trade (0–100 best)	OBI (0–100 best)	Internet users (% share of population)	Broadband (% share of population)	Judicial independence (1–7 best)	Press freedom (0–100 worst)
2004	39.72			11.92	0.11		68
2005	40.05		19	12.75	0.19		61
2006	43.24	48.32		13.65	0.35	4.82	62
2007	48.52	54.09	43	16.03	0.64	4.86	59
2008	82.89	63.10		18.01	1.01	4.95	60
2009	86.32	64.74	49	20	1.40	3.87	60
2010	86.70	65.82		21.60	1.85	3.91	65
2011	87.92	69.45	13	25.60	2.32	4.76	57
2012	87.99	70.06		26.39	2.83	4.14	62
2013	87.99	70.65		29.39	3.26	3.45	68
2014	88.08	71.14	16	31.70	3.67	4.00	73

Sources: **EB SB** : World Bank's (WB) Ease of Doing Business: Starting a Business Index; **EB Trade**: WB Ease of Doing Business: Trading across Borders Index; **Internet users**: WB Internet Users score; **Broadband**: WB fixed broadband subscriptions; **Judicial independence:** World Economic Forum's Judicial Independence score; **OBI**: Official Open Budget Index score; **Press freedom**: Freedom House's Freedom of the Press score. The cells higlighted in red show the year during which the most sudden change occured for each indicator. Legend: Sudden change signaled in pink.

Once a governance order reaches a certain equilibrium, it is extremely difficult to alter even when regime change occurs (Mungiu-Pippidi 2014). Despite, the opportunity window created by the revolution that has clearly upset the equilibrium and President Al-Sisi's pledge to make the fight against corruption one of his top priorities, control of corruption has indeed stagnated and even worsened since 2015. Over the past decade, *constraints* have remained weak and *resources* not been substantively reduced.

Under resources, major progress in each of the three indicators was induced by the economic liberaltion initiated by the Nazif government. The World Bank praised the tax and property-registration reforms and ranked Egypt as one of the world's top reformers (Ramalho 2007, Haidar 2008). However, the de jure improvements in the area of tax administration did not affect the pace of implementation, and Egypt's then Minister of Finance himself observed that "it was easier to change laws than the attitudes of those implementing them" (Fayyad 2010). It is specifically the "marriage between wealthy businessmen and corrupt politicians in the ruling party" and the resulting economic policies of the Nazif government that further led to state capture by the governing elite and increased the rich–poor divide (Essam El-Din 2008). The same nepotistic patterns ultimately pervaded the lower echelons of the public administration, where recruitment and promotion were not based on merit but rather on particularistic criteria (Moussa 2013). It was in this context that the cabinet passed resolution No. 24 in February 2007, thereby placing the fight against administrative corruption high on the government's agenda in an attempt to buttress Egypt's anticorruption machinery. The government created a smokescreen of administrative reforms leaving grand corruption, the core of particularism, unimpaired.

As regards budget transparency, progress was made in 2008 by making available the executive's budget proposal, but fiscal transparency plummeted after the revolution. The transparency deficit further indicates that resources for corruption have not been substantially weakened and may even have increased in some areas. Many public bodies, including anticorruption agencies, have a special budget called "special funds" that can be spent without any accountability (Puddephatt 2012). Two investigative journalism reports suggest that billions were lost in these special funds by 2013 and uncovered the involvement of anticorruption agencies (Manek and Hodge 2015a and b). Numerous illegal practices in the allocation of public contracts have also surfaced post-January 25th to the point where public procurement is regarded as an instrument of extraction and one of the most corrupt fields in Egypt (Moussa 2013, Egyptian Lawyer 2015). However, far from improving transparency and accountability, a 2013 presidential decree granted the state the right to "directly award government contracts in cases of emergency" (El Dahshan 2014). In practice, it allowed the army to progressively take control of the bidding process for major public procurements – where calls for tender are now virtually absent – and to expand its non-defense-related activities to private sectors, which were conventionally the big business preserves (European Diplomat 2015, Adly 2014).

On the *constraints* side, improvement in e-citizenship was counterbalanced by Egypt's underperformance in freedom of the press and judiciary independence. While the revolution opened up the public sphere, the Freedom of the Press indicator rapidly deteriorated to reach its lowest score in 2014 despite the abolition of the Ministry of Information (Mansour 2015). By the end of 2011, the state security apparatus had already reverted to curtailing the capacity of civil society actors by imposing restrictions on civil liberties, while repression under the cover of the war on terror intensified (Sika 2012). The crackdown culminated in November 2016 with the Parliament passing a controversial law on NGOs that many deem unconstitutional.

Egypt's fair performance in Judicial Independence has to be taken with caution. For one, the country launched its first National Anti-corruption Strategy in 2014 and has a relatively strong anticorruption legal framework. However, it has largely been ineffective due to the courts and anticorruption agencies' lack of independence and the absence of real scrutiny (Johnson and Martini 2012). Anticorruption bodies have been closely linked to the executive and the legal framework, which further deters the reporting of corruption cases as no whistle-blowing protection is in place. The independence of the judiciary has been further undermined by the successive post-revolution governments. For instance, a presidential decree granting the president the power to remove the heads of supervisory bodies – among them the Central Auditing Organization (CAO), was passed. Less than a year later, the head of the CAO was removed from office and jailed for publicly estimating EGP 600 billion were lost in corruption between 2012 and 2015. Secondly, the 2016 Global Corruption MENA survey shows that Egypt has the second highest bribery rate in the region and the sector the most affected is the judiciary followed by the permits and the police (Pring 2016). Finally, while the Index for Public Integrity indicator shows that judicial independence increased since 2014, there has concurrently been a surge in military trials of civilians (Human Rights Watch 2016).

Despite President Al-Sisi rhetorically placing the fight against corruption as one of his priorities, Egypt is, in practice, still deprived of an effective system of checks and balances with too many public bodies neither accountable to the citizens nor independent from the executive. While a national anticorruption strategy was launched and 22 corruption cases involving state officials (including ministers) were investigated during the first year of Al-Sisi's presidency (El-Fekki 2015), recent developments indicate the regime is repeating a pattern observed in other countries that have not yet reach ethical universalism: a crackdown on "anticorruption heroes" who try to challenge the status quo (Persson, Rothstein and Teorell, 2010, Mungiu-Pippidi 2015). Laws expanding *resources*, particularly in the field of public procurement, and curbing *constraints* on corruption have proliferated.

Promoting governance reforms: A top priority in the EU-Egypt ENP Action Plan

Started in 1966, EU–Egypt relations have evolved against the backdrop of Euro-Mediterranean cooperation, which resulted in the 1995 creation of an all-encompassing strategy, the Euro-Mediterranean Partnership (EMP). With the rather daunting experience of the EMP, the European Commission revamped its regional strategy and incorporated the Mediterranean into its new initiative, the European Neighbourhood Policy (ENP), initially designed for its neighbours to the East. The primarily financial and economic relationship took on a more political dimension with the goal-oriented ENP, which has sought to boost reforms in partner countries by adopting a differentiated approach.

1. Funds allocations

Under the ENP, financial assistance depends on the commitments to reform that the recipient countries have jointly agreed upon with the EU in the bilateral action plans (APs). With the shift to positive ex-ante conditionality, recipient countries can be rewarded economically or politically for achievements in the reform process, while benchmarks or pre-defined indicators help measure and evaluate progress (Del Sarto and Schumacher 2013).

Egypt began negotiations with the EU in 2005, and the EU–Egypt Action Plan entered into force in 2007. The 2007–2013 Country Strategy Paper (CSP) for Egypt further details the financial plan, and good governance became a priority area for the first time rather than just an issue to be discussed within the political dialogue. Following the 2005 Paris Declaration on Aid Effectiveness, the EU has undertaken a shift in aid modality towards budget support, considered to be an effective mechanism to boost reforms in partner countries, and has become the only international donor to provide Sector Budget Support (SBS) to Egypt (European Court of Auditors 2013b). The EU and Egypt, to which ownership is transferred and is responsible for implementing reforms, participated in a policy dialogue to negotiate the wording of the general conditions, the timing of the implementation, the disbursement method, and the specific provisions that determine the disbursement of the various tranches and against which progress is assessed (European Commission 2007a).

Table 2 NIPs' planned allocations, 2007–2010/2011–2013

Priority areas	NIP 2007–2010		NIP 2011–2013	
	Total NIP (EUR million)	% budget	Total NIP (EUR million)	% budget
I-Supporting Egypt's reforms in the areas of democracy, human rights, justice	40	7%	50	11.1%
Support for political development, decentraltion and promotion of good governance	13		5	
Promotion and protection of human rights	17		15	
Support for moderntion of administration of justice	10		10	
Upgrading of regulatory, institutional and legislative environment			20	
II-Developing the competitiveness and productivity of the Egyptian economy	220	40%	189	42.2%
Support for implementation of the Action Plan Programme (SAPP)	220			
Technical support	70			
Targeted support for sector reforms	150			
Transport sector reform			85	
Energy sector reform			84	
Trade enhancement			20	
III-Ensuring the sustainability of the development process with better management of human and natural resources	298	53%	210	46.7%
Support for education reform	120			
Support for public health reform	120			
Support for investment in the transport, energy and environment sectors	58			
Support for education reform as well as technical and vocational education and training (TVET)			105	
Water-sector reform			50	
Solid waste management			20	
Local community development			35	
Total	558	100%	449	100%

Source: Bauer, 2011.

In the post-revolution context, the EU organised a task force meeting with Egypt in November 2012. Here, several EU institutions committed to provide Egypt with a EUR 5 billion additional aid package, most of it conditioned on approval of a stand-by agreement between Egypt and the International Monetary Fund (IMF), a EUR 90 million grant from the Support to Partnership, Reform and Inclusive Growth (SPRING) programme, and €163 million from the NIF (Delegation of the EU in the USA 2013, Burke 2013). Following the revolution and given the constant political instability, the EU–Egypt Action Plan was extended until March 2014 and a single framework agreement for 2014–2016 was implemented. However, since 2012 no payments for SBS programmes have been approved due to a lack of reform implementation.

2. EU assistance in the fight against corruption: An ill-designed approach to Egypt's corruption problems

Within the Action Plan, the EU followed its standard promotion of external governance, although only few programmes and projects tackling indirect and direct anticorruption reforms were envisaged in the NIPs.

While the assessment of the state of corruption control in Egypt has shown major shortcomings on *constraints,* the EU's activities have mainly been focused on limiting *resources* for corruption. With the shift to budget support, the EU undertook a Public Expenditure and Financial Accountability (PEFA) study to evaluate the state of Public Finance Management (PFM) reforms, which praised Egypt's progress since 2005 but also underlined shortcomings particularly in relation to the special funds, the lack of independence of budget oversight bodies, the opacity of public procurement awards and lack of a complaint mechanism during the bidding process (Biggs 2010). Building on the PEFA, the EU planned in its 2010 Annual Action Programme (AAP) the Support to Public Administration Reform and Local Development project aimed at ameliorating civil service and enhancing PFM. The EU's "eligibility criteria" for approval of SBS programmes itself seeks to foster indirect anticorruption reforms as it requires "a well-defined sectoral policy", "a credible and relevant programme to improve public financial management" and "a stability-oriented macroeconomic policy" either in place or under implementation, and more recently "budget transparency and oversight". Three out of the five SBS – Energy, Water and Education – included PFM elements targeting fiscal transparency and accountability enhancement and the SBS Education envisaged the undertaking of a Public Expenditure and Tracking Survey (PETS).

On the *constraints* side, the EU foresaw the Modernization of Administration of Justice and Enhancement of Security project – also planned in the AAP 2010 – aimed at enhancing the efficiency of the judiciary rather than its independence, which entailed two anticorruption related objectives, namely "capacity building of the Ministry of Justice (MoJ) and court professionals to increase the quality and reduce delays within the public service of Justice" and "capacity building of the Ministry of Interior (MoI) to fight against new forms of crime". The only EU project directly addressing corruption, Supporting Measures to Combat Corruption and Money Laundering, and to Foster Asset Recovery in Egypt, implemented by the United Nations Office on Drugs and Crimes (UNODC) entailed four main objectives, namely "Institutional capacity to combat corruption and money laundering and to recover stolen assets enhanced"; "National anti-corruption strategy developed and implemented including anti- money laundering and asset recovery"; "National legal framework on anti-corruption, anti-money laundering and asset recovery established"; and "Public awareness on the negative effects of corruption and money laundering raised" (UNODC 2015).

The mismatch between the EU's intervention and Egypt's corruption problems becomes evident in that the EU did not seek to increase *normative constraints* on corruption with the involvement of civil society, instead limiting it to only one component of the anticorruption project. While none of the programmes targeted public procurement nor directly addressed the issue of special funds, the EU's efforts at establishing a sound framework for the disbursement of SBS programmes could have yielded positive results in the area of PFM. However, as the next section demonstrates, the EU scrambled to uphold its own conditional approach during the implementation phase.

Diagnosis and conclusions

This section assesses the impact of the EU projects and programmes on the balance between *resources* for and *constraints* on corruption before proceeding to explain the reasons behind the EU's failed intervention according to Mungiu-Pippidi's four-step intervention logic.

1. Impact of EU projects and programmes on the particularist status quo

With its overly ambitious roadmap, the EU has in practice failed to uphold governance as a key priority. None of the three governance-related projects were launched before January 25th and the "softly softly" approach, which has seen the EU be too flexible on tying its aid to reforms, has proven to be ineffective. The EU's absence of country-specific approach furthered Brussels' lack of impact on the balance of *constraints* on and *resources* for corruption.

On the *constraints* side, the EU has either not addressed the key areas of concern and/or failed to sufficiently involve the relevant stakeholders. For instance, the real obstacle to an efficient judiciary in Egypt is rooted in its lack of autonomy and law enforcement as well as its bribery problem. However, the EU's attempt at modernizing the administration of justice, which was delayed only to officially commence in 2015, mainly revolved around activities such as trainings and assistance to the improvement of strategies.

The implementation of the mere EUR 3-million direct anticorruption project was also delayed and delegated to UNODC and its anticorruption toolkit. From the onset, the objectives of the project – and their vagueness – denote an evident lack of tailor-made approach, which the Egyptians strongly criticised:

There were actually ongoing national anticorruption projects but the real problem was that the EU did not look into a proper assessment of these projects and see how they could build on them or boost them. (Egyptian official 2015)

The issue with the objectives targeting the establishment of a national anticorruption strategy and the legal anticorruption framework relates to the implementation. In practice, the adoption of new laws does not necessarily translate into their actual enforcement, especially when the recipient country is incited to import international legislation. The insistence of UNODC to be involved in the drafting of the strategy is precisely what led the project to almost being called off (Egyptian official 2015). Furthermore, the decision to include the assets recovery component in response to the growing post-revolution public interest for retrieving the Mubarak and his cronies' stolen assets was not the most appropriate in that it could have arguably increased resources for corruption. In practice, however, the activities for achieving "institutional capacity to combat corruption and money laundering and to recover stolen assets" have mainly revolved around trainings – on how to prepare requests for mutual assistance and on investment techniques – which, in a context of particularism may not compel the trainees to actually use this knowledge. The Egyptians themselves criticised the lack of expertise of the lecturers and the trainings for being too theoretical overall, where the same people were giving presentations and the same people were being trained. Another major issue was the strong inter-governmental dimension of the project and the lack of direct involvement of civil society even though the role and engagement of civil society organisations (CSOs) was highlighted as a priority in the project's action plan (UNODC 2013). CSOs have largely remained confined to a spectator role and having their "awareness raised" on the negative effects of corruption for the general public according to the fourth component of the project. Beyond the inadequacy of the objectives, the independent mid-term evaluation of the project highlighted the weakness of the performance indicators (enhanced, improved, supported, strengthened) "achievable with very minor effort" (ibid.).

While the EU does not appear to have affected the *constraints*, its impact on *resources* for corruption is more problematic. The Support to Public Administration Reform and Local Development project was officially launched in 2015 but the PFM sub-objective is not even mentioned by the agency in charge of implementing the project (VNG International 2015). As a result, the EU's intervention is unlikely to produce substantial results in transparency and accountability. Even when the EU funded effective projects or programmes, it has not built on those successes to further reforms. For instance, the Egyptians were very pleased with the undertaking of the PETS for the SBS education (Egyptian expert 2015). Other ministries were interested, but there was no follow-up; and, as a result, Egyptians considered this exercise to be merely another procedural requirement for receiving the second tranche of the SBS allocation (ibid.).

In the case of SBS programmes, the EU's assistance may even have increased opportunities for rent seeking through its overly flexible application of conditionality. The corruption risks associated with SBS in Egypt have not only been raised at the European Parliament, which believes the "Commission is throwing the EU money out of the window", but also by the 2013 special report of the European Court of Auditors (ECA) particularly blaming the EU for its soft application of conditionality and the slow implementation of the SBS programmes. The latter suggested that not all the EU funds could be traced because the EU had not used SBS to address major issues such as the lack of transparency regarding military and presidential expenditures, the "special funds", and the lack of transparency and independence of the supervisory bodies (European Court of Auditors 2013, 23). Furthermore, it underlined that the EU did not use budget support to address corruption despite the country's serious problems in this area and the fact that it did include specific conditions on corruption for such SBS in other ENP countries (ibid.). In its response to the ECA, the EEAS attributed the SBS's slow implementation to Egypt's low absorption capacity, and argued it had addressed the "special funds" with the inclusion of transparency and accountability-related indicators in the SBS Energy and Water (ibid.). However, during the behind-closed-doors policy/political dialogue that preceded the launch of the programmes, the EU substantially diluted the conditions in face of the resistance of their Egyptian counterparts. Former EU ambassador to Egypt, Marc Franco, recalls the negotiations on the SBS Energy, for which the EU pleaded very strongly:

> We were unable to put in clear binding wording on this issue so we put in something that was more "wishy-washy". In the end you can always say yes it fulfilled the conditions. In the end of the negotiations the conditions were so watered down that of course it didn't really have an impact. (2015)

The means of verification on which progress has been assessed further hindered the traceability of EU funds because monitoring was based on reports by the same Egyptian ministries in charge of implementing SBS programmes.

Following the addition of "budget transparency and oversight" as eligibility criterion and in the absence of an Egyptian Parliament, the EU suspended the ongoing SBS programmes in 2012 and extended their closing date to the end of 2017. The EU is not inclined to abandoning budget support despite the inherent corruption risks associated to this aid modality in Egypt, however, on the grounds that major external donors such as the World Bank, the IMF, the African Development Bank, Germany and France also have or are planning budget support operations in the country.

Flawed or Eurocentric intervention logic?

Given the short-term EU interventions that have relied almost exclusively on inter-governmental cooperation, targeting administrative corruption but turning a blind eye on the grand corruption issue, it is hardly conceivable that the EU established a full diagnosis of Egypt's state of governance. Even the indirect anticorruption reforms the EU undertook were too apolitical to have an impact on the deficient system of checks and balances in Egypt. For instance, the activities envisaged for the Modernization of the Administration of Justice project were ill-suited to effectively foster judicial empowerment from the executive. The lack of pre-assessment of the governance context in Egypt also seems evident in the direct anticorruption project, whereby the EU addressed corruption from a principle-agent perspective – rather than a collective action problem – and therefore downplayed the role of the state in the problem (Persson, Rothstein and Teorell 2010, Mungiu-Pippidi 2016). Following the principal-agent logic, the EU conceives corruption as a uniform problem irrespective of the country in which it operates and despite the ENP adoption of a differentiated approach.

The revolution provided the EU with both a window of opportunity for action and potential agents of change. Not only have civil society actors burgeoned, but corruption was also one of the drivers behind the uprising and many street campaigns calling for the end of corruption erupted (Sika 2012). At first, the EU lingered to support the Egyptian people's revolutionary demands, but later on it issued three important communications stressing the need to thoroughly review the ENP by "strengthening conditionality, engaging more with civil society, and offering a more attractive package of incentives" for those partners who engage in "deep democracy" (Isaac 2012, Aydin 2012). These communications in line with the SPRING programme emphasised the need for greater accountability and fighting corruption. The EU's pledge to expand its support to CSOs and "increase their ability to monitor reform and participate effectively in policy dialogues" fell short when CSO representatives were ultimately denied participation in the main meeting of the 2012 EU–Egypt Task Force (European Commission 2011b, Pinfari 2013). Once again, the EU missed an opportunity to foster collective action. The volatile political environment and the EU's highly bureaucratic nature, which, for instance, requires prior government approval to involve civil society, prevented the EU from acting swiftly. Furthermore, the Egyptian well-known reluctance to any interference in its domestic affairs has also been a drag on the effectiveness of Brussels' intervention. On several occasions, Egypt has warned the EU not to intervene in the country's political affairs, the latest being last January in response to EU's criticisms of the new law regarding NGOs (Ahram Online 2017).

Perhaps, most importantly, the EU's failure in positively influencing the particularist status quo had less to do with a lack of assessment than a real interest in genuinely addressing corruption. In the ENP action plan, the fight against corruption was not included among the "Priorities for Action". The EU allocated as little as EUR 3 million to the only anticorruption project and delegated the entire implementation to UNODC. This was strongly criticised by the Egyptians who complained about the EU's lack of involvement in the project (Egyptian Official 2015). With the shift to SBS the EU did conduct a PEFA study and was well aware that, if conditionality were not enforced, the huge SBS allocations would do "more harm than good" by providing further resources for corruption, since Egypt's low capacity of absorption was raised by the EEAS (Johnston 2011). The latter has in fact been far from unanimous about the use of SBS but an EU official (2015) stated "in order to spend the money, we had to do budget support". The reasons for the EU's overly flexible application of its own conditionality are two-fold. First, the effectiveness of EU conditionality rests on the political cost of implementing governance reforms for the recipient governments, which in authoritarian context triggers regime change and therefore explains Egypt's resistance to conditionality (Lavenex, Schimmelfennig 2011). Second, corruption has never truly undermined the core of EU-Egypt relations primarily grounded in economic and geostrategic interests. In 2012, bilateral trade between the EU and Egypt reached its highest level ever since the inception of the Association Agreement in 2004 and has been the main source of FDI. While the revolution did not impact trade, the power vacuum it left increased security and migration concerns of the EU, which had suddenly found itself in dire need of a stable ally. Hence, it is unlikely that the EU did not assess the impact of its intervention, but rather it did so according to its own priorities. Simply put, the political and economic costs of pushing the new regime to implement good governance reforms would have overridden the benefits the EU may have derived from standing as a governance promoter.

The EU's assistance to Egypt best exemplifies the limits of its influence and its highly bureaucratic nature. Following the revolution that has created a disequilibrium on the balance on *resources* and *constraints*, the EU's rhetorical enthusiasm for bringing about change in the region and adopting a new approach contrasted with its actions, which did not substantially depart from the planned NIP for 2011–2013. While the constant political instability in the country has been a major impediment, the financial rewards provided by Brussels have remained extremely low, especially compared to those of other external actors such as the Gulf countries or China that do not attach any political conditions to their assistance unlike traditional Western donors. The EU included "cooperate in combating and preventing corruption" in the 2014–2016 Single Support Framework. Yet, no concrete measures or projects are planned in the near future, while the execution plan for Egypt's national anticorruption strategy, which has remained undisclosed, will end in 2018. Despite significantly improved action programmes with more references to corruption introduced with the European Neighbourhood Instrument (ENI), the current EU priorities are geared towards security and migration concerns, as evidenced by the highly eurocentric 2015 review of the ENP. With the wave of terrorist attacks that have since taken place, the EU sees its interests currently lying in supporting an ever-expanding military regime that virtually has the control of both the political and economic spheres, rather than the promotion of governance reforms.

References

Ahram Online. (2012). Egyptian Presidential Candidates Choose symbols for May Vote. Available at: http://english.ahram.org.eg/NewsContent/36/122/40083/Presidential-elections-/Presidential-elections-news/Egyptian-presidential-candidates-choose-symbols-fo.aspx (access December 2016).

Ahram Online. (2014). Egypt's new investment law ignites controversy. Available at: http://english.ahram.org.eg/NewsContent/3/12/98980/Business/Economy/Egypts-new-investment-law-ignites-controversy-.aspx (accessed July 2015).

Ahram Online. (2017). Egypt says EU and UK statements on NGO assets freeze shows "double standards". Available at: http://english.ahram.org.eg/NewsContent/1/64/255056/Egypt/Politics-/Egypt-says-EU-and-UK-statements-on-NGO-asset-freez.aspx (accessed January 2017).

Ashour, Omar. (2015). Collusion to Crackdown: Islamist-Military Relations in Egypt. *Brooking Doha Center Analysis*, Paper 14, March 2015. Available at: https://www.brookings.edu/research/collusion-to-crackdown-islamist-military-relations-in-egypt/ (accessed October 2016).

Aydin, E. Sare. (2012). European Neighbourhood Policy; The Case of Egypt, Jordan, Lebanon, Occupied Palestine and Tunisia. *The Journal of International Social Research*, 5 (22):233–245.

Bauer, Patricia. (2011). The transition of Egypt in 2011: A new springtime for the European Neighbourhood Policy? *Perspectives on European Politics and Society,* 12 (4):420–439.

Biggs, David F. (2010). The Arab Republic of Egypt. In: *Public Financial Management Reform in the Middle East and North Africa: An Overview of Regional Experience*. World Bank. pp. 94–100.

Burke, Edward. (2013). *Running into the sand? The EU's faltering response to the Arab revolutions,* Centre for European Reform.

Campos, Edgardo J. and Vinay Bhargava. (2007). Introduction: Tackling a social Pandemic. In: Campos, E. J. and S. Pradhan (eds). *The Many Faces of Corruption: Tracking Vulnerabilities at the Sector Level*. The World Bank. pp 1–26.

Council of the European Union. (2003). A Secure Europe in a Better World: European Security Strategy. Available at: http://www.consilium.europa.eu/uedocs/cmsUpload/78367.pdf (accessed January 2015).

Comelli, Michele. (2010). Dynamics and Evolution of the EU-Egypt Relationship within the ENP Framework. *Istituto Affari Internazionali: Documenti IAI/10/02.*

Crawford, David and Mike Esterl. (2007). Siemens Ruling Details Bribery Across the Globe. *The Wall Street Journal*. Available at: http://www.wsj.com/articles/SB119518067226495200 (accessed November 2016).

Del Sarto, Raffaella A. (2006). *Contested State Identities and Regional Security in the Euro-Mediterranean Area*. London: Palgrave Macmillan.

Del Sarto, Raffaella A. and Schumacher, Tobias. (2013). From Brussels with love: leverage, benchmarking, and the action plans with Jordan and Tunisia in the EU's democratization policy. In: Sandra Lavenex and Franck Schimmelfennig (eds.) *Democracy Promotion in the EU's Neighbourhood*. Abingdon: Routledge, pp. 48–71.

El-Fekki, Amira. (2015, June 14). Al-Sisi's failed policies to fight corruption spread in local government: report. *Daily News Egypt*. Available at: http://www.dailynewsegypt.com/2015/06/14/al-sisis-failed-policies-to-fight-corruption-spread-in-local-government-report/ (accessed October 2015).

———. (2016, November 19). Press Syndicate President Jailed for First Time in Egypt's History. *Daily News Egypt*. Available at: http://www.dailynewsegypt.com/2016/11/19/598915/ (accessed November 2016).

El Dahshan, Mohamed. (2014). *The Egyptian Army Collects Billions in Government Contracts*. Available at: http://eldahshan.com/2014/01/03/army-contracts/ (accessed July 2015)

ENPI Info Center. (2011). Perceptions of the EU in Egypt: Evolving Attitudes (2009–2010). Available at: http://www.enpi-info.eu/library/content/perceptions-eu-egypt-evolving-attitudes-2009—2010 (accessed January 2015).

Essam El-Din, Gamal. (2008). Nazif under fire. *Al Ahram Weekly* No. 878, 3–9. January 2008.

EU-Egypt Association Agreement. (2004). Available at: http://eeas.europa.eu/egypt/aa/06_aaa_en.pdf (accessed December 2014).

European Commission. (2007a). Support *to Sector Programmes: Covering the three financing modalities: Budget Support, pool Funding and EC project procedures*. Tools and Methods Series: Guidelines No. 2.

———. (2007b). *Commission decision of 14/12/2007 approving the Annual Action Programme 2007 in favour of Egypt to be financed under Article 19 08 01 of the general budget of the European Communities*. Action Fiche. Available at: https://ec.europa.eu/europeaid/sites/devco/files/aap-financing-egypt-af-2007_en.pdf (accessed February 2015).

———. (2007d). EU/Egypt Action Plan. Available at: http://www.enpi-info.eu/library/simple_search?field_all_titles_value=EU+Egypt+Action+Plan (accessed December 2014).

———. (2007e). *Annual Action Programme financing education sector policy support programme Egypt*. Action Fiche 2007. Available at: https://ec.europa.eu/europeaid/sites/devco/files/aap-financing-education-sector-policy-support-programme-egypt-af-2007_en.pdf (accessed March 2015).

———. (2010). *Annual Action Programme for Egypt (Public Administration and local development)*. Action Fiche. Available at: https://ec.europa.eu/europeaid/annual-action-programme-egypt-public-administration-and-local-development-action-fiche_en (accessed August 2015).

———. (2011b). Joint Communication to the European Council, the European Parliament, the Council, the European and Social Committee and the Committee of the Regions – *A Partnership for Democracy and Shared Prosperity with the Southern Mediterranean*. Available at: http://eeas.europa.eu/euromed/docs/com2011_200_en.pdf (accessed January 2015).

———. (2011d). Commission Implementing Decision of 08/11/2011 on the Annual Action Programme 2011 in favour of Egypt (part I) to be financed under Article 19 08 01 01 of the general budget of the European Union, Anne – Action Fiche Energy Sector Policy Support Programme ENPI/2011/22763.

———. (2011e). *Financing Agreement between the European Union and the Arab Republic of Egypt – Water Sector Reform Programme Phase II ENPI/2010/022-905*. Available at: http://www.asktheeu.org/en/request/europeaid_water_reform_in_egypt?unfold=1 (accessed November 2015).

———. (2012). *Budget Support Guidelines – Programming, Design and Management: A modern approach to Budget Support*. Tool and Methods Series Working Document. Available at: https://ec.europa.eu/europeaid/sites/devco/files/methodology-budget-support-guidelines-201209_en_2.pdf (accessed April 2015).

———. (2013). *Memo EU-Egypt relations*. Available at: http://europa.eu/rapid/press-release_MEMO-13-751_en.htm (accessed February 2015).

———. (2014a). *Implementation of the European Neighbourhood Policy: Statistical Annex*. Available at: http://eeas.europa.eu/enp/pdf/2014/stats/statistical_annex_2014.pdf (accessed January 2015).

———. (2014b). *European Neighbourhood and Partnership Instrument 2007-2013: Overview of Activities and Results*. Available at: http://ec.europa.eu/enlargement/neighbourhood/pdf/20141217-enpi-results-2017-2013.pdf (accessed March 2015).

———. (2014c). Neighbourhood South Civil Society Facility (European Neighbourhood Instrument) ACTIONS IN EGYPT. Available at: https://webgate.ec.europa.eu/europeaid/online-services/index.cfm?ADSSChck=1405075311600&do=publi.detPUB&searchtype=AS&Pgm=7573838&aoet=36538%2C36539&ccnt=7573876%2C7573877&debpub=&orderby=upd&orderbyad=Desc&nbPubliList=15&page=1&aoref=135984 (accessed January 2016).

———. (2015a). *European Neighbourhood and Partnership Instrument (ENPI)*. Available at: https://ec.europa.eu/europeaid/funding/european-neighbourhood-and-partnership-instrument-enpi_en (accessed March 2015).

———. (2015b). *European Neighbourhood Policy and Enlargement Negotiations: Egypt,* Available at: http://ec.europa.eu/enlargement/neighbourhood/countries/egypt/index_en.htm (accessed March 2015).

———. (2015c). TAIEX Library. Available at: http://ec.europa.eu/enlargement/taiex/dyn/taiex-events/library/index_en.jsp?EventTypes=&LibMonths=&LibCountries=81&Keywords=&Speakers=&submit=Submit# (accessed August 2015).

European Court of Auditors. (2013a). "EU Support for Governance in Egypt – "well-intentioned but ineffective"", Press Release. Available at: http://europa.eu/rapid/press-release_ECA-13-18_en.htm (accessed January 2015).

———. (2013b). *EU Cooperation With Egypt In The Field of Governance*, Special Report No. 4. Available at: http://www.europarl.europa.eu/document/activities/cont/201306/20130624ATT68309/20130624ATT68309EN.pdf (accessed January 2015).

European Parliament, Council and Commission. (2006). *Joint Declaration by the Council and the representatives of the governments of the Member States meeting within the Council, the European Parliament and the Commission on the development policy of the European Union entitled "The European Consensus on Development"*. Available at: http://ec.europa.eu/development/body/development_policy_statement/docs/edp_statement_oj_24_02_2006_en.pdf (Accessed March 2015).

European Research Center for Anti-Corruption and State-Building. (2016). *Index of Public Integrity* Available at: http://integrity-index.org (accessed January 2017).

European Union. (2007). *Egypt Country Strategy Paper 2007-2013*. Available at: http://eeas.europa.eu/enp/pdf/pdf/country/enpi_csp_egypt_en.pdf (accessed January 2015).

European Union. (2014). Annual Action Programme 2013 for the EIDHR to b financed under budget line 19 04 01 of the general budget of the European Union. Available at: http://www.eidhr.eu/files/dmfile/AAP2013.pdf (March 2015).

Fayyad, Salam. (2010). Implementing Reforms in Public Financial Management: AN emerging Set of Promising Practices in MENA? In *Public Financial Management Reform in the Middle East and North Africa: An Overview of Regional Experience*. World Bank. pp. 34–57.

Füle, **Štefan**. (2011). Speech on the Recent Events in North Africa. 28 February 2011. Available at: http://europa.eu/rapid/press-release_SPEECH-11-130_en.htm (accessed February 2015).

Gamal. Wael. (2016a). Did Hesham Geneina's study exaggerate Egypt's corruption? *Mada Masr*. Available at: http://www.madamasr.com/opinion/economy/did-auditor-hesham-geneinas-study-exaggerate-extent-egypts-corruption (accessed August 2016).

Haidar, Jamal H. (2008). Egypt: How to Raise Revenues by Lowering Fees *The World Bank Doing Business – Celebrating Reforms 2008*. Available at: http://www.doingbusiness.org/reports/case-studies/2008/property-registration-reform-in-egypt (accessed October 2016).

Hamama, Mohamed. (2016). Sisi says military economy is 1.5ù of Egypt's GDP, but how accurate is this? *Mada Masr*. Available at: http://www.madamasr.com/en/2016/11/02/feature/economy/sisi-says-military-economy-is-1-5-of-egypts-gdp-but-how-accurate-is-this/ (accessed December 2016).

Hassan, Hussein M. (2009). *The Legal and Institutional Framework of Combating Administrative Corruption in Egypt*. Social Contract Center Research, Monitoring and Governance Unit. Available at: https://www.academia.edu/7383118/the_legal_and_institutional_framework_for_combating_corruption_in_Egypt_-_English (accessed April 2015).

Human Rights Watch. (2016). Egypt: 7,600 Civilians Tried In Military Courts. Available at: https://www.hrw.org/news/2016/04/13/egypt-7400-civilians-tried-military-courts (accessed October 2016).

International Commission of Jurists. (2016). *Egypt's Judiciary: A Tool of Repression – Lack of Effective Guarantees of Independene and Accountability*. Available at: https://www.icj.org/wp-content/uploads/2016/10/Egypt-Tool-of-repression-Publications-Reports-Thematic-reports-2016-ENG-1.pdf (accessed March 2017).

Isaac, Sally Khalifa. (2012). Europe and the Arab Revolutions: From a Weak to a Proactive Response to a Changing Neighborhood. KFG Working Paper Series 39, Kolleg-Forschergruppe (KFG) *The Transformative Power of Europe*, Berlin: Freie Universität Berlin.

Johnson, Elizabeth annd Martini, Maira. (2012). *U4 Expert Answer: Corruption trends in the Middle East and North Africa Region* (2007-2011), U4 Anti-Corruption Research Centre. Available at: http://www.u4.no/publications/corruption-trends-in-the-middle-east-and-north-africa-region-2007-2011/ (accessed March 2015).

Johnson, Jesper, Niels Taxell and Dominik Zaum. (2012). *Mapping Evidence Gaps: Assessing the State of the Operationally Relevant Evidence on Donor's Actions and Approaches to Reducing Corruption*. U4 Anti-Corruption Resource Centre. Available at: http://www.u4.no/publications/mapping-evidence-gaps-in-anti-corruption-assessing-the-state-of-the-operationally-relevant-evidence-on-donors-actions-and-approaches-to-reducing-corruption/ (accessed October 2016).

Johnston, Michael. (2010). *First Do No Harm Then Build Trust: Anti-corruption Strategies in Fragile Situations*. World Bank.

Kleemann, Kristof. (2010). "The European Neighbourhood Policy – A reality Check", *European Research Centre for Anti-Corruption and State-Building Working Papers,* Working paper No. 16.

Lavenex, Sandra and Franck Schimmelfennig. (2011). EU Democracy Promotion in the Neighbourhood: from leverage to governance? *Democratization*, 18(4): 885–909.

Lynch, Marc. (2012). Egypt's Brilliant Mistakes, *Foreign Policy*. Available at: http://foreignpolicy.com/2012/05/22/egypts-brilliant-mistakes/ (accessed April 2015).

Mada Masr. (2016b). "Egypt's Parliament passes new NGO law". Available at: https://www.madamasr.com/en/2016/11/29/news/u/parliament-passes-new-ngo-law/ (accessed December 2016)

Manek, Nizar and Jeremy Hodge. (2015a) Opening the Black Box of Egypt's Slush Funds. *Africa Confidential – The Angaza File*. Available at: http://www.africa-confidential.com/angaza-file#5.6_billion_accounting_trick (accessed June 2015).

Manek, Nizar and Jeremy Hodge. (2015b). Sisi and His 40 Thieves: Why Corruption Lingers in Cairo. *Foreign Policy*. Available at: https://www.foreignaffairs.com/articles/egypt/2015-06-26/sisi-and-his-40-thieves (accessed June 2015).

Mansour, Sherif. (2015). Stifling the Public Sphere: Media and Civil Society in Egypt. *National Endowment for Democracy: International Forum for Democratic Studies*. Available at: http://www.ned.org/wp-content/uploads/2015/10/Stifling-the-Public-Sphere-Media-Civil-Society-Egypt-Forum-NED.pdf (accessed January 2016).

Marquette, Heather, Rachel Flanary, Sumedh Rao and Dominic Morris. (2011). *Supporting Anti-Corruption Reform in Partner Countries: Concepts, Tools and Areas for Action*. Europe Aid Concept Paper 2. Available at: https://ec.europa.eu/europeaid/sites/devco/files/methodology-tools-and-methods-series-anti-corruption-reform-short-version-201108_en_5.pdf (accessed October 2016).

Marshall, Shana. (2015). *The Egyptian Armed Forces and the Remaking of an Economic Empire*. Carnegie Endowment for International Peace.

Messali, Pierre. (2011). METAC Workshop on Expenditures Control and Internal Audit: A Good Example of Donor Coordination. *Public Financial Management Blog*. Available at: http://blog-pfm.imf.org/pfmblog/2011/07/metac-workshop-on-expenditures-control-and-internal-audit-a-good-example-of-donor-coordination.html (accessed August 2015).

Moran, James. (2015). Egyptian Council for Foreign Relations Presentation. Available at: http://eeas.europa.eu/archives/delegations/egypt/press_corner/all_news/news/2015/ecfr_presentation_30th_september_2015_rev_1.pdf (accessed December 2015).

Mott, Patrick. (2010). Egypt's Anti-Corruption Programme and the United Nations Convention Against Corruption. Independent Research Paper. Available at: https://humanrightsstudyproject.files.wordpress.com/2012/07/pmott_egypt.pdf (accessed February 2015)

Moussa, Ghada A. (2013). Public Administration: Improving Transparency and Accountability. BARCELONA EUROMED FORUM: Social Inclusion in the Aftermath of the Arab Spring: from Politics to Policies. *DocumentsIEMed*. pp. 109–118.

Mungiu-Pippidi, Alina. (2006). Corruption: Diagnosis and Treatment. *Journal of Democracy.* 17(3): 86–99.

———. (2008). *The EU as a Transformation Agent: Lessons learned from governance reforms in East Central Europe.* Hertie School of Governance – working papers 33.

———. (2014). The Transformative Power of Europe Revisited. *Journal of Democracy*, 25(1): 20–32.

———. (2015). *The Quest for Good Governance: How societies Develop Control of Corruption*. Cambridge: Cambridge University Press.

———. (2016). Learning from Virtuous Circles. *Journal of Democracy*, 27(1): 95–109.

Mungiu-Pippidi, Alina et al. (2011). *Contextual Choices in Fighting COrruption: Lessons Learned*. Report 4/2011. Norad. Available at: https://www.oecd.org/countries/zambia/48912957.pdf (accessed September 2016).

Mungiu-Pippidi, Alina and Ramin Dadašov. (2016). Measuring Control of Corruption by a New Index of Public Integrity. *European Journal on Criminal Policy and Research* 22(3): 415–438.

Osman, Tarek. (2011). *Egypt on the Brink: From Nasser to Mubarak*, Yale University Press.

Pace, Michelle. (2012). Egypt. In: *The European Union and the Arab Spring: Promoting Democracy and Human Rights in the Middle East*. (ed.) Joel Peters. Lanham, MD: Lexington Books, pp. 49–64.

Persson, Anna, Bo Rothstein and Jan Teorell. (2010). The Failure of Anti-corruption Policies: A Theoretical Mischaracterization of the Problem. *QoG Working Paper Series* 19(10). Available at: http://qog.pol.gu.se/digitalAssets/1350/1350163_2010_19_persson_rothstein_teorell.pdf (accessed October 2016).

Pinfari, Marco. (2013). The EU, Egypt and Morsi's Rise and Fall: "Strategic Patience" and its Discontents. *Mediterranean Politics,* 18 (3): 460–466.

Preuschat, Archibald. (2015). Siemens signs $9 Billion Power-Plant Deal With Egypt. *The Wall Street Journal.* Available at: http://www.wsj.com/articles/siemens-signs-9-billion-power-plant-deal-with-egypt-1433343667 (accessed August 2015).

Pring, Coralie. (2016*). People and Corruption: Middle East & North Africa Survey 2016 – Global Corruption Barometer.* Transparency International. Available at: http://www.transparency.org/whatwedo/publication/people_and_corruption_mena_survey_2016 (accessed September 2016).

Puddephatt, Andrew. (2012). *Corruption in Egypt*, Global Partners & Associates. Available at: http://www.gp-digital.org/wp-content/uploads/pubs/Corruption-in-Egypt-Report-new-cover.pdf (accessed April 2015).

Ramalho, Rita. (2007). Egypt: Adding a million taxpayers. *The World Bank Doing Business -Celebrating Reforms 2007*. World Bank. Available at: http://www.doingbusiness.org/~/media/WBG/DoingBusiness/Documents/Reforms/Case-Studies/2007/DB07-CS-PT-Egypt.pdf (accessed October 2016).

Rao, Sumedh and Heather Marquette. (2012). *Corruption Indicators in Performance Assessment Frameworks for Budget Support*. U4 Anti-Corruption Resource Centre.

Sika, Nadine. (2012). Civil Society and Democratization in Egypt: The Road Not Yet Traveled. *Democracy & Society*, 9(2): 29–31.

State Information Services. (2009). Egypt-EU Association Agreement. Available at: http://www.sis.gov.eg/En/Templates/Articles/tmpArticles.aspx?CatID=121#.VRfkK7oxFo4 (accessed March 2015).

———. (2012). Egypt's Foreign Policy on Europe. Available at: http://www.sis.gov.eg/En/Templates/Articles/tmpArticles.aspx?CatID=120#.VR0RB7oxFsM (accessed January 2015).

Soliman, Samer. (2012). The Political Economy of Mubarak's Fall. In: *Arab Spring in Egypt: Revolution and Beyond* (eds.) Bahgat Korany and Rabab El-Mahdi. The American University in Cairo Press, pp. 43–62.

Transparency International. (2015). *Corruption Perceptions Index*. Available at: https://www.transparency.org/research/cpi/overview (accessed November 2015).

UNODC. (2004). *The Global Programme Against Corruption: UN Anti-Corruption Toolk*it. Available at: http://www.pogar.org/publications/finances/anticor/anticorruptiontoolkit.pdf (accessed November 2016)

———. (2013). *Independent mid-term project evaluation of Supporting Measures to Combat Corruption and Money Laundering, and to Foster Asset Recovery, in Egypt.* Available at: https://www.unodc.org/documents/evaluation/Independent_Project_Evaluations/2014/EGYX49_Mid-term_Evaluation_Report_JAN2014.pdf (accessed February 2015).

VNG International. (2015). *Support to Public Administration Reform and Local Development in Egypt.* Available at: http://www.vng-international.nl/blog/projects/support-to-public-administration-reform-and-local-development-in-egypt/ (accessed August 2015).

Interviews

Franco, Marc. (2015). EU ambassador and head of the EU delegation to Egypt from 2009 to 2012, Antwerp, 20 September.

UNODC. (2015). Cairo.

Given the sensitivity of the topic and the job functions of most of the interviewees, their names have remained undisclosed. They are referred to in the text as "Egyptian official", "Egyptian lawyer" or "Egyptian expert".

7. Tunisia: Great Expectations

JANA WARKOTSCH[1]

This chapter looks the EU's strategy in supporting good governance in Tunisia, in particular, following the nationwide protests in 2010/11 leading to the ousting of President Ben Ali. It analyses the relationship between Tunisia and the EU and explain how and why the EU changed its strategy following the 2011 uprisings. The EU seems to have learned from past mistakes and began to accompany Tunisia's transition with financial and technical assistance. So far, we cannot observe a clear positive change in the country. However, the transition is young as of yet, and it will take the years to come to see whether the EU's strategy for supporting good governance and anticorruption will bear fruit.

Introduction

President Ben Ali's sudden departure from power in 2011 following nationwide protests for social justice and political freedom forced the EU to rethink and adapt its previous cooperation strategy with Tunisia, which was based on security and stability in the region. The EU has been an important international partner for the country both before and after the uprising. Both former presidents, Bourguiba and Ben Ali, maintained close political and economic relationships, and proximity to the EU has been an important political and cultural reference point for the legitimacy of both regimes. The EU is the country's most important trade partner, with up to 74% of Tunisia's exports and imports going to and from the EU (Powel 2009). Part of the Southern Mediterranean neighbourhood of the EU, Tunisia was one of five countries in the Middle East and North Africa (MENA) region to adopt a European Neighbourhood Policy (ENP) Action Plan in 2005 – as well as one of the first states to enter into a free trade area with the EU in 1998 (European Parliament 2010). However, the 2011 uprising not only disposed one of the region's longest standing dictators; it also brought some of the more problematic aspects of the close relationship between the EU and the Ben Ali regime into clear focus. This concerned especially the EU's seemingly uncritical support for the regime, as well as their lack of open criticism of the country's highly repressive political structures. Following the uprising, a chastised EU has tried to learn from past mistakes and accompany the country's, at times, rocky transition with financial and technical assistance. Nonetheless indicators on good governance and control of corruption (CoC) have stagnated. This chapter will argue that this stagnation is not an indication for absence of change, however, but for a profound transformation of the nature of corruption from the Ben Ali to the transitional period. By analysing EU good governance promotion in Tunisia throughout both the authoritarian period of Ben Ali as well as the transitional period that followed his ouster, it puts a spotlight on the EU's promotion of good governance.

Ben Ali's Tunisia and EU good governance promotion

Prior to the uprising, Tunisia, like most of its regional counterparts, was highly authoritarian with strong personalist and particularistic elements of rule. The Ben Ali regime was

---

[1] Scientific coordinator, German Institute for Global and Area Studies (GIGA), jana.warkotsch@googlemail.com

equipped with vast discretionary powers, with the president sitting atop a massive party-state apparatus supported by the regime party, the Rassemblement Constitutionnel Démocratique (RCD) and tied together by relationships of clientelism and patronage (Erdle 2010, 172). The RCD provided the organisational structure to rule, often duplicating administrative structures, and capturing administrative personnel to do so (Hibou 2011, 88). Public sector employment represented one of the most important avenues for white-collar work and social advancement, making it not only an efficient instrument for control and repression but also a considerable resource for corruption. The regime thus combined substantive resources for discretionary use of power and access, with few constraints on its exercise.

Unsurprisingly both petty and grand corruption were rampant, growing markedly during the last decade of Ben Ali's rule (Freedom House 2012). This was signified by increasingly visible predation on the part of the elites connected to the first family, which had acquired a substantial share of the country's wealth through the capture of the state's regulatory framework (Rijikers et al 2014, 24). Global Financial Integrity (2011) estimates that illicit financial activities and official government corruption caused losses of over USD 1 billion per year.

Constraints on corruption were scant in contrast. Even though Tunisia ratified the UN Convention against Corruption in 2008 (Freedom House 2012), prosecution was rare – and where it did occur, political reasons prevailed over legal ones. Within the politically controlled judiciary, most judges lacked independence, making politically motivated verdicts the norm (Paciello 2010, 2). And while anti-corruption law under Ben Ali was enforced by the National Audit Office (Cour des Comptes), which had broad powers to monitor public enterprises for financial irregularities, its independence was questionable (Freedom House 2011).

Even though societal norms against corruption and particularism did exist before the uprising, constraints to corruption could not arise out of civil society due to highly restrictive rules on freedom of association, media freedoms and participation. Most broadcasting corporations belonged to the Ben Ali-Trabelsi family and self-censorship was common (Paciello 2011, 2). Opposition parties were either loyal to the regime in exchange for a share in spoils or strongly restricted in topics and radius of operation. Within the tightly controlled parliament, a dual system guaranteed the majority party a fixed share of 88% of seats, with the remaining 12% divided among the smaller parties. This established a mechanism by which loyal opposition parties could be rewarded via their inclusion in parliament, setting up an incentive system that saw opposition parties competing for seats against each other, and not with the RCD (Fuentes 2010, 526). Nonetheless, as the uprising that started in 2010 showed, open corruption and increasingly conspicuous consumption, especially by the first family around President Ben Ali and his wife Leila Trabelsi, elicited more and more popular scorn within Tunisian society.[2]

EU–Tunisia relationship under Ben Ali

Repressive structures of rule did not deter the EU from preparing the EU–Tunisia Action Plan[3] in 2004[4]. Despite the regime's refusal to discuss issues related to political reform, the EU negotiated an action plan heavy on economic and security cooperation but light on concrete measures of political reform demanded in return for aid. Nowhere in the vaguely worded objectives did the action plan allude to the authoritarian nature of the Tunisian political regime at the time, nor indeed include concrete measures to counter these tendencies (Del Sarto and

---

[2] 06TUNIS1673, 05.07.2005, http://wikileaks.org/cable/2006/07/06TUNIS1673.html
[3] http://eeas.europa.eu/enp/pdf/pdf/action_plans/tunisia_enp_ap_final_en.pdf
[4] It remained valid until 2014

Schumacher 2011, 941). Further measures intended to strengthen good governance were leaning heavily towards more technical aspects of good governance in the area of administrative reform and public financial management reform (PFM).[5] Priorities were negotiated in tandem with the Tunisian government, aligning them with the country's objectives.

While the EU acknowledged that no discernible progress had been achieved in the promotion of good governance, subsequent allocations in the National Indicative Programme (NIP) (2007–2010) did not demonstrate a commitment towards increasing progress in this area. While good governance and anticorruption measures in the technical sense were part of budget support within the economic governance priority, no separate programme supporting good governance and anticorruption practices existed during that time period.[6]

Thus, despite the EU's commitment to good governance in the initial design of the ENP, this was not subsequently translated into its approach to aid in Tunisia. Initially, the ENP was to include conditionality in the form of "Copenhagen proximity criteria", but by the time the action plans were drafted this objective had been weakened to include only vague references to political reforms (Tocci 2007, 12). Benchmarks often lacked clear and precise definitions of core concepts, such as democracy, the rule of law and good governance, as well as enforceable timetables. This was compounded by the fact that the action plans were negotiated bilaterally, which automatically tempered any potential criticism of Tunisia's repressive climate, or the interpenetration of state and ruling party (Del Sarto and Schumacher 2011, 941). Where problematic issues were included, the vague formulation of conditions regarding democracy, the rule of law and human rights left ample room for interpretations that would allow the regime to ultimately undertake mere cosmetic reforms (ibid., 943). Negative conditionality was also not enforced when the EU found itself struggling to put forward reforms such as the EUR 2.15 million media support programme, which failed to be implemented, or the EUR 25 million justice reform programme. The former could only be implemented temporarily under the threat of payment suspension and was ultimately abandoned altogether after the Tunisian side did not fulfil an equal access condition. This played into the hands of a regime, which had been unwilling to engage in justice reform to begin with. In both cases the EU ultimately continued its economic and social programmes uninterrupted (Powel 2009, 65). Del Sarto and Schumacher describe this as a manifestation of the EU's general benign neglect towards potentially contentious political issues (2011, 947).

Three central issues can illuminate the reasons for this failure. They concern firstly the fundamental assumptions behind the ENP, secondly preferences of EU engagement and thirdly the trade-off between contradictory aid and foreign policy interests.

The ENP was an attempt to transport a logic of conditionality that had worked within enlargement of its cooperation with neighbouring countries. The ENP's principle of cooperation was based on the assumption that these partner countries shared a fundament of basic values with the EU. According to this logic, divergences in the practices of rule in recipient countries must therefore be traced back to a lack of capacity rather than to divergences in basic ruling principles (irrespective of whether this was in fact really believed to be true by the EU or not) (Tocci 2007, 5). Based on this misassumption, the EU instruments were ill equipped to deal with undemocratic partner countries, where governments lacked not only the capacity for reform but also, most importantly, the political will. The reforms favoured by the EU would often have fundamentally challenged the ability of authoritarian rulers to maintain power, a fact not reflected in

---

[5] Defined by the EU as: 'The transparent and accountable management of human, natural, economic and financial resources for the purposes of equitable and sustainable development, in the context of a political and institutional environment that upholds human rights, democratic principles and the rule of law' (EC 2007a, 58).

[6] Interview with a member of the temporary Anti-Corruption Commission (INLUCC) (held 21.12.2015).

the volume and nature of incentives. This was compounded by the fact that much of institutional and legal reform advocated by the EU was in service of approximating partner countries' rules to the acquis communautaire. However, these rules were technically complex, carrying heavy implementation costs for partner countries often lacking in adequate institutional and administrative capacity (Schimmelfennig 2012, 18). But it was also unable to offer alternative rewards, such as the free movement of goods and people that are at the heart of the accession incentives, due to the protectionist interests of individual member states.

Lack of positive incentives was complemented by an unwillingness of the EU to use the full spectrum of available punitive measures, preferring engagement – also with authoritarian rulers – over confrontation. In sync with the EU's increasing use of conditionalities to further reform in the mid-1990s, the Tunisian AA contained an essential elements clauses relating to human rights and democracy that would allow for the application of punitive measures, up to and including the suspension of aid (Tocci 2007, 3). This de facto negative conditionality has never been applied in practice, however (Balfour 2012, 16). While cooperative in the economic realm, and highly dependent on trade with the EU, the Ben Ali regime had made clear that politically sensitive issues were not on the agenda: (Del Sarto and Schumacher 2011, 941). Faced with heavy resistance regarding political issues, the EU was hesitant to use either the negotiations for budget support conditionalities, or to call on the conditionalities embedded in the action plan as leverage for the disbursement of funds (Balfour 2012, 17). In the same vein, attempts at civil-society capacity building on part of the EU remained muted, with the regime putting a stop to projects directly dealing with democracy and human rights[7] and keeping NGOs underfunded so as to render them unable to muster the necessary administrative capacity to be in compliance with EU project tenders (Voss 2010).

With a climate this hostile to political reform, the EU retreated to good governance conditionalities that remained technical and apolitical, supporting the regime's own desire to modernise certain aspects of its administration.[8] This technicalisation of conditionalities is what enabled the overall positive evaluation of reform progress. International rankings such as the Davos Competitiveness Ranking, the Doing Business surveys as well as Transparency International's Corruption Perception Index (CPI) seemed to support the narrative of an "economic miracle", one characterised by strong economic growth, an expanding middle class and a modern, tech-savvy government (Hibou, Meddeb and Hamid 2011, 12). The data that these assessments relied upon was not generally questioned, despite being provided by the regime itself. The same applied to the issue of corruption, which while not unnoted, was not something seen as unusual for the region at large. And being concentrated in the domestic private sector, corruption was predominantly seen as negatively impacting the business climate – and not EU aid itself (Hibou, Meddeb, and Hamid 2011, 42). However, a certain amount of benign negligence – whereby if one got the results that were agreed upon, one assumed the money was used correctly – in combination with standard anticorruption clauses in the agreements and regular audits in the context of budget support seems to have been favoured over looking too closely.[9] While in the aftermath of the US's democracy promotion agenda in the Middle East the Ben Ali regime did find itself under pressure to entertain more political openness and work on governance projects with donors, according to experts, this space all but closed after 2005. When the global financial crisis forced the country to seek out increased bilateral aid and closer

---

[7] As was the case with the long suffering Ligue Tunisienne des Droits de l'Homme (Tunisian Human Rights League, LTDH).
[8] Interview with EU expert (held 22.01.2016).
[9] Interview with EU expert (held 03.12.2015).

cooperation with the EU, both sides decided to engage in less confrontational matters.[10]

But more than just the EU's preference for engagement, and the country's progress in administrative reform, it was the EU's own interests in the region and in Tunisia that further reduced its leverage and granted the regime leeway to evade political reform. The EU's interest in the realm of migration control and terrorism prevention thus resulted in a securitisation of the relationship, wherein the EU perceived a stable Tunisia as an important asset (Tocci 2007, 11). Cooperation thus turned towards jointly tackling problems of migration and border management, securing reliable energy supplies or the fight against organised crime and terrorism (ibid., 12). This was reflected in the EU's more forceful approach to conditionalities in the realm of security relations. The Tunisian regime thus cleverly leveraged their stability and reformist economic orientation, as well as their cooperation on migration and security issues against good governance, with the acquiescence of the EU (Hollis 2012, 93).

The EU and post-Arab spring Tunisia

Things were to change radically with the uprising that started in December 2010 and culminated in the ouster of President Ben Ali in January 2011. These events disturbed the equilibrium on the Tunisian as well as the EU side. In a climate of political instability and uncertainty, a succession of interim governments tried to reform existing structures of rule and establish democratic ones with the help of the donor community. The transitional period considerably reconfigured both resources as well as constraints for corruption within the Tunisian system on the one hand, and the opportunities for development assistance and good governance promotion on the other. Within the political system, Tunisia saw seven prime ministers within the six years after Ben Ali's toppling. Presidential elections that same years saw Beji Caid Essebsi, also of the Nidaa Tounes take office (IDEA 2014, 62–63). In addition to the turmoil on the political stage, a series of upheavals further threatened stability – including terrorist attacks, the assassination of two opposition politicians, a decline in tourism and persistent unemployment. Nonetheless Tunisia has been continually making progress towards democracy, as evidenced by improving indicators.[11] The January 2014 constitution guarantees fundamental rights and freedoms, and introduces new rights; the influence of the president has been reduced, and the roles of the prime minister and of the parliament have been strengthened (Pickard 2014, 136–138).

A transitional justice process was initiated in 2011, leading to the conviction of former President Ben Ali and his wife to 35 years imprisonment in absentia (Al Jazeera 2015a; *Guardian* 2011). In the same year, supported by EU sanctions, the assets of 110 family members of Ben Ali were confiscated and the pursuit of their remaining finances abroad was initiated (Palazzolo 2011). With these revamped rules, Tunisia thus saw a substantive decrease in discretionary power over access and resources at the top of the political system. The transitional justice process has not been without its problems and setbacks, however. Most recently, a controversial draft organic law on special procedures concerning reconciliation in the economic and financial fields (the "Reconciliation Bill") has caused protests. It would grant a general amnesty to public officials under Ben Ali accused of corruption, in exchange for the return of stolen public money and fines (*The New York Times* 2015).

In addition, gaps in the anticorruption framework remain, and corruption persists. While Tunisia has conflict of interest rules, codes of conduct and transparent public procurement systems, there is still an implementation gap (Bertelsmann Foundation 2014, 34). Corruption

---

[10] Interview with EU expert, (held 22.01.2016).
[11] Between 2012 and 2015, the Freedom House score (2015a) for the country improved from "partly free" to "free" (after being "not free" in the period 2007–2010)

remains problematic within the private sector, where over 50% of the economy is either closed or subject to continuing entry barriers (BTI 2016, 18) and there is currently no legislation criminalizing corruption (ibid., 34). Bribery is still a common feature of everyday life, and, according to the World Bank, 24% of firms report that it is necessary to speed things up with informal payments (ibid., 19). Petty corruption has been on the rise in recent years, and a study conducted by the Tunisian Association for Public Auditors estimates an amount of at least 450 million dinars (EUR 200 million) in bribes having been given to state employees in 2013 alone. Responsible parties are rarely punished (*Al-Araby* 2015b).

Thus while the destruction of the old regime meant the dismantlement of the previous centralised system of corruption and state capture, thereby substantively reducing the resources for corruption at the top of the system, the lack of institutionalisation of the transitional period also meant a diffusion of opportunities for corruption at the individual level.

At the same time, with the help of donors, institutional constraints on corruption multiplied. In 2011 the first temporary anticorruption commission, the Truth and Dignity Commission (IVD), was created and started investigating corruption based on the former regime's archives (*The Economist* 2013; *Al-Araby* 2015b). The IVD was to be replaced by a permanent Good Governance and Anti-Corruption Commission according to the 2014 constitution (International IDEA 2014: 100). In terms of constraints arising out of civil society, much headway has been made since 2011. Tunisia has witnessed a proliferation of NGOs, many of whom boast an anti-corruption agenda. The number of magazines, newspapers and television channels has multiplied (Schäfer 2015, 11).

EU intervention 2011–13

The 2011 uprising threw into disarray not only the domestic political scene but also the donor landscape forcing the EU to reverse its previous approach. These endeavours were further complicated by the fact that, in the wake of the Lisbon Treaty, the EU was in the process of redesigning its own external representation with the launch of the European External Action Service (EEAS) had only been launched in December 2010, a mere matter of weeks before the removal of President Ben Ali.

This resulted in what has been described as a "cacophonous start" (Balfour 2012, 11), with a wide variety of voices from different EU institutions and Member States adding their own proposals and opinions to the mix.[12] The EU responded by acknowledging past mistakes (ibid., 11) and by launching a number of immediate measures – as well as foreign policy instruments. It also doubled its aid budget to Tunisia for the period 2011–2013, reaching some EUR 445 million (Youngs 2015). Its new approach was to be based on more incentives, as well as more differentiation ("more for more") whereby countries that engage in reform are rewarded with greater EU support (2011, 5). Mobility partnerships were launched as instruments for migration control, and negotiations started for a Deep and Comprehensive Free Trade Area (DCFTA) to facilitate economic exchange. Catharine Ashton, the High Representative of the Union for Foreign Affairs and Security Policy at the time, subsumed the underlying tenets of cooperation under the so-called three Ms – money, markets and mobility.[13] The

---

[12] Interview with EU expert (held 03.12.2015).
[13] "Money – resources that can go into the region to help support the transition to democracy, the support for civil society and of course the economic needs of countries. Market access – the importance of making sure that we give advantages in trade, and that the people can take advantage of that by being able to export and import properly. Mobility – the ability of people to move around, for business people to be able to conduct

SPRING programme was introduced as part of the positive incentives to countries willing to embark on reforms, and Tunisia was its main beneficiary, receiving a total of EUR 155 million in the period 2011–2013 (EC 2015).[14] In addition to more incentives, conditionalities were to become more measurable and verifiable as well, relying on a proper benchmarking approach (EC 2011a). An important new departure was the push for increased transparency.[15] Next to government publications and statistics, the EU sought greater verification through access to background reports and studies, by bringing in external experts and by quantitatively verifying reports on budget allocation.[16] Cooperation now also saw an increase in good governance conditionality as well as programmes,[17] including conditions such as implementing legislation in the media sector, greater budget transparency and improved access to information,[18] and the creation of the temporary IVD.

The ENP was complemented with funding for capacity building measures from the regional South Programme by the Council of Europe (CoE) (CoE 2015, 28).

However, funds to Tunisia were put on hold by the EU and other international partners in 2013 amid political instability. After the political climate re-stabilised with a new technocratic government and the adoption of the new constitution in 2014, funding resumed (BTI 2016, 38).

In 2014, the Privileged Partnership, which represents the most recent action plan, 2013–2017, was adopted. After the increased focus on political reform following the Arab spring, it seems to confirm a shift of EU priorities back towards strengthening economic cooperation within the yet-to-be-signed DCFTAs, as well as a focus on security issues.

How did the changed approach to conditionality and good governance promotion of the EU fare during Tunisia's transition? Did it succeeded in impacting incentives for reform? In general, it seems clear that conditionality did play an important role as a lever by which to get reforms going, key bodies institutionalised and core provisions included in the constitution. The EU successfully combined their use with legal expertise and capacity building, especially where the AC commission and the constitutional provisions were concerned, as well as the draft laws for constitutional courts.[19] Positive conditionality within the SPRING programme was also essential in getting the justice sector support programme running once again. The SPRING programme also provided important support to civil society that contributed to capacity building and strengthened their incorporation into consultation processes. Civil society participated, for instance, in the EU's dialogue on the new Privileged Partnership together with the Tunisian government.[20] Hence, the EU is nowadays making certain that demands for further reform include political reforms (Balfour 2012, 25) and the demands that the transition has placed on the Tunisian government have made it both more eager to accept help, as well as more susceptible to caving to EU pressure.

However, despite the successes of EU policy after the Arab spring, three main problems remain. They concern persistent gaps in implementation, the question of incentives, as well as the adequateness of conditionalities for the Tunisian context.

The criticism raised frequently of the international anticorruption agenda is that institution

---

business more effectively." http://www.enpi-info.eu/medportal/news/latest/24485/Money,-Market-access,-Mobility-%E2%80%93-three-Ms-to-underpin-EU-support-to-its-southern-neighbours

[14] It was replaced by new "umbrella funds" in 2014 under ENI 2014–2020.
[15] Interview with EU expert (held 28.01.2016).
[16] Interview with EU expert (held 11.12.2015).
[17] Interview with EU expert (held 11.12.2015).
[18] Interview with EU expert (held 11.12.2015).
[19] Interview with EU expert (held 18.12.2015).
[20] Interview with EU expert (held 11.12.2015).

building does not always translate into successful implementation of these frameworks (Carothers and De Gramont 2013). Tunisia illustrates the problem of "institutional monocropping", especially in a context where political will to fight corruption seems to be waning, and patrimonial practices are resurging (Youngs 2015). An example was the temporary anticorruption commission. While successfully created due to donor pressure, after its creation, the IVD continued to suffer from a lack in technical expertise, low funding and inadequate equipment. Its efforts were diluted by a duplication of structures and responsibilities, most recently by the ad hoc creation of a Ministry for Good Governance and Anti-Corruption (CoE 2015, 28). Indeed, the implementation gap in Tunisia is not only facilitated by the lack of follow up mechanisms but by a lack of clearly specified reform requirements on part of the EU. Tunisian officials thus complained that:

> … there are only generalities and we do not know exactly what programmes should result in. This also causes problems with assessment. As we have no clear expectations, the evaluation cannot be done properly. EU programmes are approved in two meetings with the Ministry of International Cooperation. And it stops there. There is no follow up whatsoever, and that is one of the reasons objectives are not met.[21]

Secondly, while incentives have improved with the upgrading of assistance, they continue to be insufficient to motivate reform in those areas where the reform interests of the Tunisian government do not align with the EU's. An important departure is the general willingness of the Tunisian administration to entertain political reforms, and to seek donor support for carrying them out. However, the change in the principle features of the incentive structures are not due to a change in the shortcomings of the instruments themselves, which persist, but of the context in which they are employed. These problems with the instruments are compounded by the necessity of having individual EU member states comply with the actual delivering of incentives (Balfour 2012, 25).

The resultant potential lack of credibility is relevant with regard to all three forms of incentives embodied in Ashton's three Ms. With regard to money, experts suggested that, with EU assistance operating on fixed budgets, more money allocated to Tunisia, means less money for another partner country and vice versa. There is thus a built in limit to how much more assistance the EU is able to offer. The "market" part continues to run according to an out-dated quota system that protects defensive interests in the agricultural sector on the part of EU member countries,[22] and similar problems apply to "mobility" too, where the EU's reluctance on offering freer movement has reduced the incentives to negotiate for their Tunisian counterparts (Youngs 2015). Thus positive conditionalities only work as long as there are actually incentives on offer that are relevant to the partner country.

Lastly, conditionalities were not always adequate for the level of administrative capacity in Tunisia due to political instability and shortcomings with regards to the staff and coordination structures necessary to deal with the complicated language, procedures and requirements entailed by EU assistance (Balfour 2012, 25). This strained the government's ability to steer development and formulate long-term strategies (BTI 2016, 37). Changes in the relationship between donors and the administration compounded these problems. Under Ben Ali, donor interaction with the administration was highly restrictive and centralised, with a few, well-regulated access points. Following the uprising, donors found open ears at different levels of the administration. While this makes some of the communication easier, these changes also resulted in a loss of coherence, and a multitude of not always well coordinated donor initia-

---

[21] Interview with member of the Tunisian administration (held 21.12.2015)
[22] Interview with EU expert (held 03.12.2015).

tives. This presents the danger of imposing unrealistic reforms.[23] Over the course of the last years, conditionalities had to be changed and adapted several times because they did not match existing administrative capacities. Performance criteria have often turned out to be too ambitious (OECD 2011, 21), and the EU saw itself forced to adapt them to a more reasonable pace that took better account of local capacities.[24]

Hence, over the course of Tunisia's transition, the EU, together with other donors, has played an important role in aiding the peaceful establishment of a new political order. It has worked to increase constraints on corruption by institution and capacity building. At the same time, it has only had sparse effects on diminishing the resources for corruption in Tunisia. Corruption thus changed, adapting to the opening up of new avenues, while others closed. This explains the relatively stable trajectory of control of corruption, despite increased EU intervention in terms of aid and programmes:

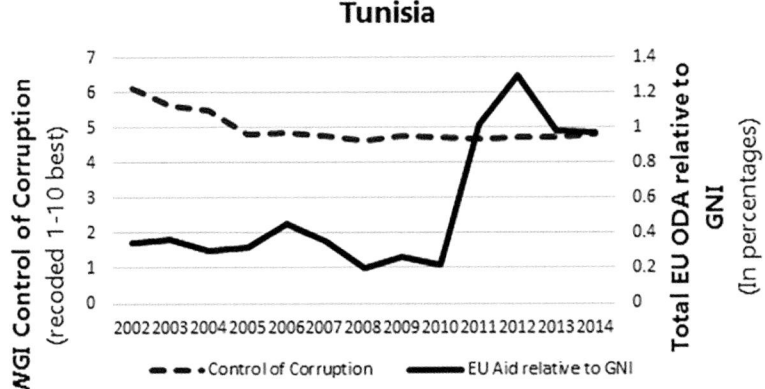

Figure 1. Stagnant governance trend against EU aid for Tunisia

The doubled-edged sword of the aid effectiveness agenda for democracy promotion in Tunisia

Many challenges remain in Tunisia's path to democracy, and the EU will need to continue adapting and improving its approach. One of the lessons of the past two periods is that EU instruments prior to the Arab spring seemed only to have worked concerning issues in which the government had a genuine interest.[25] In more contentious cases, the fact that conditionalities are jointly negotiated reduced their effectiveness, leading to the watered down and vague language employed in the ENP Action Plan of 2004. Without being linked to specific benchmarks or allocation criteria, they failed to trigger any meaningful reform in Tunisia (Voss 2010, 145).

This problem is compounded by the fact that governance, as defined by the EU, has a multitude of dimensions to it. It is thus easy to focus on the less political and more easily negotiated technical dimensions and still be able to lay claim to the promotion of good governance despite widespread violations going unpunished at the political level. On the one hand, this is in compliance with the new aid effectiveness agenda and the greater emphasis it places on country ownership. On the other, it also diminishes the room available to positively affect governance outcomes beyond the technical level.

---

[23] Interview with EU expert (held 11.12.2015).
[24] Interview with EU expert (held 11.12.2015).
[25] Interview with EU expert (held 03.12.2015).

Ownership thus proved a double-edged sword in the case of Tunisia, whose two very different phases of EU engagement over the studied time period exemplify both its advantages and shortcomings. On the one hand, it places constraints on the effectiveness of good governance promotion in country contexts hostile to reform. This is true both with respect to the demand and the supply side of reform. The transitional period during which more open and participatory governments ruled Tunisia, however, also showed, on the other hand, that ownership is necessary to negotiate reforms and conditionality that are locally led and appropriate to country context and administrative capacities. It also points to the importance of more and better donor coordination to achieve these ends.

Tunisia also showed that conditionality needs to be backed up by proper incentives, and these incentives are not to be found in additional funds but in concessions granting access to more mobility and trade.[26] The interviews conducted for this study suggested that beyond access, EU leverage lies elsewhere: in their soft power exercised through political dialogue and expertise, not through increasingly harsher conditionalities.[27] This is fundamentally at odds with the tendency in Brussels, where the direction is towards tightening conditionality in aid relationships.

However, the transition is young as of yet, and it will take the years to come to see whether the EU's strategy for supporting good governance and anticorruption will bear fruit. For these efforts to succeed it will be crucial that the government of Tunisia continues to show the political will necessary to push forward the development of anticorruption and good governance, on the one hand. But on the other, the EU will need to demonstrate its commitment to these reforms in terms of its programming, but also its willingness to punish attempts at reversing the gains made so far.

References

Al-Araby. (2015, October 4). "Petty corruption" plagues Tunisian economy. Accessed December 18, 2015, http://www.alaraby.co.uk/english/Politics/2015/10/4/Petty-corruption-plagues-Tunisian-economy

Al Jazeera. (2015): Tunisia's Ben Ali Sentenced to Life in Jail. Accessed December 8, 2015, http://www.aljazeera.com/news/africa/2012/07/20127191612311698132.html

Balfour, R. (2012). EU conditionality after the Arab Spring. IEMed.

Bertelsmann Foundation (2014). Tunisia Country Report 2014. Bertelsmann Transformation Index 2014. Accessed December 20, 2015. http://www.bti-project.org/uploads/tx_itao_download/BTI_2014_Tunisia.pdf

———. (2016). Tunisia Country Report 2016. Bertelsmann Transformation Index 2016. Accessed February 25, 2016. https://www.bertelsmann-stiftung.de/en/publications/publication/did/bti-2016-tunisia-country-report/

Council of Europe (2015). Strengthening Democratic Reform in the Southern Neighbourhood. Component 2 title: Promotion of Good Governance: Fight against Corruption and Moneylaundering (SNAC). Final Narrative Report.

Constitution of the Tunisian Republic. (2014). Unofficial translation by UNDP and then reviewed by International IDEA. Accessed December 15, 2015. http://www.constitutionnet.org/files/2014.01.26_-_final_constitution_english_idea_final.pdf

Del Sarto, R. A. and Schumacher, T. (2011). From Brussels with love: leverage, benchmarking, and the action plans with Jordan and Tunisia in the EU's democratization policy. *Democratization*, 18(4), 932–955.

Erdle, Steffen. (2010). *Ben Ali's "New Tunisia" (1987–2009): A Case Study of Authoritarian Modernization in the Arab World*. Berlin: Klaus Schwarz.

European Commission. (2004). European Neighbourhood Policy: Country Report Tunisia. SEC(2004) 570, 12 May 2004.

———. (2004). EU/Tunisia Action Plan. Published 9 December 2004. Accessed December 15, 2015. http://ec.europa.eu/world/enp/pdf/action_plans/tunisia_enp_ap_final_en.pdf

---

[26] Interview with EU expert (held 03.12.2015).

[27] Interviews with EU experts (held 11.12.2015, 18.12.2015, 03.12.2015).

———. (2007a). Aid Delivery Methods – Guidelines on the Programming, Design & Management of General Budget Support. AIDCO, RELEX, January 2007.

———. (2007b). European Neighbourhood And Partnership Instrument Tunisia Strategy Paper 2007–2013 & National Indicative Programme 2007–2010.

———. (2010). Green Paper from The Commission to the Council, the European Parliament, the European Economic and Social Committee and the Committee of the Regions: The future of EU budget support to third countries. Brussels, October 19, 2010 COM(2010) 586 final.

———. (2011a). Joint Communication "A Partnership for Democracy and Shared Prosperity with the Southern Mediterranean". Brussels, 8 March 2011, COM(2011).

———. (2011b). Joint Communication by the High Representative of the Union For Foreign Affairs and Security Policy and the European Commission, "A New Response to a Changing Neighbourhood, a review of European Neighbourhood Policy". Brussels, 25 May 2011.

———. (2011c). Joint Staff Working Paper: A Medium Term Programme for a renewed European Neighbourhood Policy (2011-2014). Brussels, May 25 2011 SEC(2011) 650.

———. (2013). Ex-ante evaluation statement on EU macro-financial assistance to the Republic of Tunisia. Commission Staff Working Document, Brussels, 20 November 2013.

———. (2012a). Commission Implementing Decision of 9 March 2012 amending Decision C(2011) 6828 adopting the Programme of Support to the Association Agreement and the Transition Process for Tunisia under the SPRING programme, Brussels, 9 March 2012, C(2012)1439.

———. (2012b). Budget Support Guidelines: Programming, Design and Management. A modern approach to Budget support. EuropeAid Development and Cooperation Directorate General European Commission, Brussels, September 2012.

———. (2014a). Joint Proposal for a COUNCIL DECISION on the Union position within the Association Council set up by the Euro-Mediterranean Agreement establishing an association between the European Communities and their Member States, of the one part, and the Republic of Tunisia, of the other part, with regard to the adoption of a recommendation on the implementation of the EU-Tunisia Action Plan implementing the privileged partnership (2013–2017).

———. (2014b). Joint Staff Working Document Implementation of the European Neighbourhood Policy: Statistical Annex. SWD(2014) 98 final, Brussels, 27 March 2014. Accessed December 15, 2015. http://eeas.europa.eu/enp/pdf/2014/stats/statistical_annex_2014.pdf

———. (2015). Tunisia Financial Assistance Fiche," Accessed December 15, 2015. http://ec.europa.eu/enlargement/neighbourhood/pdf/key-documents/tunisia/20150630-tunisia-financial-assistance-fiche.pdf

European Parliament. (2011). The Future of Eu Budget Support in Developing Countries. Directorate General For External Policies Of The Union, Directorate B, Policy Department. Briefing Paper.

Freedom House. (2011). Tunisia | Country Report | Countries at the Crossroads | 2011. Accessed December 9, 2015. https://freedomhouse.org/report/countries-crossroads/2011/tunisia Methodology | Freedom House." Accessed December 8, 2015. https://freedomhouse.org/report/countries-crossroads-2011/methodology

———. (2012). Tunisia | Country Report | Countries at the Crossroads | 2007–2012. Accessed December 8, 2015. https://freedomhouse.org/report/countries-crossroads/2012/tunisia

Fuentes, Martinez, G. (2010). Presidential and parliamentary electoral policies in Tunisia (1989–2009). *REVISTA DE ESTUDIOS POLITICOS*, (149) p.p. 123–149.

Global Financial Integrity. (2011). Corruption, Tax Evasion, Criminal Activity Cost Tunisia US$1.16 Billion Per Year From 2000–2008. Accessed December 15, 2015. http://www.gfintegrity.org/press-release/corruption-tax-evasion-criminal-activity-cost-tunisia-us1-16-billion-per-year-2000-2008/

Guardian. (2011). Ben Ali Sentenced to 35 Years in Jail. Accessed December 8, 2015. http://www.theguardian.com/world/2011/jun/20/ben-ali-sentenced-35-years-jail

Hibou, Béatrice, Hamza Meddeb and Mohamed Hamdi (2011). Tunisia after 14 January and its social and political economy. The issues at stake in a reconfiguration of European policy. Euro-Mediterranean Human Rights Network (EMHRN). June 2011.

Hollis, R. (2012). No friend of democratization: Europe's role in the genesis of the "Arab Spring". *International Affairs*, 88(1), 81–94.

Nucifora, Antonio, Erik Churchill and Bob Rijkers. (2015). Cronyism, Corruption, and the Arab Spring: The Case of Tunisia. In: The Heritage Foundation. 2015 Index of Economic Freedom Book. pp. 47–56, Accessed December 14, 2015. http://www.heritage.org/index/book/chapter-4

OECD. (2011). Application of new approach to the evaluation of Budget Support operations: findings from Mali, Zambia and Tunisia Synthesis of main results. Synthesis. November 2011 OECD DAC Network on Development Evaluation.

Paciello, Maria Cristina. (2011). Tunisia. Changes and challenges of political transition. Brussels: Centre for European Policy Studies, MEDPRO technical report, no. 3. Accessed August 19, 2014. http://www.medpro-foresight.eu/system/files/MEDPRO%20TR%20No%203%20WP2%20Paciello%20on%20Tunisia.pdf

Palazzolo, Joe. (2011). Tunisia Hires Ace to Track Down Ben Ali's Assets, *The Wall Street Journal* Law Blog (Oct. 24, 2011). Accessed December 15, 2015, http://blogs.wsj.com/law/2011/10/24/tunisia-hires-ace-to-track-down-ben-alis-assets

PEFA. (2010). Public Financial Management Reform in the Middle East and North Africa: An Overview of Regional Experience Part II Individual Country Cases. Middle East and North Africa Vice-Presidency, PEFA Report No. 55061-MNA, June 2010.

Perthes, Volker. (2011). *Der Aufstand. Die arabische Revolution und ihre Folgen.* Munich: Pantheon.

Pickard, Duncan and Todd Schweitzer. (2012). Overcoming the Binding Constraint to Economic Growth in Post-Revolution Tunisia. John F. Kennedy School of Government, Harvard University, March 2012.

Powel, B. T. (2009). The stability syndrome: US and EU democracy promotion in Tunisia. *The Journal of North African Studies*, 14(1), 57–73.

Reporters Without Borders. (2015). 2015 World Press Freedom Index. Accessed December 15, 2015. http://inReporterdex.rsf.org/#!/index-details/TUN

Rijkers, Bob, Antonio Nucifora and Caroline Freund. (2014). All in the Family: State Capture in Tunisia. Policy Research Working Paper No. 6810. Washington, DC: World Bank.

Schäfer, Isabel. (2015). The Tunisian Transition: Torn Between Democratic Consolidation and Neo-Conservatism in an Insecure Regional Context. EuroMeSCo Paper Series/Papers IEMed (25), Barcelona: European Institute of the Mediterranean.

Schimmelfennig, Frank. (2012). Europeanization beyond Europe. *Living Reviews in European Governance*, Vol. 7, (2012), No. 1.

The Arab Anti-Corruption and Integrity Network (ACINET). (2015). Official Homepage. Accessed December 21, 2015, http://www.arabacinet.org/index.php/en/home

The Economist (2013, July 25). An Uphill Struggle. Accessed December 17, 2015, http://www.economist.com/blogs/pomegranate/2013/07/tackling-corruption-tunisia

The New York Times. (2015, November 6). In Tunisia, a Mission of Justice and a Moment of Reckoning. Accessed December 19, 2015, http://www.nytimes.com/2015/11/07/world/africa/in-tunisia-a-mission-of-justice-and-a-moment-of-reckoning.html?_r=0

———. (2014). 2014 Corruption Perceptions Index – Results. Accessed December 8, 2015. http://www.transparency.org/cpi2014/results

Tocci, N. (2007). Can the EU promote democracy and human rights through the ENP? The case for refocusing on the rule of law. The European Neighbourhood Policy: a framework for modernization, EUI Working Papers, (21), 23–36.

Voss, M. (2010). Mind the gap! Assessing the implementation of the EU-Tunisian action plan in the field of political cooperation. L'Europe en Formation, (2), pp. 139–152.

Wikileaks. (2010). Troubled Tunisia: What should we do? Classified By: Ambassador Robert F. Godec, REF: TUNIS 000492, July 17, 2009. Accessed December 8, 2015, https://wikileaks.org/plusd/cables/09TUNIS492_a.html

Youngs, Richard. (2015). A New Phase in Tunisia's Transition. Carnegie Endowment for International Peace, Monday, March 2, 2015, http://carnegieeurope.eu/strategiceurope/?fa=59219

8. Tanzania: The Cosmetic Anticorruption

MAX MONTGOMERY[1]

Tanzania boasts one of the highest rates of economic growth in sub-Saharan Africa. In the last decades it also established one of the most harmonised donor frameworks. However, the relationship between Tanzania and its donors has deteriorated significantly in recent years following several high-level corruption cases and slow progress on more complex governance reform. In response, the EU has reformed the composition of its development assistance modalities, which predominantly entailed a reduction in budget support and has stopped committing further aid to Tanzania for the time being. These events indicate considerable limitations to the effectiveness of the EUs' (and other donors') measures to induce good governance through existing modi of development cooperation.

The United Republic of Tanzania[2] turned from "donor's darling" to problem child with regard to anticorruption and governance reforms in the period under review. Its status as a beacon of political stability in sub-Saharan Africa, successful democratic and economic transformation at the beginning of the early 1990s, and impressive framework for donor coordination enabled Tanzania to attract substantial development assistance from major international donors. Building on historical connections and a strategic partnership, the EU emerged as one of the major development partners and contributed considerable support to on-going national development strategies and various governance reforms.

However, a recent decline across primary and secondary governance indices, several high-level corruption cases and the prevalence of clientelistic networks within a particularistic power arrangement has resulted in friction between Tanzania and its development partners and casts doubts on the EU's strategy to promote good governance in Tanzania.

State of governance

After 30 years of adherence to a socialist model of economic development and one-party rule under the Chama Cha Mapundizi (CCM), Tanzania overhauled its political and economic system in 1992. While democratic elections have taken place every five years since 1995, the CCM-aided by its long history of rule and structural weaknesses in the political system – continues to dominate the Tanzanian government and state administration. Furthermore, a powerful executive and a relatively weak separation of powers results in a particularistic governance arrangement, characterised by a high susceptibility to corruption (von Wogau 2010, Mungiu-Pippidi 2006). This quasi-monopolistic power arrangement is reinforced by a highly politicised bureaucracy and weak corrective institutions. While political diversity has increased in recent years, the growth of major opposition parties continues to be obstructed by viola-

---
[1] German Institute for Global and Area Studies (GIGA), max.montgomery@giga-hamburg.de
[2] The United Republic of Tanzania consists of a union between mainland Tanzania and semi-autonomous Zanzibar, which merged in the process of independence in 1964. Henceforth, for simplicity's sake, this report will refer to it as "Tanzania".

tions of the right to assembly and occasional limits to the freedoms of the press (Bertelsmann Stiftung 2014). The recently introduced controversial Cybercrimes Act, which is considered to curtail freedom of speech and bestows excessive powers with little oversight to law enforcement organisations, is a further indicator of the government's current unwillingness to subject itself to a higher degree of public accountability (Goitom 2015).

Tanzania's semi-presidential system bestows excessive powers on the executive, while leaving legislative and judicial branches relatively weak. In part, this is due to the directly elected presidents wide-ranging powers of appointment. These include his cabinet members, selected from the National Assembly, the Chief Justice and Regional Commissioners. Although the National Assembly has, at times, managed to impose political constraints, for example by voting down bills proposed by the executive, it is occasionally denied its constitutional role by the government in favour of party committees. The judiciary is viewed as only partially independent[3] and lacks credibility in the eyes of the populace, with 86% of respondents to the Global Corruption Barometer 2013 viewing it as corrupt and 52% also reporting having paid a bribe when accessing judicial services (Transparency International 2016). In effect, this significantly impedes the accountability of officeholders and is considered a critical weakness by many observers (Bertelsmann Stiftung 2014, Jingu 2014).

Apart from dominating the higher echelons of government, the CCM continues to exert considerable power over the administration, as the old ties from the one-party system between party and administration continue to exist (Mukandala et al. 2005, Ewald 2011). Additionally, it wields considerable influence in the state's other executive organs, such as the army, police and security forces (Bertelsmann Stiftung 2014, Ewald 2011). This overlap between party and state administration allows the CCM to undermine political opposition in two significant ways. First, it allows the governing party to obstruct and intimidate opposition, for example by threatening arrest or revoking their rights to assembly. These tools are also used to infringe on the rights of civil society actors and the media[4] (Lindner 2014). Second, as most "political opportunities" arise within the government administration and are tied to the CCM's wider political network, it increases political opportunity cost to stand outside the party. This political environment is highly conducive to political clientilism and enshrines the predominance of informal networks, which permeate every sector of Tanzania's governance regime. As elites from different sectors have joined in complex networks of mutual dependence and favours, attracted by the administrations extensive command over resources and wealth, corruption has become a "key element linking political legitimacy with economic benefit" (Hydén and Mmuya 2008, 34; Koechlin 2013, 110; Bertelsmann Stiftung 2014; Gray 2015). As such, the distinction between public and private as well as between the CCM and the state administration is often non-transparent, resulting in a situation where access to the political system is effectively determined by clientilistic networks[5].

Recently, political opposition to the CCM's rule has grown, predominantly as a result of sluggish progress in poverty alleviation – in spite of substantial economic growth, crumbling

---

[3] Tanzania's judiciary was ranked semi-independent by the World Economic Forum's Global Competitiveness Report 2016/2017 – receiving a 3.9 on a scale from 0 (judiciary is heavily influenced) to 7 (judiciary is entirely independent), with the global median being 4.2 (Schwab and Sala-i-Martin 2015).

[4] Tanzania's press was rated as 'partly free' with a declining trend in Freedom House's Freedom of the Press Report 2016, with a score 55 on a scale from 0 (free) to 100 (un-free) (Freedom House 2016).

[5] This has been noted by several experts. For example, the Bertelsmann Stiftung (2014) and von Wogau (2010) rate Tanzania as a 'Neo-Patrimonial' state. However, considering the contested nature of this concept, this study will henceforth refer to Tanzania's power arrangements as 'particularistic' (Mungiu-Pippidi 2016; Mungiu-Pippidi 2014).

physical infrastructure – and several high-level corruption cases. However, the Chama Cha Demokrasia Na Maendelo (CHADEMA), the main opposition party, has started to pose a serious challenge to the continuation of the CCM's virtual monopoly on power in Tanzania. In response, the government has introduced several repressive pieces of legislation that effectively reduced the freedom of the press, suppress civil liberties, and which allow the targeting of the CCM's political opponents (see Goitom 2015, Lindner 2014).

Corruption and evolution of an anticorruption framework

Control of corruption has featured on Tanzania's political and public agenda for decades and resulted in a continuously expanding regulatory framework, in particular since political transformation took place in the 1990s. Nevertheless, corrupt practices continue to be considered endemic to the political system, with an estimated 20% of the government's budget lost to corruption each fiscal year, frequent high-level corruption cases and regress on core anticorruption indicators (ITAD and LDP 2011a, 3; Bertelsmann Stiftung 2014). Considerable opportunities for corruption – predominantly stemming from the particularistic power arrangement, especially the president's ability to interfere in the dealings of virtually all anticorruption institutions, and the implementation gap in anticorruption regulation – continue to exist. Tanzania's anticorruption legal framework is formally comprehensive but exhibits severe implementation gaps, which recent reforms have not been able to redress. Similarly, while key anticorruption institutions have been established, their effectiveness and independence varies greatly (Booth et al. 2014, 28). Furthermore, the lack of progress in critical areas indicates a lack of domestic agency and political will to conduct substantive improvements in anticorruption efforts. It therefore comes as no surprise that good governance and corruption issues have been a major bone of contention in the dialogue on development cooperation between Tanzania and its major donors, including the EU (ITAD et al. 2013)

Core elements of Tanzania's control of corruption framework were already established in the context Benjamin Mkapa, the first democratically elected president, and his so-called "war on corruption" in 1995 (Cooksey 2012, Lindner 2014). The primary accomplishment of this policy was the Report of the Presidential Commission of Inquiry Against Corruption,[6] which served as a fundament to the comprehensive National Anti-Corruption Strategy and Action Plan (NACSAP). However, Mkapa's ambition to combat and eliminate corruption waned after the implementation of NACSAP and his reforms ultimately proved rather unsuccessful at curbing corrupt practices (Tripp 2012).

The government's commitment to combat corruption was renewed in 2005 with the election of Mkapa's successor Jakaya Kikwete. The new strategy rested on two comprehensive and interlinked reforms: 1. the 2007 Prevention and Combating of Corruption Act (PCCA) that entailed a revision and significant expansion of the Prevention of Corruption Act and 2. a revised anticorruption strategy (NACSAP II) for the period 2008–2011. Partly, these reforms were created in response to international pressure and with support by international development partners and aimed at removing corrupt leaders, increasing synergies between existing anticorruption institutions, appointing a Minister of Good Governance, establishing an Ethics Commission and creating the Prevention and Combat of Corruption Bureau (PCCB), the primary anticorruption institution bestowed with investigative powers (Lindner 2014).

---

[6] The report is commonly referred to as the "Warioba Report" after its chairman, Joseph Warioba. It found, among other things, that public servants in the public services delivery sector engaged in petty corruption as a means of supplementing their meagre incomes and provided evidence for the existence of large-scale grand corruption among high-level officials.

However, a severe implementation gap, also due to low and decreasing judicial independence, continues to obstruct the effectiveness of these strategies and the capacity of anticorruption institutions (see figure 1). Furthermore, the majority of anticorruption institutions, including the PCCB, are considered to lack capacity and political independence to effectively constrain corrupt practices. Additionally, independent evaluations have identified considerable difficulties with the adoption of more complex, second-generation reforms to the PFM framework, in spite of initially laudable progress by the government of Tanzania in establishing budgetary and financial management regulation and practices (ITAD and LDP 2011a, ADE 2013). These issues are compounded by inadequate protection of whistleblowers, the lack of a freedom of information bill, and the recent decline in press freedom and civil liberties (Business Anti-Corruption Portal 2013, Lindner 2014).

EU development assistance to Tanzania

Tanzania's political and economic transformation quickly turned it into a "donor's darling", also as a result of its efforts towards donor harmonisation, which resulted in the Joint Assistance Strategy for Tanzania (JAST) and the Partnership Framework Memorandum in 2006. These mechanisms were designed to harmonise and align the efforts of international donors[7] with Tanzania's national development strategy, defined in the Tanzania Vision (TV) 2025 and the poverty eradication programmes MKUKUTA[8] (2005–2010) and MKUKUTA II (2010–2015). As a result, Tanzania became one of the largest recipients of development assistance in sub-Saharan Africa, usually in the form of budget support, which made up around 25% of the national budget in 2011 (Tripp 2012). However, recent cases of grand corruption, regress on a number of governance indicators and sluggish progress in PFM reform have led to an erosion of trust between Tanzania and its development partners, which withheld their support temporarily and reduced the share of budget support in their aid envelopes.

The EU has long been a key development partner for Tanzania and a major stakeholder in the JAST. The relationship is cemented in multiple agreements – which reflect the stipulations of the European Development Fund (EDF),[9] the EU approach to ACP countries[10] and Tanzania's national development strategies – with the overarching objectives to 1. support Tanzania's further political and social democratisation, 2. advocate for a pro-poor growth agenda and for improving economic governance and the business climate and 3. encourage Tanzania's continued involvement in regional economic and political integration process (Delegation of the European Union to Tanzania 2016)[11].

To this end, Tanzania received EUR 555 million, an average of EUR 92.5 million per year, under the 10th National Indicative Programme (NIP) for the period 2008–2013. The

---

[7] These include the EU and several Member States (United Kingdom, Denmark, Germany, Finland, Ireland, Belgium, Sweden, Netherlands, France, Italy), Norway, Switzerland, USAID, Canada, Japan, Korea, African Development Bank, World Bank and United Nations Agencies.

[8] MKUKUTA is the Kiswahili acronym for National Strategy for Growth and Poverty Reduction.

[9] These reflect the essential understandings of the European Consensus on Development adopted in 2006 which sets the general policy framework at the EU level. Furthemrore, the adoption of "An Agenda for Change" as a result of inernational development aid agreements, the latest from Busan 2011, resulted in the EU's commitment to disburse development assistance preferrebly through Budget Support. This aid modality that uses domestic Public Financial Management (PFM) systems and supports national development (European Court of Auditors 2010, 11).

[10] The Cotonou Agreement provides the legal basis for EC cooperation with ACP countries. Other influential understandings include the Joint Africa – EU Strategy in 2005 and regular EU-Africa Summits.

[11] A thorough description of EU-Tanzania development cooperation can be found in Montgomery (2016).

majority of this funding was directed towards macroeconomic support, with other targets being infrastructure development and support to non-state actors and governance institutions. A preliminary version of the 11th NIP (2014–2020)[12] foresees an indicative amount of EUR 626 million, EUR 104 million annually, in development assistance. This document identifies Good Governance and Development as the key target for assistance, with the remainder of the funds going to the energy sector and measures in favour of civil society organisations (CSOs). In addition, Tanzania became one of only eight countries provided with an Millenium Development Goals Contract (MDGC), which provides additional un-earmarked funds worth EUR 305 million between 2009 and 2015.

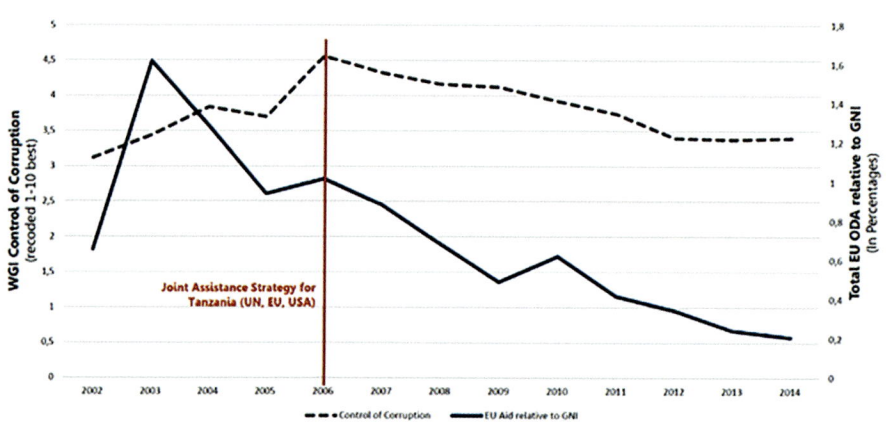

Figure 1. Control of Corruption and Total EU ODA relative to GNI 2002–2014

The high degree of donor coordination and harmonisation make it virtually impossible to assess EU measures in isolation for the policies of other donors. As figure 1 shows, the country did not progressed after a joint donor strategy was adopted. I will put particular emphasis on the EUs role within the donor harmonisation framework whenever necessary to highlight it against the donors' joint context.

The EU's role in the budget support framework

The majority of EU development assistance to Tanzania is pooled with other donors in the budget support framework. Positive evaluations of Tanzania's development performance in the context of the PAF led to significant aid disbursements to the highly aid-dependent country, predominantly in the form of budget support (Tripp 2012). The government of Tanzania's significant efforts to increase aid effectiveness through donor harmonisation further qualified it as a recipient for this type of aid modality. Conversely, Tanzania's achievements in early PFM-reforms and recent economic development are partly attributed to the influence of budget support, which has "allowed the Government to maintain a high level of development spending throughout the period, without increasing domestic borrowing, contributing to a sustained level of public investment and a fast recovery from the global financial crisis" (ITAD, Fiscus and REPOA 2013, i). Furthermore, the anticorruption components of the budget support framework are considered to have facilitated reforms of the Tanzanian governance sector (ITAD et al. 2013).

---

[12] Negotiations have not been finalised, as a result of the on-going constitutional review process, recent elections and a major corruption case in 2014.

This ostensible success story, however, is contradicted by several cases of grand corruption that were being dealt with in an unsatisfactory manner by the relevant authorities and stagnating or declining international anticorruption indicators. Under the 10th EDF NIP, budget support to Tanzania amounted to EUR 444 million – 80% of the development assistance the EU pledged to provide. Budget support continues to comprise the majority of indicative EU development assistance under the 11th EDF NIP, yet decreased significantly to EUR 360 million, or 57% of the overall amount. The relative decline in the share of budget support reflects an overall trend among donors, which have begun to reduce the share of budget support in their aid envelopes following an erosion of trust between the government and its donors after the first of several major corruption scandals in 2007[13] (Claussen and Martinsen 2011, ITAD et al. 2013)

The budget support framework severely reduces transaction costs for all parties involved and provides donors with considerable political leverage when acting united. Yet, this setup also raises a number of complications, which have proven to limit the ability of donors to monitor and enforce government commitments in the context of development cooperation (Molenaers 2012). Although donors may successfully negotiate short-term safeguard mechanisms and remedial measures, the credibility of their response to corruption will ultimately hinge on their ability to push for real actions (ITAD and LDP 2011a, 72). One of the underlying principles of the Partnership Framework Agreement states that parties will promote "[g]ood governance, accountability of the Government to the citizenry, and integrity in public life, including the active fight against corruption" (ITAD and LDP 2011a, 44). In order to ensure that this principle is upheld, donors apply both positive and negative conditionality to the disbursement of budget support.

The EU is a key partner in the development assistance framework for Tanzania. However, other actors, such as the World Bank, UN organisations and the AfDB, provide relatively higher contributions and have played a more active role in establishing key agreements underlying the development cooperation process in the past. (Delputte and Orbie 2014). In effect, the EU has taken a lead in sectors where it has comparative advantages – such as the road sector and public financial management (PFM) reform – and in the promotion and coordination of political dialogue. In particular, its efforts in in the on-going high-level dialogue (HLD) on governance and anticorruption, as well as in the design and monitoring of PFM reform programmes have received praise on several occasions (Ministry of Finance of Tanzania 2013; Delputte and Orbie 2014).

Positive conditionality: The incentive tranche and its limitations

Development assistance via budget support usually includes a fixed tranche and a variable trance, which is intended to enable the donor country to determine and enforce conditionalities in the context of development cooperation. The variable tranche in EU budget support to Tanzania through the EDF and under the MDGC, which accounts for approximately 30% of total budget support, hinges on a broad range of indicators, including governance reforms and anticorruption measures. The underlying idea is to incentivise political reforms in key sectors, as identified by the donor(s). In 2007, 2010 and 2014, failures of the Tanzanian government to comply with agreed-upon performance criteria led the EU and other donors to suspend ODA payments until action was taken by the government to comply with the stipulations of the NIP and the MDGC.

---

[13] Meanwhile, other donors, such as the UK and the Netherlands have completely withdrawn Budget Support to Tanzania.

However, the EU did not prepare an exact methodology for monitoring key indicators – a crucial component for the functioning of the variable tranche – and how these will affect the allocation of development assistance (Molenaers and Nijs 2011, 414). In fact, the 10th NIP for Tanzania simply states that the conditions for the incentive tranche will be agreed upon at a later stage. The ambiguity emerging from this has resulted in the characterisation of the EU's variable tranche as a "non-transparent process where the head of the delegation has all the discretion", limiting its predictability and clarity (Wolff 2015, 932).

Furthermore, also as a result of the absence of clear methodology attached to the incentive tranche, the EU, and other donors, have disbursed their variable tranche according to annual evaluations based on the Performance Assessment Framework (PAF). The PAF is treated as a matrix of conditions in which targets are linked to eligibility criteria and disbursement triggers. Relevant indicators in the PAF were designed to reflect Tanzania's national development strategy, MKUKUTA, and include good governance and anticorruption targets. Although Tanzania's overall performance against PAF indicators has been deemed satisfactory in the period under review, slow progress on indicators related to good governance has been recorded [14] (ITAD et al. 2013). In spite of this, the EU has disbursed the full incentive tranche to Tanzania on virtually every occasion (interview 2).

Ultimately, however, the major impairment of the performance-based tranche to induce good governance reform is that its share in the total development assistance budget is too low to provide the EU with political leverage. This shortcoming is aggravated by the progressive decline in the share of budget support in the EU development assistance envelope to Tanzania. As stated by a former member of the EU delegation to Tanzania: "It is an illusion that the [variable] tranche can be successful … Any attempt at improving domestic conditions through conditionality governance are pointless, as the share of the [variable] tranche cannot be raised to a sufficient level to extract political leverage without seriously impeding aid predictability" (interview 1). Thus, the effectiveness of the tranche to induce significant reforms in donor countries in general, and in Tanzania in particular, is highly questionable.

Political obstacles in design and application of incentive tranches

The tying of positive conditionalities to budget support is a highly sensitive, political matter. Finding agreement amongst major stakeholders on indicators that determine the disbursement of incentive tranches has proven to be difficult and often results in solutions reflecting the lowest common denominator (interview 2). Generally, the EU has prioritised political engagement over the imposition of sensitive, political conditionalities and has based disbursement conditionalities predominantly on technocratic governance criteria. These include: 1. transparent, effective and reliable public finance management; 2. well defined macroeconomic or sector policies; and 3. open and transparent public procurement. While these are important aspects of good governance, an overreliance on these indicators fails to capture the wider political context of political governance and is frequently criticised as being to restrictive and formalistic in nature (ITAD and LDP 2011b, de Vibe et al. 2013). Furthermore, the role of good governance indicators in the general PAF, which is applied by all donors, appears to have been rather marginal. For example, the 2013 Annual Review of Budget Support, conducted by Tanzania and its donors, explicitly states that it does not include discussion on matters pertaining to good governance and anticorruption. Rather, it states that partners will "seek to find other fora to continue this dialogue" (Ministry of Finance of Tanzania 2013, 130).

---

[14] This confirms the declining trend observed on major international anticorruption indicators for Tanzania (see table 1).

The reluctance to adopt and invoke these indicators as disbursement triggers can be explained by two, interlinked factors. First, performance-indicators need to reflect reasonable and attainable targets. Yet, convincing indicators for corruption are hard to come by and even harder to agree upon. Common indicators for the control of corruption are based on perceptions and often involve considerable assumptions, which severely decreases their reliability (Rhao and Marquette 2012, 2–3). Second, international donors cite the lack of government commitment to tackle corruption issues as a severe impediment to finding agreement on attainable targets. In response to the Tanzanian government's unwillingness to deepen anticorruption reforms, the EU appears to have refrained from pushing for a more comprehensive set of indicators on good governance and anticorruption measures for the disbursement of its incentive tranche (interview 2). Instead, there was an attempt to incrementally incorporate more aspects of a political-economy approach by transforming "political issues into technical and managerial problems, thereby removing them from the sphere of political decision-making and fundamental political contention" (Jaeger 2007, 260; Hout 2012). To this end, the PEFA assessments of PFM frameworks assessments were developed and pushed in the context of development cooperation.

Initially designed with to assist PFM reform formulation and monitoring as well as to serve as a risk management tool to evaluate whether countries are more or less subject to corruption and public financial management risk "over the years, PEFA standards and methodology have been de facto coupled to eligibility conditionality for EU budget support. Similarly, the EU has been trying to influence the PEFA methodology by inserting criteria that would reflect the EU's political conditionality"[15] (Wolff 2015, 931). Generally, PEFA provides a much more comprehensive view of a country's PFM system than the PAF and does not require the same degree of agreement between donor and recipient on which indicators to use. Nevertheless, as of yet, PEFA assessments do not serve as the baseline for the incentive tranche and, considering the reluctance of the government to include anticorruption indicators in the PAF, are unlikely to do so in the future (Wolff 2015).

Negative conditionality: Complete suspension of budget support

The Cotonou Agreement and the budget support framework allow for the suspension of the entire development assistance envelope in case of an extreme violation of fundamental principles. Specifically, Article 96 of the Cotonou Agreement enables the EU to suspend development assistance in the case that one of the essential elements described in Article 9, for example democracy and human rights, is violated (Del Biondo and Orbie 2014, 416). This also applies to the case of extreme corruption, in which the EU and other donors can temporarily or permanently suspend development assistance in order to exert pressure on the government to find a solution to the issue at hand. This occurred twice in the period under review, with the most recent case, following the Tegeta Escrow Scandal, still pending. In practice, the EU's political leverage stemming from this measure is limited, as it only applies to episodes of severe transgressions, impedes aid predictability and the functioning of recipient governments, and often results in considerable friction in the political dialogue. Furthermore, the effectiveness of this measure hinges on its timely execution, predictability and anchoring in a systemised effort to impose external checks on ODA recipients (Persson, Rothstein, and Teorell 2013, 6).

However, the EU's and other donors' past responses to grievances in the Tanzanian governance sector deviate from these criteria. First, there is a clear divergence between the rhetoric of

---

[15] Nevertheless, critics maintain that PEFA continues to entail a de-politicised institutional isomorphism that ignores the specificities of beneficiary domestic political systems. Therefore, in spite of transferring standards that provide legitimacy to beneficiary governments, in-depth issues of implementation sometimes remain a "black box" (Lawson 2012, Andrews 2009).

"zero tolerance to corruption" and actual practice, as only very few of the severe cases of grand corruption resulted in tangible repercussions. In fact, it appears that donors are more likely to put in place an articulated and well-communicated response when the corruption cases were too large and public to ignore, which may be attributed to an unwillingness to touch politically sensitive matters and insufficient monitoring practices (Persson et al. 2013, 6). Second, the EUs response to cases of severe corruption in Tanzania have not been fully effective in remedying the underlying issues, mainly due to the ad hoc nature of donor coordination and the protracted process of formulating common demands that need to be met by the government to reinstate budget support disbursements (interview 2). This is best illustrated in the case of the EPA scandal of 2007/08 (see Box 1).

Following the publication of massive fraudulent payments in previous years, donors failed to agree on an immediate response and instead opted to wait until a second audit of the payments was made. Furthermore, and in spite of wide acknowledgement of the scandal, the annual review of 2007/08 in the PAF made no mention of the case and awarded Tanzania a "satisfactory" rating in the good governance section at the insistence of the Tanzanian government (de Vibe et al. 2013, 11). Nevertheless, following the release of a second audit confirming the fraudulent payments, an EPA Action Plan was drafted, which, for the first time, included tangible political demands for the continuation of development cooperation. Besides strengthening the Bank of Tanzania's governance, these were predominantly aimed at extracting stronger commitment to administrative and management reforms from the government (ITAD and LDP 2011b, 64). In the following years, progress on anticorruption governance in the annual review of budget support was rated as "non-satisfactory", due to the lack of implementation of the EPA action plan. The HLD on corruption was initiated at this time as well. Although parliament and civil society had previously played an active role in annual budget support reviews, they were mostly excluded from discussions surrounding the EPA case (ITAD and LDP 2011b). Thus, while the temporary suspension of development assistance to Tanzania has helped foster an intensified dialogue, it has ultimately not been successful in leading to convictions and highlighted severe shortcomings in the structure of the Budget Support Framework: The monitoring of good governance indicators was influenced by political interests and donors were unable to respond to severe corruption in a timely manner.

The EU and other donors again decided to suspend their budget support envelopes to Tanzania in the wake of the Tegeta Escrow scandal in 2014. This time however, possibly as a result of past experience, donors chose to not respect the agreement by suspending budget support disbursements immediately and not, as stipulated, in the following financial year.[16] While this course of action contributed to a fruitful dialogue in parliament and put positive pressure on the government to solve the underlying issue, it also undermined aid predictability and the credibility of the entire partnership agreement. In effect, the EU withheld its contribution to the budget support for the financial year 2015/2016, apart from on-going support to the road sector budget, and has not completed negotiations on the indicative programme for 2014–2020.

Project-based assistance to anticorruption reforms

The EU has launched and participated in several programmes aimed at increasing institutional capacity of relevant anticorruption actors, democratic consolidation, and strengthening the media and civil society. Generally, the EU has played an important role in the development of

---

[16] See Article 21 and 22 of the Partnership Framework Memorandum 2011. Available at http://www.tzdpg.or.tz/fileadmin/_migrated/content_uploads/GBS_PFM_May_2011.pdf (Accessed January 2016).

NACSAP I and II, in particular in urging the Tanzanian government to work with civil society, the media, and private sector in the implementation of the strategy and action plan (European Commission 2011). Thus, the EU contributed to strengthening the PCCBs institutional capacity and the expansion of its mandate. Additionally, the EU has provided considerable financial assistance to the government-owned PFMRP basket fund and individual technical assistance to several rounds of PFM reform, thereby contributing to Tanzania's previous progress in strengthening its PFM systems. However, in spite of the recently stalling progress of Tanzania on various PFM indicators, the EU has declined to increase technical assistance to support Tanzania in meeting the demands of implementing "second generation" reforms – involving roll-out and consolidation rather than simple design and initiation (ITAD et al. 2013, 61).

Targeted EU Support to Tanzania's PFM reforms further entailed the provision of assistance to core institutions involved in public procurement and budget management, such as the Ministry of Finance, the NAO and parliamentary committees. Furthermore, the EU has expanded project-based assistance to the Office of the National Authorising Officer, tasked with managing budget support funds in Tanzania, after it was found that PFMRP basket money was mostly used on a plethora of workshops and training (ITAD and LDP 2011a, 61).

In an effort to promote democratic consolidation and oversight, the EU supported the multi-donor project Deepening Democracy in Tanzania Programme (DDTP), which sought to improve the electoral process and build the capacity of election management bodies and strengthen structures and institutions of governance and checks and balances (Amundsen 2010, 10). The evaluation of the DDTP has been positive, highlighting that chairpersons of parliamentary committees have become more competent at reviewing the budget and scrutinising bills, dialogue between parliament and civil society has increased. It also revealed that involvement of civil society in the review of bills has increased its influence on legislation (European Commission 2011, 130). However, these achievements are severely undermined by recently adopted legislation, such as the Cybercrimes Act 2015, and consistent government efforts to restrict civic access to political decision-making, as demonstrated in the recent drafting of a new constitution, and the lack of a comprehensive access to information bill.

Targeted EU assistance does not appear to have contributed to substantial improvements to good governance practices and a sound anticorruption framework in Tanzania. Considering the persisting lack of capacity, independence and judicial support of core anticorruption institutions, the EU appears to have failed to bolster domestic institutional capacity to effectively combat corrupt practices. Worryingly, a scaling down of targeted EU support to these institutions, CSOs and the media in recent ODA envelopes certainly will not improve their functionality in the future.

EU Aid in the nexus of Tanzania's political economy of corruption

The effect of measures aimed at inducing good governance through development assistance, including concomitant political dialogue, are, however, only effective along with high-level political will to implement anticorruption actions in recipient countries (ITAD and LDP 2011b). Ownership of the development agenda is nevertheless placed solely in the hands of the government, bypassing parliament and civil society (Tripp 2012, 17).

Political will for governance reform, which apparently existed in the early 2000s ebbed off markedly as soon as adopted legislation was to be translated into palpable action. Thus, Tanzania's regress on various control of corruption indicators demonstrates the, as of yet, cosmetic nature of anticorruption reforms. Furthermore, the government was highly resistant to actions which could upset the particularistic power-arrangement by jeopardising the CCMs quasi-monopoly on the executive and privileged access to the political system.

Nonetheless, observable progress on a number of issues can be attributed to the EU's continuous efforts to promote governance reform in Tanzania. In particular, on-going political dialogue seems to have resulted in positive effects, albeit at an incremental pace. On the contrary, conditionality and incentive stipulations have not extracted political gains, also a result of the limited financial leverage that the EU commands; instead, the result has been lengthy and conflict-filled negotiation processes with the Tanzanian government.

References

ADE. (2013). Public Expenditure and Financial Accountability (PEFA) Assessment: Mainland Tanzania (Central Government).

AllAfrica. (2013). Tanzania 24 Tanzanian District Officials Reprimanded for Corruption." *allAfrica*.

Amundsen, I. (2010). Support for Parliaments: Tanzania and Beyond. R2010: 8. CMI Report.

Andrews, M. (2009). Isomorphism and the Limits to African Public Financial Management Reform. RWP09-012. Working Paper Series. Cambridge.

Bertelsmann Stiftung. (2014). BTI 2014: Tanzania Country Report.

Biondo, K. Del, and J. Orbie. (2014). The European Commission's Implementation of Budget Support and the Governance Incentive Tranche in Ethiopia: Democracy Promoter or Developmental Donor? *Third World Quarterly* 35 (3): 411–27.

Business Anti-Corruption Portal. (2013). Tansania Country Profile. *Business Anti-Corruption Portal*.

Claussen, J., and M. Martinsen. (2011). A Brief Review of the Performance Assessment Framework for GBS to Tanzania. Copenhagen.

Cooksey, B. (2012). "Aid, Governance and Corruption Control: A Critical Assessment." *Crime, Law and Social Change* 58: 521–31.

Delegation of the European Union to Tanzania. (2012). President Barroso and Commissioner Piebalgs Visit Tanzania, *EU Tanzania News*.

———. (2016). Tanznia and the EU. *European External Action Service [EEAS]*.

Delputte, S., and J. Orbie. (2014). The EU and Donor Coordination on the Ground: Perspectives from Tanzania and Zambia. *European Journal of Development Research*, 26: 676–91.

European Commission. (2011). Annual Report 2011 on the European Union's Development and External Assistance Policies and Their Implementation in 2010. Brussels.

———. (2012). Budget Support Guidelines: Programming, Design and Management." Brussels.

European Court of Auditors. (2010). The Commission's Management of General Budget Support in ACP, Latin American and Asian Countries. 11 Special Report. Luxembourg.

Ewald, J. (2011). Challenges for the Democratisation Process in Tanzania: Moving towards Consolidation 50 Years after Independence. University of Gothenburg.

Freedom House. (2016). Freedom of the Press 2016.

Global Integrity. (2010). Global Integrity Report 2010: Tanzania. *Global Integrity*.

Goitom, H. (2015). Tanzania: Cybercrimes Bill Enacted. *Global Legal Monitor*.

Gray, H. (2015). The Political Economy of Grand Corruption in Tanzania. *African Affairs,* 114 (456): 382–403.

Hout, W. (2012). The Anti-Politics of Development: Donor Agencies and the Political Economy of Governance. *Third World Quarterly,* 33 (3): 405–22.

Hydén, G. and M. Mmuya. (2008). Power and Policy Slippage in Tanzania – Discussing National Ownership of Development. 21. Sida Studies.

ITAD, Fiscus and REPOA. (2013). Joint Evaluation of Budget Support to Tanzania Lessons Learned and Recommendations for the Future.

ITAD and LDP. (2011a). Joint Evaluation of Support to Anti-Corruption Efforts: Tanzania Country Report. 06/2011-Study. Norad Report.

———. (2011b). Joint Evaluation of Support to Anti-Corruption Efforts 2002–2009. 6/2011-Synthesis. Report.

Jaeger, H.-M. (2007). "Global Civil Society" and the Political Depoliticization of Global Governance. *International Political Sociology,* 1: 257–77.

Jingu, J. (2014). The Grand Presidency and Challenges of Accountability in Tanzania. *Tanzania Journal of Sociology,* 1 (1).

Koechlin, L. (2013). *Corruption as an Empty Signifier: Politics and Political Order in Africa.* Leiden: Brill.

Kolstad, I., V. Fritz and T. O'Neill. (2008). Corruption, Anti-Corruption Efforts and Aid: Do Donors Have the Right Approach? 3. Working Paper.

Lawson, A. (2012, July). Evaluation of Public Financial Management Reform: Burkina Faso, Ghana and Malawi 2001–2010. Joint Evaluation.

Lindner, S. (2014). Tanzania: Overview of Corruption and Anti-Corruption. U4 Expert Answer.

Ministry of Finance of Tanzania. (2013). 2013 Annual Review of the General Budget Support. Dar es Salaam, Tanzania.

Molenaers, N. (2012). The Great Divide? Donor Perceptions of Budget Support, Eligibility and Policy Dialogue. *Third World Quarterly,* 33 (5): 791–806.

Molenaers, N. and L. Nijs. (2011). Why the European Commission Fails to Adhere to the Principles of Good Donorship: The Case of the Governance Incentive Tranche. *European Journal of Development Research,* 23 (3): 409–25.

Montgomery, M. (2016). Case Study on EU Aid and Anti-Corruption and Governance in Tanzania. D8.2.6. Case Study Reports on Control of Corruption and EU Funds.

Mugyenzi, J. (2012). International Modes of Policy Influence: Does the EU Influence Good-Governance Policies in African, Caribbean and Pacific States? *Journal of Politics and Law,* 5 (1): 69–81.

Mukandala, R., M. Samuel, J. Barkan and G. Njema. (2005). *The Political Economy of Tanzania.* Washington, DC: World Bank.

Mungiu-Pippidi, A. (2006). Corruption: Diagnosis and Treatment. *Journal of Democracy,* 17 (3): 86–99.

———. 2014. The Transformative Power of Europe Revisited. *Journal of Democracy,* 25 (1): 20–32.

———. 2016. The Quest for Good Governance: Learning from Virtuous Circles. *Journal of Democracy,* 27 (1): 95–109.

Mungiu-Pippidi, A., M. Loncaric, B. Mundo, A.C.S. Braga, M. Weinhardt, A. Solares, A. Skardziute et al. (2011). Contextual Choices in Fighting Corruption: Lessons Learned. 04/2011-Study. Report. Oslo, Norway.

Persson, A., B. Rothstein and J. Teorell. (2013). Why Anticorruption Reforms Fail -Systemic Corruption as a Collective Action Problem. *Governance,* 26 (3): 449–71.

Rhao, S. and H. Marquette. (2012). Corruption Indicators in Performance Assessment Frameworks for Budget Support. 1. U4 Issue. Bergen, Norway.

Schwab, K. and Sala-i-Martin. (2015). The Global Competitiveness Report 2016–207. Geneva.

Transparency International. (2015). Corruptions Perceptions Index.

———. (2016). Global Corruption Barometer.

Tripp, A. (2012). Donor Assistance and Political Reform in Tanzania." 2012/37. WIDER Working Paper.

Vibe, M. de, N. Taxell, P. Beggan and P. Bofin. (2013). Collective Donor Responses: Examining Donors Responses to Corruption Cases in Afghanistan, Tanzania and Zambia. 2013:1. U4 Reports. Bergen, Norway.

Wang, V. and L. Rakner. (2005). The Accountability Function of Supreme Audit Institutions in Malawi, Uganda and Tanzania. 4. CMI Reports. Bergen, Norway.

Wogau, S. von. (2010). Transitions to Good Governance: The Case of Tanzania. 19. ERCAS Working Papers.

Wolff, S. (2015). EU Budget Support as a Transnational Policy Instrument: Above and Beyond the State? *Public Administration,* 93 (4): 922–39.

World Bank. 2015. Worldwide Governance Indicators.

———. 2016a. Doing Business Data. *Doing Business.*

———. 2016b. Political Stability Index. *Worldwide Governance Indicators.*

Interviews

Interview 1: European Union Expert, 05.12.2014
Interview 2: European Union Expert, 25.12.2016

Disclaimer: Given the sensitivity of the topic and the job function of the interviewees, their names will remain undisclosed.

Acknowledgments

This project is co-funded by the Seventh Framework Programme
for Research and Technological Development of the European Union

This policy report, The Anticorruption Report 4: Beyond Panama Papers, is the fourth volume of the policy series "The Anticorruption Report" produced in the framework of the EU FP7 ANTICORRP Project. The report was edited by Prof. Dr. Alina Mungiu-Pippidi from the Hertie School of Governance, head of the policy pillar of the project.

ANTICORRP was a large-scale research project funded by the European Commission's Seventh Framework Programme. The full name of the project was "Anti-corruption Policies Revisited: Global Trends and European Responses to the Challenge of Corruption". The project started in March 2012 and lasted for five years. The research was conducted by 21 research groups in sixteen countries.

The fundamental purpose of ANTICORRP was to investigate and explain the factors that promote or hinder the development of effective anti-corruption policies and impartial government institutions. A central issue was how policy responses can be tailored to deal effectively with various forms of corruption. Through this approach ANTICORRP advanced the knowledge on how corruption can be curbed in Europe and elsewhere. Special emphasis was laid on the agency of different state and non-state actors to contribute to building good governance.

Project acronym: ANTICORRP

Project full title: Anti-corruption Policies Revisited: Global Trends and European Responses to the Challenge of Corruption

Project duration: March 2012 – February 2017

EU funding: Approx.8 million Euros

Theme: FP7-SSH.2011.5.1-1

Grant agreement number: 290529

Project website: http://anticorrp.eu/

All these contributions were given as part of the European Union Seventh Framework Research Project ANTICORRP (Anti-corruption Policies Revisited: Global Trends and European Responses to the Challenge of Corruption). The views expressed in this report are solely those of the authors and the European Union is not liable for any use that may be made of the information contained therein.